Homeland Security and Private Sector Business

Corporations' Role in Critical Infrastructure Protection

Homeland Security and Private Sector Business

Corporations' Role in Critical Infrastructure Protection

ELSA LEE

CRC Press
Taylor & Francis Group
Boca Raton   London   New York

CRC Press is an imprint of the
Taylor & Francis Group, an **informa** business

Auerbach Publications
Taylor & Francis Group
6000 Broken Sound Parkway NW, Suite 300
Boca Raton, FL 33487-2742

© 2009 by Taylor & Francis Group, LLC
Auerbach is an imprint of Taylor & Francis Group, an Informa business

No claim to original U.S. Government works
Printed in the United States of America on acid-free paper
10 9 8 7 6 5 4 3 2 1

International Standard Book Number-13: 978-1-4200-7078-1 (Hardcover)

Library of Congress Cataloging-in-Publication Data

Lee, Elsa.
    Homeland security and private sector business : corporations' role in critical
infrastructure protection / Elsa Lee.
        p. cm.
    Includes bibliographical references and index.
    ISBN 978-1-4200-7078-1 (hardcover : alk. paper)
    1. Infrastructure (Economics)--Security measures--United States--Planning. 2.
Corporations--Security measures--United States--Planning. 3.
    Business enterprises--Security measures--United States--Planning. 4.
Industries--Security measures--United States--Planning. 5. Preparedness--United
States. 6. Terrorism--Prevention. 7. United States. Dept. of Homeland Security.
National infrastructure protection plan. I. Title. II. Title: Corporations' role in critical
infrastructure protection.

HC110.C3L44 2009
363.325'936360973--dc22   2008039392

Visit the Taylor & Francis Web site at
http://www.taylorandfrancis.com

and the Auerbach Web site at
http://www.auerbach-publications.com

CONTENTS

PREFACE

I started out with a vision of decoding terrorism for the private sector and providing a template for preparedness to owners and operators of our nation's 17 critical infrastructure sectors. The template would be derived from 20 years of successful counterintelligence practices securing and protecting national security assets from terrorism, espionage, sabotage, and other foreign and domestic threats.

Preparing the template would have required starting with an overview of our Homeland Security laws. They are not the best laws in the world, but they suffice. We are a young nation, and our existing laws are the best we have to work with for now. So far, we have been able to introduce laws that allow us to maintain a delicate balance between being a "free society" and not a "police state" nation. We do need laws, and I am sure our friends in the legal system will continue to draft laws that preserve our civil liberties but hopefully with enough enforceability to protect us from future 9/11s. I quickly realized that taking this approach would have taken up all the chapters of the book.

Instead, I decided to focus on my ultimate goal — to educate the private sector on terrorism preparedness by framing problems and solutions in a way that everyone can understand so that mindsets can evolve quickly to improve our security posture as a nation. My vision is to infuse current leaders, future leaders, and the 300 million or so people in America with knowledge that bends the minds, teases the brain, and stumps emotional intelligence — through rhetorical questions, lighthearted humor, anecdotal material, and tactical and strategic perspectives — to help put terrorism back where it belongs: in the Dark Ages.

Through "critical, scholarly, and intellectual thinking," we can accelerate our security evolution ... our security awakening — maybe even put ourselves in "turbo mode" and bolt into action right now. We can start by securing exploitable vulnerabilities.

Terrorist groups who conspire to carry out attacks in this country or elsewhere already know the limits of our laws and use them to their advantage. They know our laws prevent us from investigating them without solid information. We cannot investigate someone simply on the basis of a notion "in their head." This is largely due to intelligence oversight changes introduced after the Watergate events of the 1970s. Thus, terrorists are free to live among us, conduct meetings, raise funds, send funds to other plotters abroad, and engage in surveillance of U.S. facilities that they would like to target — right under our noses.

I was 39 when I retired from the U.S. Army and I could have easily stayed retired and taken up gardening, but I could not take my eyes off "the prize" — making our nation a safer place to live and preserving our way of life.

Really, how could someone like myself — who served on an international terrorism task force that captured terrorists at age 22 and who could've, would've, should've died in three different terrorist attacks in three different countries on 3 random days of my life — simply roll over and go away, all while watching events like 9/11 unfold?

I really feel that "the prize" is precious, even if no one else can. I cannot change what is. I cannot undo the political decisions or historical events that got us here, but I must do something. You must do something. For years, I saw the threat of terrorism and "tenacity" building up, but not in a way that I alone could stop. Together, we can do something. Those of us who have served in this field do it because we care. We do it because we have skills that are suited for this kind of work — it's not that we're brave or crazy ... well, maybe a little. But we are just a few, and we 10 percent of the population can no longer carry the workload of the other 90 percent — rhetorically speaking, of course.

The prize is worth fighting for, worth dying for — the prize being "a safer America." I love this country more than the blood that runs through my veins, which is why I served for 20 years in the U.S. Army — a noble and fine profession. I believe I have earned the right to grab a megaphone and communicate my message loudly and freely. Get out there and secure your vulnerabilities — train your people — and harden your facilities!

We don't want suicide bombers approaching our parking lots. We don't even want to put ourselves "out there" and see how we would react to subway attacks. Help secure tomorrow today. Don't let our government try to carry the full load. The U.S. Government needs our help regardless of our political affiliation. Government, if you need our help, please be more specific about what you need. Business owners, when there is a lull in terrorist activity, that is the time to hurry up and put defenses in place. Use the time wisely — look inward and revamp or restructure the security architecture that protects your assets. Doing so positions you to deter and effectively mitigate risk. It can also solidify market share, strengthen your brand, lower insurance premiums, and endear customers and stakeholders to you because of the confidence you will instill in them through your security actions.

There are more than 1 million action items you could probably come up with in the race to secure your assets before catastrophe strikes again, but the fastest and most prudent way to go about this is through the National Infrastructure Protection Plan (NIPP) — which the Department of Homeland Security (DHS) published in June 2006. Of all the plans, strategies, programs, and best practices observed over my 28 years in the business of preventing and deterring terrorism and managing security risks — this is the closest thing to an "oracle."

Our Government is working hard to make the nation safer. The DHS, FBI, CIA, and other state and local agencies are reaching out to private industry for assistance in technology development and advice on how to protect our critical resources — they are trying to wade through the bureaucracy and put as much effort as possible into sharing information, making informational resources available, and drafting legislation that protects us from terrorists while still keeping a delicate balance to protect our civil liberties. But they can't do the job alone, and even within government there are influences at work that hamper efforts — political agendas, the inability to self-reform, and the inability to overcome or adapt organizational cultures overnight.

This book is not the answer to all your problems — though I wish it were. It is not meant to give technical advice in one specific area or on which security technology to select. You should not readily defer a selection like that to someone communicating to you through a book. This book is meant to open your mind, and entice you to embrace other ideas and approaches so that you can solve problems with solutions that you never thought of before. Please find three things that you can change, improve, or secure, and calculate how much you saved by catching what would be an exploitable problem — early on. I want to do something measureable that will help you. Please allow me that privilege.

ACKNOWLEDGMENTS

This book is the result of my 28 years of experience in counterintelligence and security. It would not have been possible to write it without events that shaped me … serving as a Counterintelligence Agent in the Army from age 19 to 39 — personal experiences in 19 countries — living to tell about three countries in which I did not die in terrorist attacks — and being touched by those who have died horrific deaths in terrorist attacks. For that, I thank God that my name is not on that list and that I am here today with the power to infuse the world with the antidote — protective and deterrent measures against threats.

I am grateful to Mark Listewnik for spotting me in the crowd and building a path to this publishing milestone — to Stephanie Morkert and Linda Leggio for being extremely helpful and their hardwork on this project — to all my friends, family, quiet warriors, and colleagues still serving who supported, assisted, and collaborated with me to make this book possible — and to all the quiet warriors who still serve and cannot be named. Another important acknowledgment goes to the publisher, Taylor & Francis Group, who provided me the opportunity to continue with my vision of educating millions so that together — we can secure tomorrow, today.

I am grateful to Peter L. Bergen, a CNN terrorism analyst and a print and television reporter, for his works and expertise on terrorism and for permission to use material — to Stephen Emerson for his contributions to terrorism awareness, and Michael Scheuer for his research and tenacity in opening our eyes to how serious the threat is — and to each of my colleagues who took valuable time from their busy schedules to provide reviews and insight.

For the development and production of this book, I feel a deep sense of gratitude, and I wish to thank:

- Jessica Farias, my lovely daughter, for working under a tight deadline and providing me with her valuable time, expertise, and creative talent to design and create all the graphics and tables needed for this book.
- My best friend, Traci Britton, for her sacrifices, for providing nonmilitary civilian insight on security, conducting research, and

giving me encouragement to write this book, but mostly for taking on a greater workload at Advantage SCI so that I could dedicate the time needed to write this book.

- My friend Gary Berntsen, author of *Jawbreaker* and a former CIA officer with extensive experience in Iraq and Afghanistan, who provided me with the encouragement to write this book.
- My parents for teaching me the basics of survival and going the distance in everything I pursue.

To those who are currently fighting in Iraq, Afghanistan, and other places across the globe, I salute you and support you 100 percent. Another group I wish to recognize are former U.S. Military personnel who continue to serve as civilian and government employees sharing their security and intelligence expertise in protecting our nation. May God bless all of you.

And most of all to my husband and partner ... Pete Lee, who works extremely hard in this business. He knows this business better than I do. With his 24 years in the U.S. Army Special Forces, he is the best partner to help me with my mission to keep America safe and secure. Without his leadership and support, and contributions to Chapters 5, 8, and 9, this book would still be in my head and Advantage SCI would not exist. Thank you — Pete Lee.

ABOUT THE AUTHOR

Elsa Lee is a lecturer and the CEO and founder of Advantage SCI, LLC, a professional services firm based in El Segundo, California, providing corporate, homeland, and national security services to government and private industry. Lee is a retired 20-year U.S. Army counterintelligence officer who served in the United States, Europe, Central America, and Asia. She has 28 years of experience in counterterrorism, counterintelligence, and security operations. She is a recognized expert in terrorism deterrence and counterintelligence methods. Lee has been featured and quoted extensively in national and international newspapers and professional journals and has appeared on CNN, Fox News, CBS News, Voice of America, Canada Business Channel, and in international security journals.

Lee worked closely with the Federal Bureau of Investigation (FBI), the Central Intelligence Agency (CIA), the U.S. Secret Service, the National Security Agency (NSA), Great Britain's Security Service (MI-5), and Germany's Special Operations and Counterterrorist Forces (Grenzschutzgruppe — GSG-9) while in the Army, establishing strong information-sharing partnerships and conducting assessments of critical infrastructure vulnerability to terrorism. She is one of the few experts in this nation trained in U.S., British, and Israeli counterintelligence and counterterrorism methods and operations. She has provided training to U.S. and foreign nationals, including U.S. Presidential staff; White House executives; German, Russian, Central American, and U.S. military leaders; and international law enforcement and intelligence audiences worldwide.

Lee has helped clients effectively manage organizational security risks. She has taught leadership, global cultural relations, resource management, and business communications courses as an adjunct professor in Los Angeles. She speaks Spanish and German. Her education includes a Master's degree in Organizational Leadership and a graduate certificate in Human Resources, both from Chapman University, and a Bachelor's degree in Behavioral Science from the University of Maryland. Recent accomplishments include providing support to national counterintelligence programs, delivering antiterrorism training overseas for the U.S. Department of State, and conducting first-time studies on Railway, Port, and Critical Infrastructures' vulnerability to terrorism in partnership with the University of Southern California (USC) Homeland Security center "The Center for Risk and Economic Analysis of Terror Events" (CREATE), RAND Corporation, and the Los Angeles County Economic Development Corporation (LAEDC).

While in the military, she served in the Defense Intelligence Agency, the U.S. Army Intelligence and Security Command (INSCOM), U.S. Army Europe, the Pentagon, the U.S. Army Intelligence Center & School, and the Defense Nuclear Agency (DNA). At DNA, her liaison efforts with local, state, federal, and international law enforcement facilitated threat and vulnerability assessments, incident response, and contingency planning for terrorist attacks against nuclear facilities, including weapons of mass destruction (WMD) attacks.

In 1995, she served as the Chief Intelligence Officer of a joint task force in Central America directing intelligence operations for the U.S. Army. Her diplomacy skills with U.S. Embassy diplomats, senior military executives, and Central American officials facilitated timely and safe conduct for many peacetime operations, ensuring Force Protection of U.S. forces and zero incidents and fatalities on her watch.

From 1980 to 1986, at the height of terrorist attacks against Americans in Europe, Lee served on an international terrorism task force responsible for the capture of two terrorists and survived three terrorist attacks. She presented terrorism awareness, methodology, and ways to protect against terrorism to U.S. Armed Forces in Europe. Her intelligence contributions influenced U.S. Presidential policy decisions. During her 20-year career as a Counterintelligence Special Agent with the U.S. Army, Lee received numerous recognition awards and military honors, including the highest military peacetime award possible, the Legion of Merit.

1

Introduction
Homeland Security Vision

The will of God prevails. In great contests each party claims to act in accordance with the will of God. Both may be, and one must be, wrong. God cannot be for and against the same thing at the same time. In the present civil war it is quite possible that God's purpose is something different from the purpose of either party — and yet the human instrumentalities, working just as they do, are of the best adaptation to affect His purpose.

Abraham Lincoln

THE DESIRED STATE OF HOMELAND SECURITY

In the ideal world of security, society, businesses, and government work together in synchronicity as true partners. Concepts, ideas, and insights from the soft and hard sciences merge to enable remarkable capabilities in Prevention, Detection, and Response to terrorism and disasters. Whether in Washington, D.C., Texas, or California, the response is coordinated and orchestrated like a well-oiled machine — it is decisive and automatic. No one shudders at the sound of *terrorist attack* or *disaster* because everyone has been trained. They understand their roles. Everyone is accountable and owns a share of preparedness. There are documented procedures that have been tested, validated, and rehearsed across all environments and industries.

In personal and professional settings, people got past the shock, fear, and denial stages of terrorism; reached a level of acceptance; and "bought into it" emotionally and intellectually to do something about it. Everyone went through the "forming, storming, norming, and performing"[1] stages of team dynamics to collectively establish effective security and preparedness measures to ensure all operations would run smoothly. This was just one of the many great models learned over time and adopted as an effective training tool. Terrorism is managed and controlled smartly in this perfect world, so that even my grandmother knows what to do if she were to stumble upon something that remotely smelled terroristic. Members of all communities were properly trained to recognize and report suspicious behaviors in a timely manner to the right office — from recognizing a person who is seeking employment in an organization for the purposes of collecting information needed to plan an attack to an ill-intentioned culprit studying a facility's security practices to see if there is a way to exploit vulnerabilities for personal gain. Suspicious reports are received, managed, properly tagged, tracked, and acted on. They do not disappear into an abyss of backlog in an obscure basement, nor are they relegated into binary data trapped in some virtual bin.

On the off chance that a disaster occurs, people are sensitized to go into action and not slip into a psychological paralysis. This is where the soft sciences were best utilized. Psychologists and behavioral scientists introduced training and exercises that helped everyone understand how the body responds in certain situations under stress and how the release of certain chemicals in the body causes people to freeze and become immobile or kick into autoresponse because the brain's hidden potential unleashes when survival depends on it. Everyone quickly learned that immobility, shock, and a lack of confidence cause situations to quickly go from manageable to completely fatal. On the terrorism front, there are no soft targets. Public and private sector organizations successfully hardened their facilities and reinforced security just like mini "Fort Knoxes" except that they do not look like fortresses. Security designs are pleasing to the eye, safe, and environmentally friendly. Crime Prevention through Environmental Design principles are effectively used. Everywhere the eye can see, adequate technology complements layers of security, and no one broke the bank to achieve it.

---

[1] Bruce Tuckman's model of team development and behavior, introduced in 1965; in 1970, he added the fifth stage, Adjourning.

People were not always this way, though. One day everyone came together — learned to think differently — learned to change — and merged ideas from different disciplines and became highly evolved and effective at risk mitigation and disaster preparedness. People had to learn three things — Prevention, Detection, and Response. We made the learning process interesting and provided incentives that would entice people to participate. Most people were not interested in the incentives but finally realized the importance of their role. We realized that there were over 300 million in our population and each was viewed as a potential contributor if we could just get them to learn and practice basic security. We found the right methods — one of them was an interactive learning game. Though prior to the launching of the game, some felt we had to mandate that everyone register and take the training, but instead we helped most of them understand the importance, and for others we created incentives that enticed them to play. Developing the game was done through the help of psychologists, professional development trainers, and branding and marketing experts who came in after the game designers. The training became a game and a contest. It cost $25 to play the game. Everyone who played and learned was automatically entered in the contest. We gave everyone 18 months to participate or, rather, play the interactive game. We called it *Play PDR!* It was a simple concept and stood for Prevent, Detect, and Respond. The overall effort was managed on the Internet — through 10 servers that could handle the daily bandwidth of millions of participants online at any given time.

We had calculated that at least 200 million people were of age and had the ability to participate. This was determined through an organized team effort. We brought in the "numbers people," Web site administrators, lawyers, accountants, lottery commissioners, and fund administrators to help launch and manage the game. We were right; 202 million people logged on and played. When people got to the end of *Play PDR!* they were issued a number generated by the interactive game and stamped onto a certificate of graduation. At the end of the 18-month period, half the funds were set aside as a giveaway, and 5,000 people were randomly selected (through the certificate numbers generated) to receive $1,000,000. The winners were televised on local news over a 12-month period. This one-time campaign cost $900,000 (covered from the fees to participate), but it proved to be an explosive success. After the giveaways and the cost of designing, launching, and managing the game settled, the remainder of the funds were reinvested into homeland security enhancements. The game signaled a defining moment in our evolution. People changed not just because the game sparked interest and brought everyone together but also because they had an epiphany and finally understood that society could not tolerate barbaric acts of terrorism that belonged to earlier centuries — not in modern times. Survival and world order depended on society's ability to control the spread of terrorism. Security has one common meaning in this world, and now everyone is on the same page. But that is in the ideal world. To get there, we still have to chart a map.

THE CURRENT STATE OF HOMELAND SECURITY

The problem of *terrorism* is bigger than one can imagine. We often recognize that globalization, technology, and culturally diverse workforces intertwine, collide, and clash — creating situations that bring risk into our daily lives. If we take a hard look at our immediate terrorism worries, we will find that the terrorism battle we are fighting today — Al Qaeda-inspired networks — is really a conflict of epic proportions. We are two civilizations from different centuries fighting with the knowledge of our eras.[2] The "values" system of today's terrorists is centuries old — and our society has evolved too much to understand this threat. How do we begin to frame it so we can solve it? Do we try de-evolving so we can relate to the threat and properly protect against it? Or, how do we escalate the "threat's evolution" and bring them forward to the current century? What do we do with this discovery — the problem is really a phenomenon of epic proportions.

Other threats are morphing and surfacing at phenomenal rates, like out-of-control viruses, and it is not a problem that can be managed without a wide-scale community effort. Our society feels the pain of these threats intermittently and rarely is compelled to do something about it. The threat problem we face will require that our society change rapidly. Society will need to put itself into turbo mode as soon as possible to properly mitigate the resulting risks of today's threats. We need to master the ability to address threats more effectively as quickly as they surface, so that we do not scramble about chaotically when struck by terrorists or even "Mother Nature." To do so requires that we gain an understanding of

---

[2] Excerpts from Middle East Media Research Institute (MEMRI), "There Is No Clash of Civilizations but a Clash between the Mentality of the Middle Ages and That of the 21st Century," interview with Arab American psychiatrist Wafa Sultan, clip no. 1050, February 21, 2006, http://www.memri.org (accessed February 10, 2008). These excerpts also appear in Appendix G at the end of this book.

how we have evolved and then come up with an intervention to improve our threat management skills. The United States is one of the world's most advanced nations when it comes to defense, technology, and world power, but despite its omnipotence, its citizens are being dumbfounded by attacks like 9/11.

Many will argue that much has been done in the name of Homeland Security. Yes, many solutions are in place across operating environments as a result of 9/11, and the public now realizes that terrorism is something to worry about. Nevertheless, this work consists of only elementary steps — when considering the desired state. To reach the desired state, we need framers to frame the problems in ways we can understand, implementers to introduce plans that work against the threats we face, visionaries to show us how to get to the desired state, creative thinkers to pave the way, leaders and managers who are not afraid to take risks for improvement and who can stimulate execution and follow-through … and citizens primed for necessary change.

When too much time lapses between terrorist attacks and people witness no localized terrorist activity, they become complacent and drop their guard. They lose interest in threat awareness, and the momentum created by the last catastrophe quickly fades away. Managers begin to think their risk management measures are sufficient and that no further actions or security improvement expenditures are necessary, and employees begin to find ways to circumvent security measures because they are cumbersome and not needed. Imagination is no longer used to identify ways that threats might develop to attack us.

Just as it was echoed in the 9/11 Commission Report that a "failure of the imagination" made the 9/11 attacks possible, people can't seem to imagine that at times of lull where no attack has been witnessed, "the threat" is possibly taking time to train, hone skills, and plan for the next attack.[3] Maybe attacks have not occurred because security was tight and visible. Maybe, there was a sufficient "hustle and bustle" of activity relating to security scrutiny creating a perception of preparedness. Perhaps it appeared too difficult to strike. Whether there are great security programs in place or not is not so important if the program succeeds at protecting assets and deterring threats. What matters is that even if one did not have the resources to implement the most robust security program, they gave a

---

[3] National Commission on Terrorist Attacks upon the United States (9/11 Commission), 2004, *9/11 Commission Report*, http://www.gpoaccess.gov/911/index.html, ch. 11.

perception that the best security strategy was in place and appeared like a difficult target not worth attacking.

To illustrate how true this is, we simply have to look at our historical experiences with attacks.

After the first World Trade Center attack of 1993, the attacker Ramzi Ahmed Yousef explained that he worried he would not get out of the garage before the bomb he had just placed would explode. Later, as he watched from the Jersey City waterfront, he explained that he was so disappointed that the explosion did not cause the tower that had just been attacked to topple over and knock down the other tower and kill 250,000 people, as he expected.[4] He had carried out this attack in retaliation for U.S. aid to Israel. When asked why he didn't select Israeli targets, Yousef remarked that "they were too difficult therefore, if you cannot attack your enemy, you should attack friend of your enemy." The attack was meant to let Americans know they were "at war."[4] The fact that he said they "were too hard" (referring to Israeli targets) speaks volumes about what we must do.

It is difficult to buy into the idea that we are targets wherever we are. Thus we are very surprised when attacked. Terrorists train. They wait. They plan. They plot, and then they execute attacks. "All U.S citizens are legitimate targets," says Osama bin Laden and other Islamic extremists. They have repeatedly warned us since the 1993 World Trade Center attack, but we are not getting that message. How we became targets, is immaterial. We cannot erase time, political decisions, or actions that appear to have inspired today's attacks, but we must take action and be accountable for our share of Homeland Security preparedness.

Where will terrorists strike next? Probably in the locations where they have already told us they will attack — as they did repeatedly with the Twin Towers. They like to impress and embarrass us by letting us know what the target is and proving that no matter what we do, they can still accomplish their mission. If Osama bin Laden has been saying, "We are working for a big operation; namely, dragging the United States into a confrontation with the entire Islamic world,"[5] broadly speaking he is saying that terror attacks will continue to be carried out and he does not care how they are orchestrated.

---

[4] Stephen Emerson, *American Jihad* (New York: Free Press, 2002).
[5] Peter L. Bergen, *An Oral History of Al Qaeda's Leader: The Osama bin Laden I Know* (New York: Free Press, 2006).

Since he comes from a culture where the direct message does not come out — you have to ponder the thought and try to arrive at what he really meant — we should revisit what terrorists have declared to be targets in recent years and secure them. We need to discern such threats sooner rather than later and not when it is the day of the attack, as in 9/11. On that day, we just could not imagine such actions being carried out by humanity. To manager terrorism, maybe our leaders should establish a dialogue with the good people of Muslim communities and see what they have to say about those threats. If we cannot discern the threats because they are too broad in nature and the plotters are stuck in an earlier century and we do not have a time machine, we should consider enlisting the help of the good members of the Muslim community. Perhaps they can assist to prevent future acts.

In fact, why not set a goal that for the next 5 years (or fill in the blank), we will deter attacks by reviewing and acting on lessons learned — even those from Pearl Harbor? Let us put measures in place and learn to change as a society so that we are not surprised as we were on 9/11. First and foremost, this ambitious goal requires leaders and managers with superior skills in efficiency and effectiveness — and the ability to surround themselves with people who are smarter than them to execute this plan.

To do this, we must first come to terms with an understanding of the "words" being used — or "misused?" We have to agree to standard definitions. First, *security* has a broad definition that has many meanings to different people depending on what industry they come from, their background, and where they work. We are not all on the same page. Some think "security" means to invest in or buy stock, while others think it refers exclusively to information technology networks. The multiple uses of this word easily conjures an image in my mind … there is a team of rowers in a boat, each member rows in a different direction and all are unaware that the boat is not going anywhere. Each one is proud of their team contribution, but no one is aware that they are not moving.

The use of the words *antiterrorism* and *counterterrorism* has been intermixed. The words have lost their original meanings. Those who have worked in counterterrorism units for decades would never use the word "antiterrorism" interchangeably with "counterterrorism." Traditionally, "counterterrorism" has been used to describe quick reaction forces that break down doors and "take out terrorists" — so to speak. To this group, "antiterrorism" signifies another type of security professional, one who might focus on preventative measures and perhaps give advice on where to place perimeter barriers at the front gates to protect against terrorism. It would be an insult to counterterrorism forces to refer to them as "anti-terrorism forces." Conversely, a consultant advising customers on barrier placement who has only book knowledge of terrorism and who has never served on a counterterrorism unit would be receiving undue credit if he or she were referred to as a "counterterrorism expert." But the lines of definition have become blurred since 9/11, and now the words are used interchangeably by nearly everyone so that the respect that once belonged to small elite groups of specialized forces who put their lives in danger is now lost in oblivion.

There are pockets of vulnerability or weakness in many areas of Homeland Security resulting from security gaps and a lack of under-standing about today's threats. This is further compounded when you add to the equation nonexperts who are out there giving advice. After 9/11, many people surfaced as homeland security experts. Some are con-sidered experts because they are well-read, published, noted cultural experts, or perhaps were chiefs of police, but they have no real opera-tional experience in terrorism as the experts who acquired it operation-ally. A security professional may claim to have expertise gained while in the FBI, the CIA, the Secret Service, the military, law enforcement, or a security position held prior to 9/11. Do not be fooled by fancy acronyms or military and law enforcement experience. Just because they served in those organizations does not make them an expert in terrorism or coun-tering terrorism. It is important to validate where the expertise origi-nated. It could be that it was obtained from something other than an active role in counterterrorism units. While it is prudent to reach out to counterterrorism and antiterrorism professionals — American or inter-national — it is crucial to validate expertise, or people who lack field or operational experience will unwittingly put many others in harm's way through their lack of operational or practitioner experience. The number of people who served in operational counterterrorism roles prior to 9/11 was small, and by my calculation many of them will reach retirement age soon if they have not already retired. Private and public sector orga-nizations should do everything possible to reach out to them and solicit their knowledge and expertise before it becomes obsolete and loses util-ity. Even lessons from the Cold War are applicable in today's global war on terror.

HOMELAND SECURITY ISSUES AND CHALLENGES

Even though the Department of Homeland Security (DHS) and many related legislative and security programs were introduced in the aftermath of 9/11 to protect against such attacks in the future, several years later there are still many obstacles that hinder progress. They include the following:

- Lack of reliable early warning methods.
- Ineffective communication and coordination between public and public sectors.
- Confusion and ambiguity about public and private sector homeland security roles.
- Lack of trust between the government and private sector on information sharing.
- Legal impediments to sharing classified information between public agencies and between government and the private sector.
- Facing a global and stateless adversary — Al Qaeda networks.

To successfully implement Homeland Security programs, it is essential to understand security within our nation.

There are three major components that comprise our nation's security hierarchy. They are National Security, Homeland Security, and Private Sector Security or Corporate Security, as illustrated in Figure 1.1.

National Security entities are focused on protecting our nation from hostile takeovers, have the most authority in comparison with the other

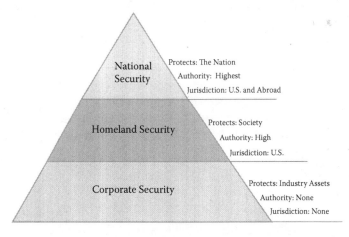

National Security
Protects: The Nation
Authority: Highest
Jurisdiction: U.S. and Abroad

Homeland Security
Protects: Society
Authority: High
Jurisdiction: U.S.

Corporate Security
Protects: Industry Assets
Authority: None
Jurisdiction: None

Figure 1.1 Our Nation's Security Hierarchy (Illustration by Jessica Farias. With permission.)

two components, and have jurisdiction in the United States and abroad. At the National Security level, workers have a greater amount of responsibility than anybody else in the hierarchy, and as far as the security of the nation goes, this group has been focused on threats since the birth of this nation. This force is responsible for ensuring that national security is preserved at all times and never compromised. Ever wonder what life would be like if another nation came into our country, overthrew the government, and took over our nation? It is not something we think of often, but ensuring that such a thing never comes to fruition is the main reason for national security programs. Our nation's survivability depends on national security being preserved. This is achieved through economic, military, and political power; the use of diplomacy; and the use of intelligence, counterintelligence, and secret agencies, and this is true of most nations. Secret agencies are the cornerstone to national defenses.

Though Homeland Security was introduced after 9/11, it previously existed in the form of multiple agencies chartered with various security functions, protecting our country's borders, and responding to natural disasters. The authority and jurisdiction were nationwide. Agencies that comprise Homeland Security have some of the same roles, responsibilities, and authority as national-level players, but jurisdiction for the most part is inside the United States — with frequent requirements to reach into collaboration with the private sector and other nations on activities related to ports, travelers, and movement of goods into the United States.

Private sector security, of course, has existed since the birth of the private enterprise, and its focus has always been on asset protection and market share protection in order to be profitable. Private sector security is a critical component of our nation's security, and many members of it do not yet recognize this. Though none report to one another among the three security components, there are points of intersection and crossover between them, yet each works independent of one another.

Within this hierarchy, there are intangible factors and interdependencies that affect Homeland Security success. There are security practices within each component that if shared among the other two could help solve some of the problems faced in Homeland Security today. Collaboration between the three would enable being on the same page, working in unison toward the same preparedness goals, and sharing methods to minimize duplicative, wasteful, and ineffective measures.

Despite all the work in Homeland Security progress, we still do not have preparedness essentials. There are three dimensions of communication that should be taking place to enable full preparedness.

A critical component of preventing terrorism is intelligence. Many organizations need to improve their intelligence and information collection capabilities — intelligence in the public sector in law enforcement; intelligence within DHS agencies, and information gathering in the private sector. A major component of this deficiency is the collection of quality data and predictive analysis — analysis that is not just "nice to know stuff" but also predictive. This includes timely analysis and proper sharing. The intelligence community has experienced losses over the years due to the following:

- Budget cuts of recent decades.
- Capabilities that diminished after the Nixon Watergate event.
- The Cold War ending.
- White House administrations forcing budget cuts to intelligence ("Everything is good in moderation ... but look where it put us on 9/11").
- Prevailing mindset after the Cold War ended that "there is no more threat."

EVERYONE HAS A ROLE IN HOMELAND SECURITY

Organizations and citizens have a tendency to blame preparedness and response on the Government, but none of those affected by an attack wants to take responsibility for their part of prevention and being prepared. To achieve preparedness, everyone plays a part and has the ability to help prevent a terrorist attack. If everyone were properly trained for this, they could really help achieve Homeland Security objectives and there would be success for unified efforts. A partnership that included society would likely produce a population where no one might feel inclined to point fingers if a terrorist attack took this nation by surprise again. With everyone practicing effective security based on common awareness and fundamental education, the target list would simply shrink. Risk would become manageable, and targets would become minimal because every facility would seem like a hard target.

According to the U.S. Census Bureau, the population of the United States in January 2008 was 303,268,282.[6] In this statistic, except of course for toddlers and newborns, nearly everyone has the potential to be a contributor to

---

[6] U.S. Census Bureau, "Population Clock," http://www.census.gov.

National Security, Homeland Security, or Corporate Security. Imagine millions of people having the same fundamental knowledge of effective security practices to enable Prevention, Detection, and Response to threats in a way that minimized damage and negative economic impact to our nation.

America's citizens — whether at work or at home — could properly respond to terrorism if they had fundamental knowledge. With a few exceptions in threat characteristics, some of the responses would be the same. Terrorism and disasters are not an "apples to apples" comparison. A primary difference is that terrorism is the outcome of a plan concocted and carried out by fellow humans who mean to inflict torturous pain in a grand display of blood and carnage. Utter awareness that fellow humans were the perpetrators is enough to catapult people into immobilizing shock. This is probably because people are so far removed from and no longer live in barbaric times, an era when such atrocities were an everyday occurrence. In contrast, in disasters, where "Mother Nature" is not acting out of malicious intent or premeditation, the shock factor is not the same even though the scale of the disaster may be the same as that generated by terrorist attacks.

If the American population were more educated on the basics of security and practiced them regularly, they could be genuine contributors — not as street-corner posses to go out and hunt terrorists but as educated people who know what they would do in a terrorist attack or other related disaster. Hopefully, they would also know how to take care of themselves, their families, and their neighbors, in that order when facing an attack or disaster. Educating 300 million people on such topics is not easy but needs to be a primary goal through fun and interesting methods.[7]

HISTORY OF TERRORISM

There are terrorism fundamentals that we should all know. Terrorism is the oldest form of warfare. On the war scale, it is the lowest form of

---

[7] J. Straw, "What's Wrong with the War on Terrorism?" interview with Brian Jenkins, *Security Management*, September 2007, http://www.securitymanagement.com/article/what-s-wrong-war-terrorism?page=0%2C2.

low-intensity conflict — in line with insurgencies.[8] Originally, terrorism was intended to be an attack tactic that a nation would use against another nation through a small unconventional force with the objective to force political changes in the other nation. The unconventional force carried no banners and wore no uniform during the attack — thereby allowing the nation that launched the attack the ability to make a plausible denial if accused. Now we all know that to say "the war on terror" is confusing because it is like saying "the war on war" — which does not make sense. The context of the original meaning seems to also be lost in oblivion, like many other things we have lost since 9/11. If we were a society where education is ongoing at all times, we would have learned this from essential fundamentals. This education should now be a priority so that we can all contribute to our preparedness.

Terrorist groups of the 1980s relied on state sponsors for support and safe haven. Today, the only countries on the U.S. Department of State sponsors list are[9] Cuba, Iran, North Korea, Sudan, and Syria. If we do not succeed at fighting terrorism abroad, we face a strong probability of doing it inside our own borders.

In the last 50 years, terrorism has expanded due to instant communications, the Internet, and quicker continental travel methods. Attacks, methods, recruitment, funding, training, and target selection have dramatically changed, and terrorism has spread uncontrollably. No human in any corner of the world is immune from it. Targets historically consisted of airplanes, people, trains, buses, cars, restaurants, shopping centers, and buildings. When they were against American interests, targets were often U.S. Government or Embassy buildings or military personnel, but again they usually took place outside of U.S. borders. In all the years that we witnessed terrorist threats against American interests, the attack profiles were the same. They took place abroad. This made most Americans feel

---

[8] U.S. Army, "Military Operations in Low Intensity Conflict," in *Field Manual 100-20* (Washington, D.C.: Government Printing Office, 1990); and U.S. Army, "Operations in Low Intensity Conflict," in *Field Manual 7-98* (Washington, D.C.: Government Printing Office, 1992). "Low-intensity conflict" is defined by the U.S. Joint Chiefs of Staff as a political-military confrontation between contending states or groups below conventional war and above the routine, peaceful competition among states. It frequently involves protracted struggles of competing principles and ideologies. Low-intensity conflict ranges from subversion to the use of armed forces. It is waged by a combination of means, employing political, economic, informational, and military instruments. Low-intensity conflicts are often localized, generally in the Third World, but contain regional and global security implications.

[9] Countries determined by the Secretary of State to have repeatedly provided support for acts of international terrorism.

safe inside the United States because the attacks seemed so far removed from our world of reality. This mindset made it impossible to imagine that anyone would ever carry out a terrorist attack inside U.S. borders. The attacks of the 1970s and 1980s era were politically motivated for the most part and were perpetrated by groups sponsored by Communist countries or Middle Eastern state sponsors. Terrorist attacks carried out today are likely to be motivated by religious ideals (Old World versus New World), and the perpetrators fit no particular profile. Physical traits or ethnic characteristics are not reliable indicators or predictors of people who engage in terrorist activities. Today it can be anyone who has been recruited for the cause. The suicide bomber of today may think nothing of taking her own life and those of others as a martyr.

There are critical infrastructures or facilities that provide public services which we have come to rely on for everyday life activities and now those are the targets. In 2007, there were hundreds of prosecutions, arrests, and foiled attacks in the United States, Yemen, India, Italy, Britain, Spain, Azerbaijan, Thailand, Romania, Scotland, Germany, Denmark, and Turkey. In the United States, there will continue to be groups — homegrown, Al Qaeda-inspired, and Jihad extremists that plot attacks against U.S. facilities such as critical infrastructures.

THE DIRECT IMPACT OF MODERN-DAY TERRORISM

Al Qaeda, global Al Qaeda affiliate networks, and homegrown terrorists will continue to present the greatest terrorist threats to America for years to come. Noted author and terrorism expert Peter Bergen states that after the

> Iraq war broke out, many fighters who fought in Afghanistan against the Soviets along side Osama bin Laden showed up in Iraq to fight against the U.S. and coalition forces and Iraq became one of Al Qaeda's prime training grounds. When the Iraqi war is over, many of these fighters can be expected to focus future attacks against the U.S. in the U.S. We once thought terrorist attacks against America would only take place in foreign soil — not in the United States. That notion proved to be wrong on 9/11. There is no reason to expect that the same won't be true of the Islamic extremists fighting in Iraq today.[10]

He also believes that

---

[10] Bergen, *An Oral History of Al Qaeda's Leader.*

several factors could make blowback from the Iraqi war even more dangerous than the fallout from Afghanistan. Foreign fighters started to arrive in Iraq even before Saddam Hussein's regime fell. They have conducted most of the suicide bombings — including some that have delivered strategic successes such as the withdrawal of most international organizations and the United Nations. They are more battled-hardened than the Afghan Arabs, who fought demoralized Soviet Army conscripts. Foreign fighters in Iraq today are testing themselves arguably against the best army in history, acquiring skills in their battles against coalition forces that will be far more useful for future terrorist operations than those their counterparts learned during the 1980s. Mastering how to make improvised explosive devices or how to conduct suicide operations is more relevant to urban terrorism than the conventional guerilla tactics that were used against the Soviet Union in Afghanistan.[11]

As America gets better at protecting assets and law enforcement interdicts plots to carry out attacks, Al Qaeda and its affiliates also look for ways to stay a step ahead and change their methods. Al Qaeda's network is very adept and able to self-fund, self-equip, and self-train on the Internet — in contrast to 1980s groups like Abu Nidal and the Red Army Faction. They are savvy in marketing and networking, better educated, and more radicalized than any other group in history. Osama bin Laden began making threats against the United States and other Western nations in the 1990s and has since delivered on them. He is in this war (Jihad) for the long run. Whether he lives or not is of no consequence. His impact is already made. Al Qaeda is no longer just a group but rather a movement that has successfully recruited people worldwide, even converted Westerners.

WHAT'S AT STAKE WITH TODAY'S TERRORIST ATTACKS

The attacks of September 11, 2001, were pivotal because commercial facilities defenseless against terrorism were attacked. Shortly after 9/11, we saw mass transit and other critical infrastructures attacked in Europe. Prior to 9/11, no one really worried about threats against infrastructures except during Y2K or when engineers raised concerns about "infrastructures" reaching capacity levels due to growing populations. Today, we still have to worry about infrastructures but for different reasons. Are we going to experience attacks to our critical infrastructures like Britain and other European countries?

---

[11] Bergen, *An Oral History of Al Qaeda's Leader.*

15

The greatest devastation from terrorist attacks can occur from attacks to critical infrastructure facilities and key resources (CIs/KRs), including public venues where masses congregate.

The greatest threat from terrorism in the United States and in most Western countries is to critical infrastructures. Preparedness across infrastructures is the area that needs the most improvement work because the public depends on them to sustain everyday life. There are 17 critical infrastructure sectors,[12] but they do not all have the same level of criticality. They are described in Table 1.1.

Of the 17 critical infrastructure sectors, DHS is most worried about a few more than others because of their potentially significant economic and psychological impacts. They include Nuclear and Energy Facilities, Chemical/Petroleum Industry, Transportation Systems, Water Systems, Food Industry, and Electric Power Grids.[13] However, historically attacks have been carried out against Commercial Facilities, Defense Industrial Bases, Government Facilities, and Transportation Systems. So essentially, there are about 10 we should all be concerned about.

Government officials approximate that 85 percent of the U.S. infrastructures are owned and operated by the private sector. This puts our country in a vulnerable position because the private sector does not have its own armies, fortresses, or intelligence resources like the federal government. The federal government has an assumption that given the guidance published by DHS, private sector security professionals know exactly what they need to do to help protect infrastructures. There are many ambiguities and assumptions on both sides that place infrastructures and the private sector in vulnerable positions. For example, in addition to assumptions, what are the compliance requirements, and what are the consequences if the private sector does not meet them? We are a young nation compared to European countries that have been dealing with terrorism for decades. There's much that we can learn from them. Again, caution should be exercised as some of their practices may not be appropriate for our nation, our

---

[12] "Critical infrastructures" are systems and assets, whether physical or virtual, so vital to the United States that their incapacity or destruction would have a debilitating impact on national security, national economic security, national public health or safety, or any combination of those matters. Key resources are publicly or privately controlled resources essential to minimal operations of the economy or government, including individual targets whose destruction would not endanger vital systems but could create a local disaster or profoundly damage the nation's morale or confidence.

[13] Robert McCreight, "Soft Targets in Your Backyard: Building Our Own Hometown Readiness," *Homeland Defense Journal* 5, no. 10 (October 2007).

Public Sector <> Private Sector
Public Sector <> Public Sector
Private Sector <> Private Sector

Figure 1.2 Homeland Security and Sector Communications

way of life, or our Constitution. Collectively, we need to quickly grasp the fundamentals of terrorism and master the ability to Prevent, Detect, and Respond so that we can help prevent another 9/11 ... so that we will not be taken by surprise ever again ... so that our infrastructures can be properly secured and protected to sustain everyday life as we know it and expect it. Effective communication is not taking place at various levels of response to share threat knowledge and warnings — or properly handle recovery efforts in the face of a disaster. Figure 1.2, "Homeland Security and Sector Communications," depicts the formal and informal relationships that currently exist between and among government and industry.

There are various types of relationships that exist among these groups — from formal to informal to nonexistent. An example of a public-to-public relationship would be government to government at any level, in any state. Public-to-private would be all critical infrastructure owners and DHS (as well as other government members), and private-to-private would be all critical infrastructure owners and operators communicating with each other and with other private sector community members to share information. Dynamics that affect these relationships are the authority and regulator role of government and the political, technical, and organizational barriers that are ingrained in various organizations. Some of the obstacles that need to be overcome include understanding organizational cultures and rules, removing distrust, and placing aside egos and jealousy, to name a few.[14]

---

[14] Kumar, Amir. Unabridged version of doctoral dissertation "Developing Homeland Security Partnerships: Comparative Analysis of the Development of Homeland Security Partnerships." *HIS Journal of Homeland Security*, August 2007. http://www.homelandsecurity .org/newjournal/Articles/displayArticle2.asp?article=163 (accessed March 2008).

Table 1.1 Critical Infrastructure Sectors

Sector-Specific Agency	Sector	Infrastructure Description
Department of Agriculture, Department of Health and Human Services, and Food and Drug Administration	Agriculture and food	Supports food needs; feed and crop supply chains; harvesting of food; food processing and retail sales
Department of Defense	Defense industrial base	Supplies military means to protect nation through weapons, aircraft, ships, information technology, supplies, and maintenance
Department of Energy	Energy	Provides electrical power; oil and gas refining, storage, and distribution; includes electricity, oil, and natural gas
Department of Health and Human Services	Public health and healthcare	Mitigates disaster and "attacks" risk; provides recovery; includes health departments, clinics, and hospitals
Department of Interior	National monuments and icons	Represents monuments, physical structures, objects, and geographical sites widely recognized as important on a national, cultural, religious, historical, or political level
Department of Treasury	Banking and finance	Provides for nation's finances; includes banks, insurance companies, mutual funds, government-sponsored enterprises, pension funds, and all other financial institutions
Environmental Protection Agency	Drinking water and water treatment	Provides safe drinking water from more than 53,000 community water systems and properly treated wastewater systems from more than 16,000 publicly owned treatment works
Department of Homeland Security: Office of Infrastructure Protection	Chemical	Transforms natural raw materials into products for health, safety, and productivity; produces more than 70,000 products essential to automobiles, pharmaceuticals, food supply, electronics, and other necessities

Department of Homeland Security: Office of Infrastructure Protection	Commercial facilities	Prominent commercial centers, office buildings, sports stadiums, theme parks, and sites where masses of people congregate for business, commerce, or recreation
	Dams	Manages water retention structures and levees; 77,000-plus conventional dams, navigation locks, and canals (excluding channels); includes other similar or symbolic infrastructures
	Emergency services	Provides for fire, rescue, emergency medical services, and law enforcement
	Commercial nuclear reactors, materials, and waste	Provides nuclear power; includes commercial nuclear reactors; nonpower nuclear reactors for research, testing, and training; nuclear materials for medical, industrial, and academic uses; nuclear fuel fabrication facilities; decommissioning of reactors; transportation, storage, and disposal of nuclear materials and waste
Office of Cyber Security and Telecommunications	Information technology	Includes information technology, hardware manufactures, software developers, Internet, and service providers
	Telecommunications	Provides wired, wireless, and satellite communications for business and government
Transportation Security Administration	Postal and shipping	Delivers private and commercial letters, packages, and bulk assets; includes U.S. Postal Service and other carriers
Transportation Security Administration, U.S. Coast Guard	Transportation systems	Enables movement of people and assets vital to the economy, and vital to mobility and security; includes aviation, ships, rails, pipelines, highways, trucks, buses, and mass transit
Immigration and Customs Enforcement, Federal Protective Service	Government facilities	Ensures continuity of functions for facilities owned and leased by the government; includes federal, state, territorial, and local and tribal government facilities in the United States and abroad

Source: Department of Homeland Security, *National Infrastructure Protection Plan* (NIPP) (Washington, D.C.: Government Printing Office, 2006); and George W. Bush, "Homeland Security Presidential Directive HSPD-7" (Washington, D.C.: White House, 2003).

COUNTERING TERRORISM WITH DHS HELP

Many applicable Homeland Security laws and directives were introduced since 9/11 to help guide preparedness and protective efforts. The key roadmaps for critical infrastructure protection (otherwise referred to as CIP) are Homeland Security Presidential Directive 7 (HSPD-7) and the National Infrastructure Protection Plan (NIPP) prepared by the Department of Homeland Security. The NIPP is designed to bring infrastructure protection under one national unified effort. HSPD-7, signed by President George W. Bush in December 2003, established a national policy for federal departments and agencies specific to identification, prioritization, and protection of the CIs and KRs in the United States, and this led to the creation of the NIPP. The NIPP was published in June 2006 by DHS and "provides the coordinated approach to critical infrastructure and key resource protection roles and responsibilities for federal, state, local, tribal, and private sector security partners." A snapshot of the 196-page plan is included in Appendix A, "National Infrastructure Protection Plan Table of Contents."

Countering the threat of terrorism requires that all facets of society and communities of teams come together to manage the problem. No nation or government agency alone can fight terrorism. To effectively manage or control terrorism requires a basic understanding of terrorism and how we got to this point — worrying about our infrastructures being attacked. The attacks of September 11, 2001, began to unfold in the 1990s, when Islamic extremists began to focus on the United States as a focal target. Within a matter of years, attacks would cross over into U.S. borders and 9/11 would come to be marked indelibly in everyone's mind as the worst terrorist attack in history. Would a cruise ship attacked in the middle of the ocean have caused the same psychological effect as the Twin Towers and Pentagon attacks? Probably not, because the cruise ship would need to be close enough for media and news cameras to capture and broadcast the attack in order to achieve the desired mass reaction. The cruise ship attack might affect the cruise industry, but it would not have the same effect that the 9/11 targets had on the economy. The message to the world was clear — here is a super world power that was brought to its knees, not in some remote part of the world, but here in America. In the mastermind's view, this was a plan conceived and executed by "low-tech" means, not by a high-tech Army of a rival nation. "Wow! It was successfully carried out to fruition, and was not that hard to pull off — imagine that" — say Osama bin Laden's cohorts as they give each other the "high five" after the attacks.

What does it take for us — the targets — to heed these messages? Are we smart enough to detect the next attack? Are we taking the time to read their literature and attempt to understand where they are coming from? Are we enlisting the help of other Muslims who may be able to offer a helpful perspective that we simply do not possess? Have our listening abilities diminished to the point where we no longer have basic functioning senses — like listening? Osama bin Laden has sent out several messages, and his followers are inspired to do what he asks — "kill Americans anywhere."

The problem is not that we all could die tomorrow in an attack. The problem is that we cannot seem to perform the basic functions of diagnosing and treating the problem so that it is manageable. Public and private sector partnerships are critical to the success of this management and should already be further along than they are to create partnerships and information-sharing collaboration. Under the NIPP, this collaboration is absolutely required.[15] Government officials believe that collaboration between the private sector owners of critical infrastructures and key resources and the government sector councils exist for the most part but they are not yet efficient or effective with timely sharing of information. The NIPP is a starting point for ensuring that we execute a unified approach to terrorism preparedness, but there are too many obstacles hindering progress between the government agencies and the private sector. For example, the private sector is uncertain about the steps that follow risk and vulnerability assessments. The private sector is afraid to share risk or vulnerability results for fear that information will not be protected by the government and will be leaked to competitors or to the media. This is due in part to past experience, where allegedly the government inadvertently leaked information. The government is not perfect but has its heart in the right place and has apologized for such leaks. All actions called for in the 196-page NIPP may seem daunting and intimidating, but it is possible to work within the framework by dissecting and working on issues one at a time. This book can be used as a decoder to roll out actions called for in the NIPP because in my 28-year career I have witnessed or carried out successfully the activities in the NIPP at many agencies, organizations, and private sector companies at reasonable costs.

---

[15] Department of Homeland Security, *National Infrastructure Protection Plan (NIPP)* (Washington, D.C.: Department of Homeland Security, 2006).

Addressing terrorism smartly requires growing, nurturing, and updating public and private sector preparedness programs. Both sectors need to work together with a strong spirit of collaboration, but the cultures are so different that often this barrier hinders their endeavors. It is essential to understand the differing natures of government and business in order to capitalize on what they can achieve together to contribute to homeland security.

Businesses exist to provide a product or service in exchange for fees, thus producing profits. Governments also exist to provide services but also enforce rules, maintain order, and ensure the well-being of the people. Private industry is driven by profitability, and businesses take risks in the hopes that they will be profitable. New and innovative approaches can be tried easier than in government organizations. Generally, the worst that will happen in a business is that the effort may not prove to be profitable. When it comes to Homeland Security, government must implement preparedness plans and counter terrorism through proven measures — this fits in with government's risk-averse nature. Government expects that businesses will do the same — implement proven methods.

In order to establish true partnerships, government and private industry need to take time to learn about each other's organizational traits as they build relationships. Their differences often result in misunderstandings and frustrations about each other. Every catastrophe in the last few years has shown that these huge differences have a way of impeding response and recovery efforts — as well as prevention measures. Both sectors have to interact, but the methods for coordinating and communicating are disjointed. Both sectors must get past the misconceptions and frustrations and simply bolt into action to achieve Homeland Security objectives.

Having attended hundreds of security conference events over the last 5 years has provided me with a unique opportunity to hear the concerns of public and private sector leaders. Private sector workforces have often declared that they do not know whom to trust or what to do when it comes to Homeland Security requirements. For example, when the Homeland Security Advisory system is elevated due to threat information that becomes known, many private sector organizations still do not know what escalation measures to implement. If they are not completely passive, they tend to be very reactive, and it ends up being terribly costly for them.

DHS HELP IS NOT ENOUGH

The United Kingdom, Germany, Italy, France, Israel, and Ireland have been dealing with terrorism since well before 9/11. The FBI, the U.S. Military, CIA counterintelligence, and U.S. Military Special Operations Forces have been preventing, detecting, and responding to terrorist threats since the 1960s. This nation is missing out on the ability to infuse Homeland Security programs with their expertise. These experts should be rounded up and debriefed. We would find that counterterrorism forces can tell us how they breached security just before they kick the door down to neutralize terrorists. We would then take that information and implement appropriate security countermeasures to harden our critical infrastructure facilities. The counterintelligence professionals who have monitored, surveilled, and investigated terrorists could provide information on the terrorist behaviors to look for when the terrorists are in the plotting stages. We should then take that information and present it to critical workforces in training and education. We need to put their expertise in "offensive tactics" to work to develop "better defensive measures" against terrorism threats. Their job was once to neutralize or capture the "threat." Today, everyone's job is to protect America from the same threats.

Terrorism will be around for centuries, but societies must not get to the point where they can tolerate it. In contrast to crime — which we deal with and tolerate — terrorism can affect world order and turn our world upside down. We may not be able to wipe out terrorism, but we can, and we must, work to control it. Our history with terrorism shows that in the 1970s and 1980s, U.S. interests were attacked abroad. The attacks of 9/11 crossed over, and compared to interests abroad, attacks inside the United States threaten not just homeland security but also national security. We can strike at terrorists abroad where U.S. interests are at stake, but in the United States we are limited in what we can do. If the only evidence of a planned attack is the "intent" in the mind of a "would-be" terrorist, given our laws in this country, there's not much we can do with mindful intent.

2

Essential Threat Factors

The so called religious awakening has turned everything upside down ...
the dead have taken control of the living.... Arab society and culture are
regressing in a superstitious and unreasonable manner ... living in a
world of the supernatural — not today's world of logic.

Saudi author and reformist Turki Al-Hamad

THE PROBLEM WE FACE WITH THREATS

We live in a world of ever growing threats that we cannot seem to foresee
or stop. The war against terrorism is taking its toll on us all and taxing our
resources. One reason that we are overwhelmed is that all problems with
terrorism aspects appear to be rolled up under one label, the *Global War on
Terror*. It includes an insurgency in Afghanistan, an insurgency in Iraq, the
chase on Bin Laden, disabling Al Qaeda, bringing all Jihadist extremists
responsible for 9/11 to justice, tracking militant Islamists plotting attacks
against us, and controlling homegrown radicalized groups that are plotting attacks inside our borders.[1] No wonder we have grown weary.

To properly address these concerns requires seeing them in new
ways than what we are used to — or facing a world with more 9/11s.
Through proper anticipation and recognition, painful experiences could
be avoided. While the threat of terrorism is real and 9/11 proved that we
were no match for what hit us that day, it is possible to live in a state of

---

[1] J. Straw, "What's Wrong with the War on Terrorism?" interview with Brian Jenkins,
Security Management, September 2007, http://www.securitymanagement.com/article/
what-s-wrong-war-terrorism?page=0%2C2.

preparedness without fear and panic. The average American has a 1 in 8,000 chance of dying in a car accident, about a 1 in 18,000 chance of being a victim of a homicide, and a less than 1 in 500,000 chance of dying in a terrorist attack based on figures charted from the deaths of 9/11.[2]

Other problems we face are identifying and reporting individuals who perform the acts without stereotyping. If everyone reporting suspicious activities focused strictly on Middle Eastern men or Muslims, we would open ourselves up to being completely oblivious of valid threats. There is no profile for terrorists that we can rely on today. History has shown that terrorists change many of their tactics as soon as they determine that their methods can be countered including their appearance. Over the last few years, we have noted that Al Qaeda successfully recruits Westerners, Europeans, blue-eyed men, women, and even professionals like engineers and doctors. In observing terrorists during activities that lead up to an attack, the only attribute that has been reliable at all times is behavior. Behaviors translate into actions, and action is required to carry out attacks. That is a reliable attribute that has not changed throughout history. There are essentially three stages in terrorist attacks — planning, preparing, and executing the attack. The planning and preparation stages are the only points in the attack timeline with a high probability of detection because they require physical access to the target location by the terrorists to confirm information for the attack. If activities are not detected in these stages, it will be nearly impossible on the day of the attack to detect and stop the terrorist. On that day, it will involve different role players than those involved in the earlier stages.

Because of the major impact that a terrorist attack would have on our economy, our infrastructures, and our physical and psychological well-being, everyone (government, private businesses, employees, and citizens) needs to take on an active role in helping to prevent them. One way to do this is to look at successful ways that it has been done in other organizations and countries and mimic successful practices that would apply in the United States. Why reinvent the wheel? Using the best practices of others will put us in a position to better respond to threats and to Department of Homeland Security (DHS) compliance. It also helps pace us because the road to preparedness is a long way off and we will be dealing with terrorism for years.

---

[2] J. Straw, "What's Wrong with the War on Terrorism?" interview with Brian Jenkins, Security Management, September 2007, http:/www.securitymanagement.com/article/what-s-wrong-war-terrorism?page=0%2C2.

GENERAL THREATS TO SECURITY
HIERARCHY COMPONENTS

Threat can be defined as anything that can cause, or aims to cause, losses, harm, or damage. Threats are viewed, defined, and perceived in various ways across industries. However, we will all feel the impact of the blow if the most deadly of threats — terrorism — strikes one of our critical infrastructure facilities. All components of this nation's security hierarchy face threats but with a few differences in the characteristics of the threats faced by each. Many organizations across the hierarchy have very good methods for addressing them. Let's compare and put into contrast some of the threats faced in the United States. The threats the U.S. government is most concerned about at a national level are as follows[3]:

1. *Terrorism*: Premeditated, politically motivated violence perpe-trated against noncombatant targets by subnational groups or clandestine agents to influence an audience.

2. *Proliferation*: The provision of chemical, biological, radiological, or nuclear weapons and/or technology by states that have controls in place and possess them to states that do not.

3. *Chemical warfare*: The military or terrorist use of toxic substances such that the chemical effects of these substances on exposed per-sonnel result in incapacitation or death.

4. *Biological warfare*: The deliberate use of pathogens or toxins for military or terrorism purposes; more toxic than chemical warfare nerve agents on a weight-for-weight basis, and potentially pro-viding broader coverage per pound of payload than such agents; attacks can be masked as naturally occurring epidemics due to the presence of anthrax in the environment.

5. *Information infrastructure attack*: Political activism on the Internet ranging from using e-mail and Web sites to organize for purposes of attacking the United States, to Web page defacements and denial-of-service attacks or hacking for political activism.

6. *Narcotics trafficking*: A chronic problem created by drug depen-dence and related activity; it is a chronic problem and a relapsing disorder that exacts an enormous cost on individuals, families, businesses, communities, and nations. Addicted individuals fre-quently engage in self-destructive and criminal behavior. Illegal

---

[3] U.S. Intelligence Community, http://www.intelligence.gov/2-threat.shtml (accessed January 2008).

drug trafficking inflicts violence and corruption on our communities.

7. *Foreign intelligence services*: Identifying, understanding, prioritizing, and counteracting the intelligence threats from foreign powers from espionage, sabotage, assassinations, or international terrorism. It involves more than simply the capture of spies (counterespionage); neutralizing, all aspects of the intelligence operations of foreign nations. U.S. counterintelligence activities are governed by executive order, and "information gathered" as well as "activities conducted" undergo extensive oversight.

At the Homeland Security level and across the 17 critical infrastructure facilities, owners and operators face some of the same threats as the national level but with slight differences. The threats to the community level also apply to businesses and corporations that are not associated with critical infrastructures. Here are some of the most common threats faced by critical infrastructures:

1. *Terrorism*: Activities ranging from undue interest to full-force attacks. Undue interest includes surveillance of facilities for the purposes of identifying security program effectiveness or vulnerabilities that could be exploited at a later time to carry out an attack.
2. *Sabotage*: A deliberate act of perpetrating physical damage to a facility or its assets to inflict losses or damage, or to disrupt operations.
3. *Workplace violence*: Acts originating from employees or others whereby the employer and its employees are threatened; this includes incidents of abuse, threats, assaults, or an explicit or implicit challenge to their safety, well-being, or health.
4. *Theft*: Involves acts of stealing, larceny, or the taking of property of employees or the facility or employer without authorization or consent.
5. *Espionage*: Involves a human physically stealing or taking information without permission from the holder of the information for uses other than what the owner intended or would consent to.
6. *Bomb threat*: An effective means of disrupting business operations by claiming that a bomb will explode in the facility; the threat may be telephoned or physically brought to the site by any means; used by terrorists, extortionists, and disgruntled employees.
7. *Cyber-threats*: Threats to information systems that could disrupt or bring down operations, including online masquerading;

password and identity theft; phishing, spyware, malware, and theft of hardware; criminal use of botnets; cyber-terrorism; spying and theft of data by governments, industry, terrorists, other criminals, or insiders; denial-of-service attacks; and organized cyber-attacks capable of causing debilitating disruption to the critical infrastructure, economy, or national security.

GENERAL THREAT EFFECT ON HOMELAND SECURITY

Despite the differences in the threat characteristics to National Security and Homeland Security components, the one that both have to really worry about is terrorism. It is the one we are least prepared to deal with. Terrorist threats have a way of emerging from nowhere with little warning. A new threat comes up on our radar but only as a mere "bleep." Like faint sonar, it is often too far off the radar to pinpoint and act on. The "threat" involves individuals who probably know our Homeland Security deficiencies and aim to successfully plan attacks and incapacitate infrastructure facilities. The critical infrastructures that we rely on most are transportation, commercial buildings, defense industrial bases, and government facilities. They have historically been targeted by terrorists and foreign intelligence services for exploitation for classified information.

A terrorist attack to our critical infrastructures would have a tremendous impact on the public and this nation. We all are dependent on the various modes of transportation and their nodes to get to and from work. Goods we use daily are also delivered through these nodes. We conduct all business using the financial sector. We depend on government and defense to protect the nation. We visit public venues and theme parks with our families. We are totally dependent on critical infrastructures, and even if we do not work at critical infrastructure facilities, we have access to them and frequent them often. That means that we have the potential to witness threats, report them, deter them — or be present when the full blow of an attack is already in progress.

The sooner we remove the aura of fear or strangeness from the word *terrorism*, the sooner we can all help to implement solutions. This would also enable us to "think out of the box" so that we can face Homeland Security challenges head on — or save our own lives if caught in the middle of an attack. When a word sounds scary, we resist having anything to do with the subject. But we must get past the shock, fear, and denial stages

- At yourself for having been blind to the way threats work
- At the government for being too bureaucratic and slow at times
- At everyone who remained blind to the threat instead of acting proactively
- At the threat for knowing your weaknesses and using them against you
- At all the funds wasted on technology instead of investing in the human factors

Figure 2.1   Emotional Anger and Blame

and reach the acceptance stages of "terrorism" to avoid being passive or pessimistic about this topic.

When assigned to an organization where the risk of attack is high, or, an attack has been experienced people experience all of those emotions. Ordinary, decent people would not find anything comforting, fun, or exciting about such an assignment. They would simply be scared at first. Then, upon witnessing something short of an attack or the attack itself, the first logical reaction would be shock. If people do not recognize that all the emotions they are likely to feel are part of a logical progression, they might get stuck in the stages of shock or fear.

When they finally get to acceptance, they realize that they must take action … learn everything possible to avoid ever having that experience again. They would buy into it emotionally and intellectually, but at some point, as addressed in Figure 2.1, they would even get mad.…

THREAT MANAGEMENT THROUGH INTELLIGENCE

Properly managing risk in all work environments requires a thorough understanding of the "cause and effect" of threats. Threat variables must be viewed objectively and subjectively by diverse threat review teams with the objective to highlight information that would otherwise be missed. Even when the information is right in front of us, sometimes we cannot see it; however, critical information we are likely to miss can be brought to our attention through the use of "intelligence" and threat assessment processes used by national security resources.

Our nation's first line of defense to fight against adversarial threats occurs through something called the *intelligence process*.[4] It take the rawest form of collected data and converts it to useful information so that policy makers can make decisions on the diplomatic, economic, and military

---

[4] U.S. Intelligence Community, http://www.intelligence.gov/2-business.shtml.

actions needed to maintain national security. If the intelligence process fails and our first line of defense becomes compromised or ineffective, the steps that would follow could involve surprise attacks, a "low-intensity conflict," a full-scale war, or an invasion. This is why it is critical that the "first line of defense" capability not be compromised. The intelligence process involves five steps that are highly formal and heavily scrutinized by oversight committees.[5]

1. *Planning and direction*: Management of the entire intelligence cycle, from identifying the need for data to delivering an intelligence product to a consumer.
2. *Collection*: Gathering of raw data from which finished intelligence is produced.
3. *Processing and exploitation*: The synthesis of raw data into a form usable by the intelligence analyst or other consumers.
4. *Analysis and production*: Integration, evaluation, and analysis of all available data, and the preparation of a variety of intelligence products.
5. *Dissemination*: Delivering the products to consumers who request them through categories of finished intelligence available to consumers.

The private sector could develop and model an "early-warning" capability based on similar concepts: the ability to have a program that looks at threats and how they would impact the company — and what options exist for dealing with identified threats. To some degree, this already happens in companies through risk management strategies, business intelligence, and competitive intelligence; however, the focus rarely includes the gathering and analysis of terrorism information — groups, methods, tactics, and so on. The focus tends to be how to protect assets, how to protect market share, and how to protect company secrets and trademarks.

The intelligence process steps involve activities that often warn us of threats before they become imminent — making them "early warnings" and "indicators" which then enable leaders and managers to make timely tactical decisions.[6] The U.S. Intelligence Community has two primary challenges: determining the capabilities that an opponent can muster, and fathoming the intentions of the opponent to use those capabilities against

---

[5] U.S. Intelligence Community, http://www.intelligence.gov/2-business.shtml.
[6] U.S. Intelligence Community, http://www.intelligence.gov/2-community.shtml.

us — the who, what, when, where, and how. As shown in Figure 2.2, this is an ongoing, round-the-clock process.

The keys to good U.S. intelligence are cooperative arrangements among the various U.S. agencies and bilateral and multilateral exchanges with friendly governments. But collection is only the beginning of a successful intelligence effort toward preparedness; more critical is how analysis turns data into useful information and then into an understanding about what opponents or the enemy is planning.[7] There are limitations and constraints, requiring the prioritizing of resources. When the Soviet military was no longer a threat, security and control of Russia's nuclear arsenal became a greater threat concern because of known accountability issues. Development of chemical and biological weapons by any nation or any group without a nation and the means to deliver them also are significant priorities. The farther away we get from the Cold War, the greater the

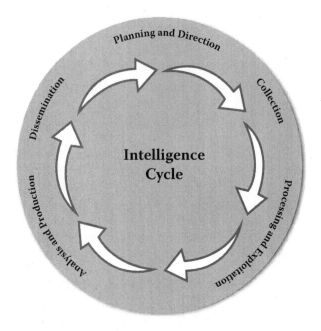

Figure 2.2 The Intelligence Cycle

---

[7] U.S. Intelligence Community, http://www.intelligence.gov/2-business.shtml.

possibility that nuclear, chemical, or biological materials will get into the wrong hands — or, worse, this may already be the case.[8]

Using these dangerous materials for attacks could be launched by nonstate terrorist groups or individuals. In contrast to countries, these groups operate much like an intelligence entity and are difficult to track and monitor.

TERRORISTS' OPERATIONAL METHODOLOGY

Modern-day terrorists linked to Al Qaeda or inspired by Al Qaeda follow a template for attacks. They learned their methods from the Al Qaeda manual, Web sites, or other "how-to manuals" that they circulate among themselves and on the Internet. Several decades ago, all of them were recruited and trained through face-to-face contact but only after being sponsored and vetted by someone in the group. Control was tight and centralized, and each one had a role to play in an attack. Today, there is flexibility. Many of them are loosely affiliated to Al Qaeda and trained through methods that make their detection difficult — through the Internet, extensive marketing campaigns, exchange of underground manuals, or face-to-face meetings in mosques, prisons, or any other gathering places where they can feel comfortable to plan and plot. Though a lot has changed in the way they are recruited, trained, and organized, there is no longer centralized, "top-down" control. Instead, Al Qaeda and its affiliate networks operate similar to a star network typology, as depicted in Figure 2.3, with affiliate groups and cells worldwide — each country may have its own *recruitment, training, support, planning, target selection, attack methods,* and *decision making authority.*

An example of a terrorist centralized command is the Hezbollah. It is a Lebanese umbrella organization of radical Islamic Shiite groups and organizations. It operates in a traditional structure of centralized command where activities and operations are controlled by the top leadership. Hezbollah also opposes the West, seeks to create a Muslim fundamentalist state modeled on Iran, and is a bitter foe of Israel. Hezbollah, whose name means "party of God," is a terrorist group believed to be responsible for nearly 179 attacks since 1982 that have killed more than 1,535 people, according to the Terrorism Knowledge Base.[9]

---

[8] U.S. Intelligence Community, http://www.intelligence.gov/2-business.shtml.
[9] MIPT Terrorism Knowledge Base, http://www.tkb.org/IncidentGroupModule.jsp.

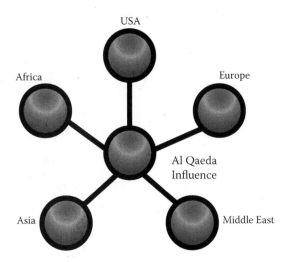

Figure 2.3 Al Qaeda Global Network Reach (Rendering by Jessica Farias, 2008. With permission.)

In general, these terrorist groups share expertise and revel in each other's success — often watching videos afterward and taking notice of what worked and what didn't. Most terrorist planning cycles include the following steps:

1. Broad target selection
2. Intelligence and surveillance
3. Specific target selection
4. Preattack surveillance and planning
5. Attack rehearsal
6. Actions on objective
7. Escape and evasion

Selection of a target for actual operational planning often includes the following factors[10]:

- Does success affect a larger audience than the immediate victim(s)?
- Will the target attract high-profile media attention?

---

[10] U.S. Army, *A Military Guide to Terrorism in the Twenty-First Century*, TRADOC G2 Handbook no. 1, 2007, http://www.maxwell.af.mil/au/awc/awcgate/army/guidterr/app_a.pdf, app. A.

- Does success make the desired statement to the correct target audience(s)?
- Is the effect consistent with the objectives of the group?
- Does the target provide an advantage to the group by demonstrating its capabilities?
- What are the costs versus benefits of conducting the operation?

These groups work in networks of compartmented cells to increase the success of the mission if an individual or cell is compromised. The groups are well-known to each other, but to prevent compromise of the network, only one member may know someone in another cell. Groups like Al Qaeda have been trained in military, special operations, and intelligence tactics. So while they may not operate under the banner of one nation, they employ tactics as if they did. One of Al Qaeda's trainers was Egyptian American Ali Mohammed. In Peter Bergen's "The Osama bin Laden I Know," Mohammed, a former U.S. Army green beret, explains what his training role was at a training camp in Afghanistan.[11]

> I was capable of making explosives from a pile of aspirins. The science is in knowing how to separate the acids and then mix them with other substances. I also learned how to make explosives with the mercury of thermometers. I even managed to make nitroglycerine, the handling of which is very dangerous. Very often as a result of copies of manuals intended for the American Green Berets! (U.S. Special Forces manuals provided to Al Qaeda by its main military trainer, the Egyptian-American Ali Mohammed, who was a U.S. army sergeant at Fort Bragg, South Carolina, the headquarters of the Green Berets between 1986 and 1989.) [I arrived in Afghanistan in March 1990 and left in] October '91. My group used my services on several occasions because I had a clean European passport and could therefore travel and contact certain people. I went to India, Egypt, Turkey as part of my work.[12]

Another recruit, in Peter Bergen's "Osama bin Laden," details the methodology about their surveillance training and working independently without knowing other cell members.[13]

> We started [surveying] small things, like bridge, like stadium, like normal places in which nobody is, and then in the second stage we went to

---

[11] Peter L. Bergen, *An Oral History of Al Qaeda's Leader: The Osama bin Laden I Know* (New York: Free Press, 2006).
[12] Peter Bergen, with copyright permission granted.
[13] Bergen, *An Oral History of Al Qaeda's Leader.*

police stations, for example, and in my group we were trained to go to Iranian consulate and Iranian cultural center in Peshawar.

The trainer [Ali Mohammed] explained how to make surveillance of targets and how to collect information about these targets. We trained how to use different cameras, especially small cameras, and how to take pictures in the guesthouse in which we were living. After taking pictures we go back to our place and we develop that film, using a machine, fixer and developer and water.[14]

During the training, Mohamed explained [to] us that this job is the first part of [the] military part. You collect the information about this certain target, and whenever you finish your work, our group, we just leave, we send our reports to our bosses and we leave. Those people they go through this report and they read all the information, and everything. Then they make some decisions how to attack that target, and then they send another group who supply everything so as to attack that target. Whenever that third group finish[es its] job, [it] has to leave. At the end the fourth group who can do the job come so as to do the final job.[15]

An early Al Qaeda recruit and Portuguese convert to Islam was Paulo Jose de Ameida Santos — he met bin Laden in 1991. After his training he was dispatched to Italy to assassinate Zahir Shah, the 77-year-old king of Afghanistan who lived in exile in Rome. It appears this was the first time Al Qaeda engaged in international terrorism.[16] Santos posed as a journalist, gained access to the highly guarded villa, and stabbed the king in the heart with a dagger, but a tin of cigarettes saved the king. He served 10 years for the attempted assassination. Santos confirms what has been known for years about working in cells with specific independent yet supporting missions[17]:

We had been divided into several groups. There was a technological group. I did a test to become part of that group, but the person in charge, who was an Egyptian electronics engineer, did not like what I did and failed me. They put me in the analysis group where I had to read all the newspapers and give my analysis about what to do.[18]

The accounts above support the fact that terrorist cells operate independently in an effort to not compromise each other or the plot itself. Therefore, if terrorist activities such as "surveillance of an attack target" are not discovered while they are in the planning stages, the attack

---

[14] Bergen, *An Oral History of Al Qaeda's Leader.*
[15] Bergen, *An Oral History of Al Qaeda's Leader.*
[16] Bergen, *An Oral History of Al Qaeda's Leader.*
[17] Bergen, *An Oral History of Al Qaeda's Leader.*
[18] Bergen, *An Oral History of Al Qaeda's Leader.*

is not likely to be preempted or stopped on the day it occurs because a different set of role players will be on the scene. There is no chance of recognizing them if their first time on the scene is "to carry out the bad deed." Nevertheless, the potential exists to gather "intelligence" or "critical information" from terrorists' reconnaissance activities if we are vigilant and lucky enough to detect them early on.

Sometimes the most reliable intelligence comes from clandestine operations — the secret undercover gathering of information. For these operations there are many aspects that need to work well together to be successful, and if the capability does not exist, it can take several years to create the capability. Where an indigenous capability is either inadequate or nonexistent, intelligence sharing with friendly governments that might have a capability becomes imperative but dangerous. We never know to what extent trust exists or whether the information being provided to the United States has been effectively vetted, but in the absence of any other reliable capability, the United States may have to consider this option.

Because we are dealing with terrorist threats in a way that we have never had to before, constant education is critical. The terror networks we are dealing with can be highly organized and centralized, or can be highly decentralized — but the networks are well connected across many world regions. Sometimes critical intelligence comes from investigative journalism. In Steve Emerson's *American Jihad: The Terrorists Living among Us*,[19] a picture emerges on just what kind of threat Ali Mohammed was. He volunteered to serve as an FBI source to report on illegal activities of cross-border Mexicans to move the focus away from his "terrorism role." By working for the FBI, he was insulated and protected from any scrutiny from other agencies. He also tried to serve as a CIA source at the same time but was not successful. Unbeknownst to the FBI, the man who was at one time responsible for moving bin Laden from Afghanistan to Sudan and setting up training camps in New Jersey and Connecticut was using them while operating as their source.

LIMITATIONS OF EARLY WARNINGS

When threat warnings surface, they are almost always broad in nature — not enough to identify where the blow will be or what, "if anything," can be done

---

[19] Steven Emerson, *American Jihad: The Terrorists Living among Us* (New York: Free Press, 2002).

to prevent it.[20] The sources that report them sometimes cannot be verified because of various limitations — intelligence and law enforcement investigators are not authorized to investigate without cause, or the source has not been vetted. In nearly all investigations that followed terrorist attacks, information has always surfaced indicating that warnings of the attacks were issued but were too broad to act on. This happened with the 9/11 attacks,[21] the Khobar Towers attack of 1996,[22] and the 2000 USS *Cole* attack.[23]

Broad threats cannot be analyzed to any degree of success to provide details about a specific time and location of an attack. What we can count on with absolute certainty is that regardless of which government, law enforcement, or intelligence agencies announce or make mention of a terrorist threat warning, they will always receive criticism for the manner in which they did it. This is unfortunate because it is a "no-win" situation. If they make an announcement based on limited details on hand, they get criticized for not providing enough details. If they do not make an announcement because the information is too sketchy to be of value, they will get criticized for not sharing it publicly.

"They are overreacting" is what critics say about the Government if no terrorist attack is witnessed after an alert or warning has been shared with the public. This occurred in the summer of 2007, when Secretary of Homeland Security Michael Chertoff announced that he had a "gut feeling" that terrorists were planning to attack the United States in the summer.[24] Reporters thought it was an odd statement. To his credit, the truth about most terrorist attacks is that when people notice that something is wrong or is out of place, their stomachs will always tell them before their brains do. This is true even of people who apparently have no intuitive or instinctive abilities whatsoever. This is what people who have witnessed precursors to disasters have said in the post incident debriefings. Experts say that the funny feeling in the pit of the stomach or the feeling of the hairs standing on the back of the neck is the body's way of telling us that

---

[20] National Commission on Terrorist Attacks (hereafter, 9/11 Commission), *Final Report of the National Commission on Terrorist Attacks upon the United States* (hereafter, *9/11 Commission Report*), 2004, http://www.gpoaccess.gov/911/pdf/sec11.pdf (accessed March 2008).

[21] 9/11 Commission, *9/11 Commission Report*, 347.

[22] Rebecca Grant, "Khobar Towers," *Air Force Magazine Online* 81, no. 6 (June 1998): http://www.afa.org/magazine/june1998/0698khobar.asp (accessed February 2008).

[23] CargoLaw.com, "USS Cole Attack," http://www.cargolaw.com/2000nightmare_cole.html#disaster.

[24] ABC News, "Chertoff Explains 'Gut Feeling' about Terror Attack," http://abcnews.go.com/WN/LegalCenter/story?id=3367404 (accessed March 23, 2008).

something is very wrong.[25] The body gets a shot of adrenaline because the brain determines that there is danger. The subconscious mind, which operates 10 times faster than the conscious mind, picks up on signals of danger that the conscious mind has not yet processed. The queasy stomach feeling is simply the body's first reaction to adrenaline entering the bloodstream. At that time, the digestive system shuts down to allow more blood to flow to the muscles so that you can take the physical actions needed to survive if you have to bolt out of there very fast. Apparently, there is nothing magical about this phenomenon. It is not paranoia or imagined fear. It is real, and survival depends on it.

"The threats are not specific enough," say private sector businesses about DHS threat information provided through critical infrastructure information-sharing networks. Before the USS *Cole*, Khobar Towers, and 9/11 attacks took place, general warnings were circulated within the intelligence community in the United States, and unilaterally between the United States and allied nations, but nothing specified a date, time, or location.

No matter how significant the "threat warning" or how skilled the intelligence analysts are — threat warnings issued did not prevent the attacks, and here are some reasons:

- People suspend belief and imagination.
- People generally don't think "it" will happen to them.
- The warning is too ominous to take specific action to prevent it.
- The warning gives a false sense of control.

Before the Twin Towers were attacked, engineers, builders, and tenants strongly believed that nothing could bring the Twin Towers down — not wind, not airplanes, not fire, not earthquakes. "The effect of a bomb on the Twin Towers was likened to that of a flea on one's leg.[26] The general consensus was that those buildings were indestructible. They were built to withstand almost anything. To try to blow these buildings up was seen as pure folly."[27] The size of the bomb required would be so conspicuous, they would never be able to smuggle it in. They could not possibly imagine that the bomb would come from the air. The prevalent mindset never allowed any other thought process to dominate — such as the possibility of another attack.

---

[25] Scott Flint, "Learn to Trust That 'Gut-Feeling': It Just Might Save Your Life,:" http://www.selfgrowth.com/articles/Flint2.html (accessed March 23, 2008).

[26] Edward Jerlin, "My Twin Towers Experience," http://www.geocities.com/ejerlin/ (accessed March 23, 2008).

[27] Jerlin, "My Twin Towers Experience."

CREATING YOUR OWN THREAT-WARNING CAPABILITIES

Owners and operators of critical infrastructures need to adopt similar practices as the national security–level resources to establish their own methods for "first line of defense" capabilities. They need to develop their own methods of "information collection" but not use the same descriptors as the intelligence agencies. They must develop good analytical and threat assessment capabilities. Seeing threats on a closed-circuit television (CCTV) monitor does not qualify as "early warning." If you are seeing a terrorist threat on your monitor — it is already too late to move your assets elsewhere, and now you have to go into "react" mode.

Establishing effective "information" gathering and analysis and using appropriate "threat assessment" methodologies to meet Homeland Security objectives that mimic those of "national security" can be challenging for the private sector. They are not methods that would ordinarily be performed because they are not within the mission or focus of the private sector. Knowing where to start to mimic those practices may be difficult. Generally, when the private sector "collects information," it is for the purposes of protecting its market share or trade secrets from competitors — not to determine which country or terrorist organization is interested in spying against them or putting them on a terrorist target list. Private sector assessments, sometimes performed by human resources, are usually aimed at identifying and mitigating potential workplace violence by disgruntled employees. The scale of damage that an employee can inflict rarely eclipses that which can be inflicted by Al Qaeda- or Osama bin Laden-inspired terrorists. So, they should rethink who performs them.

In order to establish analytical practices aligned with National Security and Homeland Security objectives, the private sector can consider adopting and adapting what is already in use at the national level. Through checklists, templates, and repetition of new practices, a new method of collecting and assessing information would soon become second nature. At first, it will seem difficult because the tasks that need to be performed will feel awkward. Perhaps it will require using skills or behaviors (legal and ethical) that stretch people out of their comfort zone. But it must be done because the federal government cannot carry the load of terrorism prevention alone. Additionally, the information provided through private sector–DHS partnerships will be too strategic to drive private sector decisions about capital expenditures for security that may — or may not — be needed.

In the threat assessment process of risk management, all information must be brought together to determine if there are imminent threats or just general broad threats. The analysis must determine if the threats are realistic and if they are directed at the organization. Fundamentally, we should all understand how threats work, what constitutes a threat, and how to address them at work and at home. At the organizational level, all organizations need to periodically perform threat assessments. If not, they risk operating in the blind, so to speak — and being completely surprised when an attack breaks out in their work environment. Threat assessment processes have to be bulletproof through quality information gathering and comprehensive threat analysis. People best suited for this endeavor tend to come from security, intelligence, and law enforcement professions. They have a keen sense of threats and a strong ability to naturally perform functions related to threat analysis — it is almost second nature to them.

PAINFUL LESSON: THE USS *COLE* ATTACK

The boat that attacked the USS *Cole* on October 12, 2000, in the Yemen harbor of Aden appeared ordinary. The two guys on the boat appeared friendly. Therefore, they aroused no immediate suspicion upon sight. The USS *Cole* intended to get in and out as quickly as possible when it went into the Yemen harbor to fuel. Given that no dates or specific locations came with the warning they had been informed of, that was the only logical precaution they could seem to exercise.

This attack is difficult to recall because it was not an attack against any ordinary Navy ship — it was one of the U.S. Navy's guided missile destroyers, and the resources needed for recovery were intensive. Imagine the scene — the USS *Cole*, a 505-foot destroyer, suffers damage — a 40-foot by 40-foot hole from the blast to the ship's hull, killing 17 sailors and injuring 39.[28] The first naval ship to arrive on the scene to assist the *Cole* was the Royal Navy Type 23 frigate, HMS *Marlborough*, which had full medical and damage control teams on board. The first U.S. military support to arrive was a small group of U.S. Marines from the IMCSF Company, Bahrain. Assistance also came from a U.S. Marine platoon with the 2nd Fleet Antiterrorism Security Team Company (FAST), based out of Yorktown, Virginia. The Marines from 4th Platoon, 2nd FAST arrived on October 13

---

[28] Associated Press and Reuters, *U.S. Official Sees Similarities between USS Cole Blast and Embassy Attacks*, http://archives.cnn.com/2000/US/10/23/uss.cole.01/ (accessed March 23, 2008).

from a security mission in Doha, Qatar.[29] The FAST platoon secured the *Cole*. The USS *Donald Cook* and USS *Hawes* arrived that afternoon, providing repair and logistical support. The *Catawba, Camden, Anchorage, Duluth,* and *Tarawa* arrived some days later, providing watch relief crews, harbor security, damage control equipment, billeting, and food service for the crew of the *Cole*. LCU 1666 provided daily runs from the *Tarawa* with hot food and supplies and ferrying personnel to and from all other naval vessels supporting the *Cole*.

Two weeks before the attack, a popular satellite TV channel in Qatar broadcast an ominous message from Osama bin Laden. The broadcast shows Osama bin Laden and his top lieutenant, Ayman al-Zawahiri. Zawahari warned that it was time to "take action" against the "iniquitous and faithless" U.S. forces in Yemen, Egypt, and Saudi Arabia. Osama bin Laden looked on approvingly.[30] The Navy was criticized for possibly overlooking important information that could have foiled the attack that killed 17 American sailors. Officials always contended that the general warning provided to the United States of a possible attack on an American warship prior to the USS *Cole* attack lacked detail and did not specify the country in which to expect the attack, and therefore could not be acted on — except to exercise precautions, fuel quickly, and get out of there as fast as possible.

Since the early 1990s, there have been broadcasts of terrorist plans to attack the United States from bin Laden and other groups. In 2005, the British government warned that the United States could potenitally see its own share of surprise attacks such as those carried out in London and Spain. British citizens were shocked that their own citizens — and even doctors — were attacking them, and thought the United States had time and should take action to increase efforts to deter such attacks.

Let's stop for a moment to ponder a question. Has any U.S. company or government agency ever taken Osama bin Laden's or any terrorist groups' messages to heart and successfully predicted where and when an attack would occur to be able to preempt it? Can the private sector act on the strategic information provided by DHS through "information-sharing partnerships" currently in place? The information provided by DHS at quarterly or annual meetings or through the DHS private sector pipeline is no different than warnings provided to the U.S. government by other nations or sources, such as the USS *Cole* warnings.

---

[29] Wikipedia, "USS Cole Bombing," http://en.wikipedia.org/wiki/.
[30] Wikipedia, "USS Cole Bombing."

In 2004, targeting activities revealed that terrorists had conducted surveillance for years on the International Monetary Fund, the Prudential Building, the New York Stock Exchange, as well as facilities in Las Vegas, Nevada. The discovery of these activities would then imply that those facilities have received a warning.

IMPLICATIONS OF NOT UNDERSTANDING THREATS

The implications of not understanding threats can produce grave consequences. Organizations could miss threats when the threats are heading straight for them and thus not get a chance to respond because the threat could be deadly and instantaneous. Other implications include the following:

- Failure to properly invest in the right security technology and preparedness training.
- Implementing insufficient security measures to protect assets.
- Not knowing how to respond to threats when they emerge.
- Not being able to recover, and being put out of business for good.

If the organization is high on the critical infrastructure list of services that the public depends on, it could have an adverse impact on the economy and society to such a degree that such recovery is not possible.

One of the critical gaps of preparedness is that no one seems to be performing trend analysis from the findings of previous attacks to determine what clues were missed — in the way of a threat or early warning. In 2005, many accounts were reported about suspicious activities in major U.S. cities' metro systems where "men" were observed taking covert photography. In one incident, four men who appeared to be Middle Eastern were caught taking pictures of the undercarriage of a metro train by a metro maintenance employee. When asked what they were doing, they left the scene in a hurry. The men appeared to be Middle Eastern but could easily have been Hispanic or any other race. The "look" is not a reliable way to describe or profile a suspicious person. We are a society of poor and faulty methods of identification. Our powers of observation are not reliable — this is based on the outcome of many witnesses identifying the wrong suspects in lineups and the high number of wrongly accused people who erroneously get sent to prison for someone else's crime.

In the same city in 2005, on a different metro line, a man who appeared to be Middle Eastern held a small camera at his waist in a covert manner and snapped many photos of the tracks and the scenery behind the train as the train was in motion. The individual was not interrupted; the witness stayed on the train until the individual got off the train. The witness rode with the individual from the start of the line to the end of the line. The man appeared nervous and looked around often to see if anyone had noticed him taking photos. The witness reported that he felt "a sick feeling in his stomach and reported that the hair on the back of his neck stood up," but remained calm, and when he exited he went straight to the nearest law enforcement officer on site at the station. The information was not well received, and the individual had to make several attempts to file a report on this activity. Thus, it would appear that in this particular city, certain law enforcement officers are in denial and do not have the capacity or the cognitive processes to perform critical analysis that yields information of value to make strategic decisions or possibly qualify as early warnings.

It would have been invaluable to replay CCTV video in an attempt to identify the people involved and properly investigate the matter — as any good law enforcement officer would do in a "terrorist interdiction investigation." The two events described above happened within a month of the London train bombings of 2005, yet it was quite difficult for the witnesses to file law enforcement reports on these incidents. It would possibly have pointed to an "indicator" of a terrorist intelligence cell gathering information for an attack; a probe — testing our security and reactions; or a dry run.

This could be the link to prevent a possible future attack, but we will never know such things until after the fact-finding of an attack. The other possibility was that many networks in the world were sharing the same plot and racing against each other to see who would successfully attack first — much like hackers who are prideful of their technical abilities and brag to others. There were two attacks in progress in London at the time of their transit attack. The second one did not succeed because the bomb-making techniques were sloppy, but the procedures for carrying out the attacks were identical. Why would this be the case — unless the two were plotting unbeknownst to each other, and the second group saw no reason to abort their attack? The other possibility of why activity was occurring in the American city described above is that it was for the purposes of probing to test security responses and citizen awareness, or a possible dry run for an imminent attack that was aborted.

LESSON LEARNED: FIRST WORLD TRADE CENTER ATTACK, 1993

Ramzi Yousef, arrested for the 1993 attack of the World Trade Center, was also discovered to be linked to another terrorist plot in the Philippines. The plot was uncovered in January 1995, when a fire broke out in his apartment. The plot called for blowing up a dozen U.S. airliners over the Far East as part of an operation he called *Project Bojinka*. When 9/11 occurred, everyone was shocked and in total disbelief that four U.S. airliners were flown into buildings by men willing to follow an order and fly the planes to destination "death."

If everyone had fundamental education and our leaders and management were not in denial that such an event could ever occur, we would not have been extremely surprised about the method in which the airplanes were used on 9/11. This was not the first time a plane was considered for a terrorist attack, nor was it the first time a plane was hijacked in America.

LESSON LEARNED: FIRST AMERICAN HIJACKING, 1961

On August 1, 1961, a 40-year-old American male hijacked a commercial airliner at Chico Municipal Airport, Butte County, California. Armed with a switchblade and a Colt 2-inch 6-shot blue steel revolver, he stormed his way into the plane. A ticket agent tried to stop him from getting on the airplane without a ticket. "This is my ticket," the man said, pulling out his gun and shooting the ticket agent in the back. He then fired a shot at a stewardess and missed. Next he announced that he would begin killing the passengers unless the pilot did as he said. "You are first," he said, as he turned the gun on a nearby seated passenger and fired. Again, he missed. He then headed for the cockpit. He stood over the pilot and copilot as they taxied the plane onto the runway but they told him the plane could not leave until the cockpit door was closed. Through confusion or anger (or both), the man shot the pilot in the head. The copilot knocked the gun from his hand, then the man pulled out a knife but was quickly overpowered by three passengers. Reportedly, no one died in the attack. He had been chased in a high-speed pursuit by police prior to arriving at the airport. He was very late and would've missed the plane, but the plane was very late in departing. The man only had a gun, a knife, and a car, and he was trying to get home to his wife after working away from home. It is not known why he did not consider other, less drastic measures. It appears he had been inspired by recent news accounts of passenger planes in other countries that had been hijacked to Cuba.

1. Department of Homeland Security: Manage the Nation's overall CI/KR protection framework and oversee NIPP development and implementation.

2. Sector-Specific Agencies: Implement the NIPP framework and guidance as tailored to the specific characteristics and risk landscapes of each of the CI/KR sectors designated in HSPD-7.

3. Other Federal Departments, Agencies, and Offices: Implemented specific CI/KR protection roles designated in HSPD-7 or other relevant statutes, executive orders, and policy directives.

4. State, Local, and Tribal Governments: Develop and implement a CI/KR protection program as a component of their overarching homeland security programs.

5. Regional Partners: Use partnerships that cross jurisdictional and sector boundaries to address CI/KR protection within a defined geographical area.

6. Boards, Commissions, Authorities, Councils, and Other Entities: Perform regulatory, advisory, policy, or business oversight functions related to various aspects of CI/KR operations and protection within and across sectors and jurisdictions.

7. Private Sector Owners and Operators: Undertake CI/KR protection, restoration, coordination, and cooperation activities, and provide advice, recommendations, and subject matter expertise the the Federal Government.

8. Homeland Security Advisory Councils: Provide advice, recommendations, and expertise to the government regarding protection policy and activities.

9. Academia and Research Centers: Provide CK/KR protection subject matter expertise, independent analysis, research and development (R&D) and educational programs.

Figure 2.4 Homeland Security Partners

HOMELAND SECURITY ROLES AND MISCONCEPTIONS

The National Infrastructure Protection Plan (NIPP) states that private sector owners and operators of critical infrastructures are primary security partners of the nation's critical infrastructure protection framework, as highlighted in Figure 2.4. These security partners are responsible for undertaking "CI/KR protection, restoration, coordination, and cooperation activities, and providing advice, recommendations, and subject matter expertise to the Federal Government" for terrorism preparedness.[31]

There are many myths regarding homeland security roles and responsibilities. My interaction with Federal Government personnel and private sector security partners across the nation over the last 5 years has revealed that much of the private sector is not fully aware of their homeland security responsibilities or their linkage to the nation's critical infrastructures. This creates a dangerous environment filled with ambiguities and assumptions on the part of both Government and the private sector. The Government truly believes that the private sector understands their role and envisions that all necessary steps for terrorism preparedness are being carried out. The private sector hears what the Federal Government — DHS, in particular — is saying about "needs" but is not actively listening and does not seem to understand how critical a piece they are to the nation's overall preparedness. On the periphery it appears that the private sector has measures for preparedness, but they tend to be "ad hoc" and generally are not enough to make the organizations compliant with all existing DHS mandates — including the NIPP. Most private sector organizations linked to critical infrastructures do not even recognize that they are mandated to "do something" in the way of protection and preparedness. That "something" just seems to elude them.

Protection and preparedness against terrorism also require effective measures to response, resiliency, and recovery — through both Business Continuity Plans (BCP) and security plans. It has been interesting to hear the views of private and public sector individuals at security conferences when asked how they would respond to terrorist attacks. Members of the private sector (financial, energy, ports, airports, commercial buildings, water, and transportation) often say that if they were to experience a terrorist attack, their security guards would know how to respond and they would rely heavily on their guards. The idea of prevention is rarely mentioned and does not seem to be a thought that enters their minds.

Security guards working at private sector facilities often say that responding to or stopping an attack is not within their scope of work, nor are they trained for it. They say that under such circumstances, they would call law enforcement because law enforcement is trained to respond. Several law enforcement officers I have spoken with over the years have often said that terrorism is just another crime to respond to in

---

[31] Department of Homeland Security, *National Infrastructure Protection Plan (NIPP)* (Washington, D.C.: Department of Homeland Security, 2006) p. 2.

addition to all other crimes within their purview. They do not have the resources to focus exclusively on terrorism or the resources to specialize in antiterrorism tactics. They expect that guard forces and facility managers would already be at the scene of the attack and would have to serve as first responders until law enforcement and emergency responders arrive to assist. Depending on how widespread the attack is or the impact of the attack, this could take a while. The misconceptions and false expectations that result from these views can be attributed to one theory: there is a large communication gap between the public and private sectors — as large as the one between modern-day western nations fighting the Stone Age mentalities of the Jihad extremists.

SHARING INFORMATION

With a strong commitment to improving communications between the private sector and public sector — one of the things that has not been addressed by law enforcement is the ability to access a databank of known threats and conduct trend analysis. Various public and private sector organizations have their own internal logs of incidents and events. What would be useful for the owners and operators of the 17 critical infrastructures would be for them to have an ability to look through the window of other infrastructures' incidents and learn about attempted attacks, probing, or surveillance — and share information, what a concept! It would cue them that the same suspicious activities may be going on at other like facilities or even in the local area. Threats can change overnight. That's why threat gathering, analysis, assessment, countermeasures, and reviews need to be continuously ongoing. The goal is to be able to see the threats before they become imminent, actively engaged against your facility, or inside your building creating catastrophe.

One area that the private and public sectors share in common is the inability to perceive true threats to the company or organization. In 2000, an employee of a public sector company was reportedly caught breaching network security and accessing unauthorized files. The event took everyone by surprise because the individual held the highest government clearances and had undergone extensive background screening and polygraphs. For years, the individual had been entrusted with the nation's top secrets in a position where he focused on external threats.

Similarly, a Fortune 100 company overlooked an external threat because it was lulled into a sense of security due to its high rate of happy employees. As such, there was no urgency to incorporate a recommended risk mitigation measure for workplace violence. Just 3 weeks after the recommendation, workers were held hostage by an outsider, someone who had previously been turned down for employment.

It is not so important to ask why critical infrastructures are targets or when the next attack will occur. The answer to "why" can be best answered when one develops a deep understanding of religious conflicts and world politics. The answer to "when" is in accordance with the terrorist's time table — not ours. The question to focus on is "how." How will we detect and respond, or how can we be best prepared? Having no plan in place or no sense of potential threats puts facility owners in a vulnerable position on so many levels. They may find that they are in noncompliance with Homeland Security mandates. They may find that they are spending more than is necessary on security. Last, implemented solutions may not be designed to do what the owners need in order to mitigate risks. Without a focused look, owners could end up doing a lot of dangerous guessing and wasteful spending.

Department of Homeland Security leaders across the nation simply trust that the private sector will properly use the NIPP to develop plans and put compliance measures in place. Unless a disastrous incident occurs, it is likely that no one will come to inspect those plans. If an incident occurs, however, a facility owner's plan could end up being scrutinized as material evidence in a court of law. Even worse, what about the lives that were at stake or the ones that were lost? Therefore, it is prudent to comply with the NIPP and have a plan that has been diligently prepared.

THREAT TRENDS

It helps to see what others are experiencing in their operating environments. It may clue us to check our activities for anything similar internally. Sometimes, this is the best warning you can get — you see it happen to someone else, and then you find that it was an imminent threat waiting to happen to you. Here are some identified threats in different operating environments in 2008:

Employees born after 1980 pose a great threat to workplace technology, according to a Symantec study. The millennial generation has a freer attitude toward using the Web at work, frequenting social-networking sites, or downloading software onto company computers — 75 percent admitted adding personal applications to their office computers. With baby boomers nearing retirement, the millennial generation is the future of controlling the information technology sector and — somewhere down the road — our IT critical infrastructures.[32]

Of the National Institutes of Health's (NIH) patient records, 2,500 have been stolen, and now NIH has to answer to legislators on why it waited nearly 1 year to inform 2,500 patients that their unencrypted medical data were in a laptop that was stolen from the locked trunk of a researcher's vehicle.[33]

Hackers target small businesses with e-commerce capabilities, but many of these businesses do not have the same protections in place as large corporations. Almost 60 percent of small company managers do not believe they need a plan to secure business data. Because cyber-criminals constantly change their tactics, experts recommend that small businesses and others invest in a security officer within the IT department or hire a consultant with around-the-clock availability.[34]

Terrorists continue to fund activities, despite the best counterterrorism efforts of the United States. In the years since September 11, 2001, support from other countries has waned, and experts say some of the United States' biggest allies now lack the political will to continue to follow money trails. Even in instances when large sums of money trade hands among Al Qaeda sympathizers, intelligence experts cannot easily differentiate legitimate transactions from nefarious ones. A 2008 report by the Paris-based Financial Action Task Force said the international community must change its tactics to fight money laundering and terrorist financing, but U.S. Department of Defense officials admit that U.S. agencies are mired in infighting and have not given due diligence to cooperation.[35]

Politicians want Internet Service Providers (ISPs) to crack down on online terror sites, but this is hard without restricting free speech. "Those

---

[32] B. R. Ballenstedt, "Younger Employees Present Challenge to Information Security, Study Shows," http://govexec.com/story_page.cfm?articleid=39569&dcn=todaysnews (accessed March 25, 2008).

[33] Associated Press, "US Airways Pilot's Gun Accidentally Goes off on Plane," 2008, http://www.startribune.com/nation/16964491.html (accessed March 25, 2008); and Reuters, http://www.reuters.com/article/domesticNews/idUSN2428054820080324?feedType=RSS &feedName=domesticNews, March 24, 2008 (accessed March 25, 2008).

[34] J. E. Gaskin, "Small Business Technology: Alert Hackers Target Small Businesses," *Network World Online*, 2007, http://www.networkworld.com/newsletters/sbt/2007/0730smbtech1.html?page=1.

[35] Josh Meyer, "Terrorism Money Is Still Flowing," *Los Angeles Times*, March 24, 2008, p. A1.

who think that we can stop online terrorism by removal of Web sites are either naive or ignorant about cyberspace and its limitations for interference," says Haifa University professor Gabriel Weimann. Multilateral agreement on fighting Web terror is lacking because of legal ambiguities, such as who ultimately has authority over the determination of terrorist sites. ISPs' efforts to develop filter and block technologies of malevolent parties are being met by Jihadists' improvement of work-around strategies.[36]

Several paintings stolen from the Isabella Stewart Gardner Museum in Boston over a year ago. The Museum is now receiving tips as a result of a new Web site publicizing data about the thefts and asking individuals to provide comments and clues. Also, a $5 million reward was available for the return of all the paintings in good condition — tips were attributed to the World Wide Web's power to help solve the thefts.[37]

CONCLUSION

Misreading threats or being oblivious to them in this day and age is not just risky business but also simply irresponsible work behavior. Assessing threats is an essential part of managing risk. When the threat posture of an organization is known, it is possible to choose how much risk to take on. Risk can then be mitigated, eliminated, transferred, or managed. Taking proactive measures to mitigate risk generally results in regulatory compliance, reduced risk exposure, reduced liability, and stakeholder confidence in the organization's response measures. A confident workforce is likely to respond successfully and minimize the consequences of a terrorist attack because people know exactly what to do and are able to go into response mode without freezing. On the other hand, an organization whose workforce has never exercised its response plan, has not been trained or educated in security and threat identification or is unaware of the response procedures, and has never taken proactive steps to understand threats and manage such risks would have a high probability of failed outcomes.

---

[36] Greg Goth, "Terror on the Internet: A Complex Issue, and Getting Harder," *IEEE Distributed Systems Online* 9, no. 3 (March 2008).

[37] T. Mashberg, "Gardner Getting New Tips in Search for Stolen Art," *Boston Herald*, March 18, 2008, 12.

3

Threat, Vulnerability, and Risk Components

No one should be surprised when Osama bin Laden and al Qaeda deto-
nate a weapon of mass destruction in the United States. I don't believe in
inevitability. But I think it's pretty close to being inevitable.

Michael Scheuer

OVERVIEW

Industry has many roles in Homeland Security. One of the major roles it
plays is researching, developing, and implementing technology solutions
to help protect our nation's infrastructures.

Industry also has another role — ensuring that it has protective
measures in place to protect against terrorist attacks at their facilities —
they comprise an important component of the Department of Homeland
Security's (DHS) plan — they are critical. DHS plays a couple of roles in
its interaction with industry. It is a partner to industry, but sometimes it
assumes an authoritarian role — expecting industry to comply with its
mandates. DHS has rallied the best resources in the country to establish
all the programs in place in the short time that it has been in existence — it
has been a daunting and overwhelming task, but the work and quality of
the work are high. For the most part, it does assume a role of collaboration
— more than the other role. DHS has many industry partners working in

partnership to develop standards and guidelines. Many industries have developed their own standards and guidelines, which may be similar to DHS's or perhaps even exceed DHS requirements. ASIS is working to promote education, standards, procedures, and much more to assist industry in their homeland security role. ASIS International (also known as ASIS) is the largest organization for security professionals, with more than 35,000 members worldwide. Founded in 1955, ASIS is dedicated to increasing the effectiveness and productivity of security professionals by developing educational programs and materials that address broad security interests, such as the ASIS Annual Seminar and Exhibits, as well as specific security topics. ASIS also advocates the role and value of the security management profession to business, the media, governmental entities, and the public. By providing members and the security community with access to a full range of programs and services, and by publishing the industry's number one magazine — *Security Management* — ASIS leads the way for advanced and improved security performance.[1]

Chapter 2 was about essential factors on threat. This chapter is about identifying threats, methods for identifying threats, methods of identifying vulnerabilities, and determining risk and countermeasures through three models. This chapter is designed for organizations that have very little in place for preparedness and for audiences that require security education related to DHS risk management and critical infrastructure and key resources (CI/KR) protection requirements. With today's threats, it is clear that tactical and strategic approaches are needed to address our nation's threats — but mainly those that will help protect and secure critical infrastructures from terrorism threats. There is an abundance of information and resources to assist industry on preparedness — there is no possibility of getting just one set of simplified instructions. In this book, I have attempted to chart a path for understanding threats, helping industry see their threats, helping identify vulnerabilities — and then taking measures to secure assets to a level of preparedness and compliance using as many simplified and proven approaches as possible. You don't have years to collect all the resources and get all the certifications that would be nice to have, but if you just need to launch your protective efforts, this book will help you achieve your objectives.

Because threats are in a constant state of change, it is difficult to keep up with security measures to prevent, detect, and respond to all of them — or is it? Security measures that are in place and working effectively today

---

[1] ASIS, "About ASIS," http://www.asisonline.org/about/history/index.xml.

may no longer be appropriate 6 months from now. By assessing and updating the threat picture, an organization can determine if it is investing enough and focusing sufficient resources to keep up with the threats. The full extent of vulnerabilities cannot be known without a regular snapshot of the threat environment to assist in identifying the risk exposure.

Threats and vulnerability, among other elements, determine the level of risk exposure organizations face. The process of determining threats and vulnerabilities should be performed periodically because the environment is fluid and constantly changing. After the threats and vulnerabilities are reviewed, measures and countermeasures should be considered and implemented. Before that step is taken, though, current measures need to be reviewed to see if they are adequate and effective against newly discovered threat activity.

This process is a team process and not to be performed by one or two individuals, even though this is usually the most common way it is done by organizations today. The importance of using members with different abilities in the organization to form the team that performs threat, vulnerability, and risk assessments is discussed in more detail in Chapter 7 ("Human Factors and Team Dynamics").

Risk management is needed to properly protect critical infrastructures against terrorism — as DHS requires and expects — and warrants that your risk management efforts include business continuity, IT, security, and emergency services risk managers. Then, collectively determine the best courses of action for solutions to respond to the threats. By involving these other resources, the organization's moves begin to demonstrate that it can execute a fully integrated approach that includes physical security, information systems security, and emergency response, which is absolutely necessary and critical.

Threats have many dimensions and aspects that are important, and once threats are identified they need to be weighed against known vulnerabilities so that risk can be determined and risk management decisions can be made.

Models for risk analysis, risk management, and risk economic assessment are available through DHS, Homeland Security Centers of Excellence (established in 2003), and private industry. DHS has invested heavily in developing frameworks to unify protective and preparedness measures for public and private sector users and for individual consumers. It has not, however, done a good job of educating the end users on the wealth of resources available through DHS. For example, the Critical Infrastructure Partnership Advisory Council (CIPAC) represents a partnership between government and CI/KR owners and operators and provides a forum in which they can engage in a broad spectrum of activities to support and coordinate critical infrastructure protection.[2] A related program exists to enable information-sharing efforts, but it is not well publicized, and private sector audiences have not been given an understanding of how their information will be protected once they share it or report it. DHS's Homeland Security Centers of Excellence bring together leading experts and researchers to conduct multidisciplinary research and education for homeland security solutions. The University of Southern California evaluates the risks, costs, and consequences of terrorism, and guides economically viable investments in countermeasures that will make our nation safer and more secure. The research that they conduct is valuable and will be useful for the next generation of Homeland Security leaders, but it is not clear how current owners and operators of critical infrastructures could tap into the research material to help transition it to a user level, and DHS has not advised infrastructure owners on how they can access the research. In addition to the research efforts, the Homeland Security Centers of Excellence also offer degrees in homeland security programs.

The academic and research center communities play an important role in enabling national-level CI/KR protection and implementation of the National Infrastructure Protection Plan (NIPP), including the following[3]:

- Establishing centers of excellence (i.e., university-based partnerships or federally funded R&D centers) to provide independent analysis of CI/KR protection issues.
- Supporting the research, development, testing, evaluation, and deployment of CI/KR protection technologies.
- Analyzing, developing, and sharing best practices related to CI/KR protection efforts.
- Researching and providing innovative thinking and perspectives on threats and the behavioral aspects of terrorism.
- Preparing or disseminating guidelines, courses, and descriptions of best practices for physical security and cyber-security.
- Developing and providing suitable security risk analysis and risk management courses for CI/KR protection professionals.

---

[2] Department of Homeland Security, http://www.dhs.gov/xprevprot/committees/.
[3] Department of Homeland Security, http://www.dhs.gov.

- Conducting research to identify new technologies and analytical methods that can be applied by security partners to support NIPP efforts.

DHS RISK MODEL AND NATIONAL INFRASTRUCTURE PROTECTION PLAN (NIPP)

One of the best models for risk management and the one that the private sector should use if they are owners and operators of critical infrastructure is a framework provided by DHS, the NIPP. The NIPP is part of DHS's overall protection effort to ensure a steady state of protection within and across all sectors. This DHS model includes a step for the "consequences" — the negative effects on public health and safety, the economy, public confidence in institutions, and the functioning of government, both direct and indirect.

The private sector often makes decisions about security investments based on (1) what is known about the risk environment, and (2) what is economically justifiable and sustainable in a competitive marketplace or in an environment of limited resources. Having said that, the private sector probably already uses processes from its business continuity and emergency-planning processes to identify what type of security expenditures need to be made and have been made over time — and what it will need to do to be in compliance with government regulations. DHS will not offer any expenditure and budgeting advice for Homeland Security preparedness. The private sector will have to determine if the security measures and technology are sufficient to protect their critical assets, and it will have to perform its own cost-benefit analysis and determine what — if any — return on investment can be expected. At any rate, it can

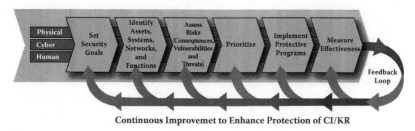

Continuous Improvemet to Enhance Protection of CI/KR

Figure 3.1 Department of Homeland Security (DHS) Threat Model

continue to use successful risk assessment practices as long as they meet the standards and requirements of the NIPP.

DHS offers the model (Figure 3.1) with detailed instructions for performing all the steps that it feels are warranted in the effort to assess and control risks to critical infrastructures. To properly apply the model would require reading the 196-page NIPP document, whose table of contents has been included in this book as Appendix A, "National Infrastructure Protection Plan Table of Contents."

The DHS risk management framework can be applied on an asset, system, network, or function basis, depending on the fundamental characteristics of the individual sectors. For sectors primarily dependent on fixed assets and physical facilities, a bottom-up, asset-by-asset approach may be most appropriate. ASIS International offers several education opportunities — they even have the NIPP online at their Web site (http://training.fema.gov/EMIWeb/IS/is860.asp). They urge members to take a free online course on the NIPP. Developed by DHS and the Federal Emergency Management Agency (FEMA), the course is offered with options for those who want to take it for credit or review the information on an informal basis. Those completing the course for credit must take a final exam and will receive a certificate from DHS.[4] The course covers the following:

- Explain the importance of protecting critical infrastructure and key resources.
- Identify the relevant authorities and roles for CI/KR protection efforts.
- Describe the NIPP unifying structure for the integration of CI/KR protection efforts, including:
  - Sector security partnership model.
  - Risk management framework.
  - Information-sharing process.

A common approach based on a robust understanding of existing methodologies is needed to enable the setting of protection priorities across sectors. The first element of this approach is to establish a common definition and process for analysis of the basic factors of risk for CI/KR protection. In the context of homeland security, the NIPP framework assesses risk as a function of consequence, vulnerability, and threat:

$$R = f\ (C,V,T)$$

---

[4] ASIS, http://www.asisonline.org.

For sectors with diverse and logical assets, such as Telecommunications and Information Technology, a top-down, business continuity, or mission continuity approach that focuses on networks, systems, and functions may be more effective.

Each sector can choose the approach that produces the most actionable results for the sector and work with DHS to ensure that the relevant risk analysis procedures are compatible with the criteria established in the NIPP. Below are a few of the NIPP's risk management framework activities:

Set security goals: Define specific outcomes, conditions, end points, or performance targets that collectively constitute an effective protective posture.

Identify assets, systems, networks, and functions: Develop an inventory of the assets, systems, and networks, including those located outside the United States, that comprise the nation's CI/KR and the critical functionality therein; collect information pertinent to risk management that takes into account the fundamental characteristics of each sector.

Assess risks: Determine risk by combining potential direct and indirect consequences of a terrorist attack or other hazards (including seasonal changes in consequences, and dependencies and interdependencies associated with each identified asset, system, or network), known vulnerabilities to various potential attack vectors, and general or specific threat information.

Prioritize: Aggregate and analyze risk assessment results to develop a comprehensive picture of asset, system, and network risk; establish priorities based on risk; and determine protection and business continuity initiatives that provide the greatest mitigation of risk.

Implement protective programs: Select sector-appropriate protective actions or programs to reduce or manage the risk identified; secure the resources needed to address priorities.

Measure effectiveness: Use metrics and other evaluation procedures at the national and sector levels to measure progress and assess the effectiveness of the national CI/KR protection program in improving protection and managing risk.

RESPONSIBILITY AND ACCOUNTABILITY PER DHS

The NIPP says owners and operators of critical infrastructures will be responsible for taking action to support risk management planning and investments in security as a necessary component of prudent business planning and operations. The NIPP does not dictate what specific actions to take for security investments or how much to spend, but expects that activities listed in the 196-page NIPP document will be conducted. Here are a few of the action items that the private sector is expected to perform:

- Reassess and adjust continuity of business and emergency management plans.
- Build increased resiliency and redundancy into business processes and systems.
- Protect facilities against physical attacks and cyber-attacks, natural disasters, and insider threats.
- Create networks among utility regulators and other federal, state, local, and private sector entities to address cross-sector issues.
- Explore and recommend solutions to cost recovery issues associated with key water, gas, telecommunications, and energy infrastructures.
- Implement protective actions and programs to reduce identified vulnerabilities appropriate to the level of risk presented.
- Promote CI/KR protection education, training, and awareness programs.

HOW TO PERFORM YOUR OWN THREAT ASSESSMENT

A safe practice is to take a hard look at threats regularly. The first time should be based on a thorough comprehensive effort. Then, thereafter, it can be in "snapshot" mode two to four times a year. Once threats are known, vulnerabilities need to be identified to determine how risky it will be to conduct business in the face of those threats and vulnerabilities. Are the vulnerabilities exploitable? What if they are not? Do facility owners still expend time and resources to eliminate them? What is the worst-case scenario if the identified threats were to be exploited? Threat assessments often show that certain perceived threats were not valid. Most organizations would want to know this before continuing to fund the activity. What if their security programs were "over the top" and the value of the assets was one-fourth the cost of their security expenditures? Or, what if the allocated security budget was insufficient compared to the value of the material assets? Without going through a process of assessment — formal or informal — an organization would have no idea where they stood in terms of preparedness or whether they were doing any wasteful spending. There is no correct answer to this dilemma because many times organizations do not take into consideration assets that do not seem to have material dollar value — like employees. If the only thing at risk is human life, then security investment still needs to be made — all life is worth protecting.

Organizations are often very lucky. After threat assessments are performed, a picture emerges, people are immediately surprised at the threats and vulnerabilities discovered, and it is common to hear remarks such as "Oh my God! We were so lucky!" At one financial institution during a non-routine check of the servers, the IT team discovered that they had four Web servers operating outside the firewall in the open with unrestricted access to the public. The servers contained customer credit card numbers and Social Security numbers. These servers had been replaced by other servers, but someone forgot to disable these four from the network, or at least secure them inside the firewall. They had been accessible by people on the Internet for 4 months. If someone had stolen the information that was stored on those servers, the organization would have suffered from lawsuits due to identity theft of customer information, penalties for failing to meet basic security requirements, negative publicity, and loss of customer confidence. After the company overcame the immediate shock reaction, they found themselves in an ethical dilemma — what to do about the discovery? Report it to management? Report it to the customers? Or never say anything about it? The answer for them was not to report anything until customers complained about identity theft, and then let the company's public relations and legal departments handle it. No one reported any incidents, so it appears this organization was lucky. This is not the right answer. It seems to be a common approach, though, to risk mitigation in several companies. Standard operating procedures in security and periodic vulnerability assessments could have prevented this event from happening in the first place.

The NIPP and Homeland Security Presidential Directive 7 (HSPD-7) mandate that measures be taken to ensure that the 17 critical infrastructure sectors are protected against terrorism and other threats. The sectors are all different, and not all aspects of infrastructures are critical. What works for one sector may not work for the rest. Also, the cost of protecting one facility may be much lower than what is required at others. The threat of terrorism may not be imminent across all infrastructures, and some of them will never see the early phases of terrorist planning (surveillance) or an attack, but terrorism is a solid threat. As you read this book, plots are in progress and some terrorist cells may even be collecting information and identifying their next target while others are being successfully deterred by effective security programs or are being successfully identified and captured by police in the United States, Europe, Asia, Central America, and the Middle East. The average worker does not see the magnitude of the threat that is visible from such arrests. Nor is he aware that terrorist cells have been living among us since the 1970s. This became known and publicized in 2002, as displayed in Figure 3.2 (Islamic Fundamentalist Networks operating within our borders).

The map in Figure 3.3 provides an overview of the threats to the United States since 1970 and demonstrates how they migrated from Europe and the Middle East to the United States over the decades.

NIPP AS A TEMPLATE

Now that we know that a first line of defense capability is possible through intelligence analysis and threat assessment, we can look at a third approach

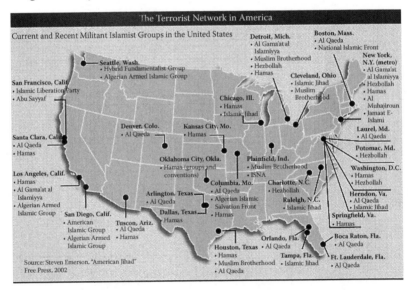

Figure 3.2 Islamic Fundamentalist Networks (As excerpted from Steven Emerson's "American Jihad," Free Press, 2002. With permission.)

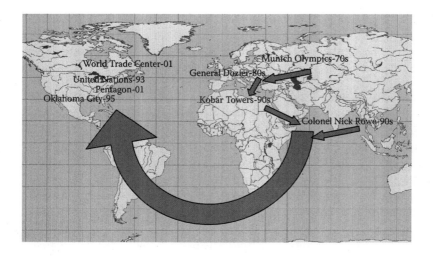

Figure 3.3 Terrorist Threats to the United States, 1970s to Present (Elsa Lee, 2008.)

for effective threat and risk mitigation. If there is no preferred method for assessment in place or it is too difficult to select an approach, the National Infrastructure Protection Plan is a good one-stop shop for the many steps that lead to preparedness, including threat assessment. Without a clear understanding of threats faced, the subsequent security steps that follow for risk management could end up being performed in a sequence that is counterproductive or inadequate to achieve preparedness. The NIPP went through a few rewrites before it became final in June 2006. It is designed primarily for the government sector of critical infrastructures, but DHS expects that the private sector can use it as a guideline to contribute to the national unified effort to secure and protect infrastructures that they are in control of. The NIPP provides an approach for integrating the nation's many CI/KR protection initiatives into a single national effort. This collaborative effort between the private and public sectors will result in the prioritization of protection initiatives and investments across sectors. It will "ensure that resources are applied where they offer most benefit for mitigating risk by lowering vulnerabilities, deterring threats, and minimizing the consequences of terrorist attacks and other incidents."[5]

---

[5] Department of Homeland Security, *National Infrastructure Protection Plan (NIPP)* (Washington, D.C.: Department of Homeland Security, 2006).

Establish Program
and Workgroup

Security and Response
Plans Are Updated

Upgrades Are
Implemented

Plans Are Reviewed
and Updated Using
the Workgroup

Workgroup Reviews
Security Plan and
Response Plans

Exercises Are
Conducted

Threat, Vulnerability,
and Risk Assessment
Is Performed

Plans Are
Reviewed and
Updated Using
a Workgroup

Figure 3.4 Security Process Model

A FRAMEWORK FOR TAKING THE NIPP APPROACH

Figure 3.4 illustrates the steps involved in organizing teams to develop and implement plans to mitigate risk. In assessing threats to eventually mitigate risks, the approach I would take would be to assemble a team consisting of all business units, physical security, IT security, risk managers, security managers, and continuity and disaster recovery planners. I would have a copy of the NIPP for each member. I would send a memo (Outlook Invite) ahead of time on what to expect and schedule a required meeting. I would plan to meet during lunch as it would make sense to meet for 2 to 3 hours. The meeting room would be a large room where everyone could sit in a circle. I would have note takers present and large easel pads ready (the type that can be torn and hung around the room). I would have one member knowledgeable on the NIPP briefly explain what it calls for. I would have another member briefly explain what emergency plans have been completed and their current status. We would also want to know if they have been rehearsed and tested or are they dusty. I would turn every section in the NIPP's table of contents into an action item or checklist to start with something manageable. I would task the group to compare the DHS action items to the current plans, then convene the group again after giving them time to report what actions they felt needed to be performed to complete the NIPP checklist. I would assign a project manager and allow the team to help establish a timeline and goal date for completion. By stepping through the process this way, people get a chance to buy into the whole effort — instead of viewing this as a project that was dropped on their lap with no guidance on something that seems overwhelming.

A FRAMEWORK FOR ASSESSING THREAT

The threat assessment process should never take place in a vacuum and should never be a low-priority task assigned to a sole individual. The process is best served when performed by a team as a dedicated effort with a start and end date and clearly defined objectives, scope, and purpose.

The way this assessment is conducted varies across industries. Sometimes organizations are lucky enough to have employees with experience in assessing government, military, and corporate facilities. In such cases, all of that experience translates into having the ability to use combined methods tailored to the organization's needs.

For assessments conducted at nuclear weapons facilities, the procedures for all methods have to be performed "by the numbers." For example, during the conduct of one assessment, when team members first showed up for the introduction meeting, they were met by the guards at the front gate ... with weapons pointed at their head. They were expected to, and had been told exactly how to approach the front gate and what to do until their identity was validated. All of their movements were "by the numbers," precisely orchestrated and followed by the guards' gaze as preinstructed before their arrival. They were warned that there was zero room for errors. This experience is not like anything the average worker goes through in his or her everyday job. However, it was clear that the facilities' owners and operators took their business seriously and did not monkey around.

This meticulous attention to threats is not the norm across all sectors. Though it is arguably the most important component of risk management, the process is often overlooked, misunderstood, and performed by inexperienced personnel. In government settings, threat assessments frequently focus on external threats — terrorism, espionage, and sabotage — while the private sector focuses more on Human Resources (HR)-related workplace violence and information technology issues.

Threat assessments do not have to be like those performed at highly restricted defense facilities, but they need a dedicated and focused effort

Figure 3.5 Lee's Simplified Risk Model

and need to become part of the organizational culture. The fact that no organization really has the resources to keep up with constantly changing threats or the expertise to perform assessments, does not make it any less excusable for not performing them. It is true that anyone obsessed enough to do harm will find a way to do it regardless of how much security is in place, but there is much that can be done to discourage the bad deed. It happens through strategic security measures developed from realistic perspectives of threats.

Taking the time to compile and analyze threats and security event trends, enables security teams to visualize the potential threat picture which can then translate into possible *early warnings*. In the national security arena, "early warnings" often come from intelligence resources, and thus "intelligence" is often considered to be the first line of defense. It affords time to respond protectively and harden the security of assets further or move the asset to a safer location. When threats are identified, they can be mitigated or discouraged through deterrence methodologies and more effectively from human intervention than technology.

There are many models for assessing risk. Figure 3.5 is a simple three-step model for mitigating the risk of terrorism when time is critical and there is only a short period to perform essential steps.

In this model, Step 1 involves collecting information about the threats the organization faces and making sense of those threats. Are they imminent? Are lives in danger? Is the organization in compliance with applicable industry mandates? What is the worst thing that will happen if these threats are not addressed now? What is the deadline for completing Step 1? Is it in relationship to a DHS deadline? Did someone make a terrorist threat against the company? Are there other factors that warrant timely completion of the process? After threat information is collected, Table 3.1 ("Threat Ratings"), can be used to identify and rank the threat information using the following criteria:

- High = It has occurred one or more times at this location, and correlating security vulnerability exists.

Table 3.1 Threat Ratings

Threat	Negligible	Low	Medium	High
Terrorism				
Suicide bomber (male)	X			
Suicide bomber (female)	X			
Truck or vehicle bomb		X		
Letter bomb			X	
Assassination	X			
Kidnapping	X			
Improvised explosive device		X		
Hijacking/airplanes	X			
Siege/hostage taking		X		
Remote triggered bomb		X		
Time-fused bomb		X		
Chemical attack	X			
Biological attack	X			
Radiological attack	X			
Nuclear attack	X			
Espionage			X	
Sabotage				
Vandalism				
Disgruntled person			X	
Cyber-attack				
Civil unrest	X			
Telephone bomb threat				
Hazardous material incident			X	
Letter bomb		X		
Earthquake				
Flood			X	
Fire				
Tornado				
Hurricane			X	
Tsunami	X			

- Medium = Someone has articulated a desire to conduct the act, no correlating security vulnerability exists, and a threat or event has occurred at other similar facilities.
- Low = No one has articulated a desire to conduct the act, no correlating security vulnerability exists, but the act has been carried out at other similar facilities.

- Negligible = It has no possibility of occurring, and no correlating security vulnerability exists.

There are several methods, templates, and published opinions as to recommended methods and sequential orders for establishing preparedness plans. But assessing the threat is a crucial first step for establishing preparedness plans through either internal teams or outsourced professionals, and the input of each functional unit are important. At a minimum, the following resources should be included in the process:

- Legal
- Public relations
- Security
- IT
- Human resources
- Finance
- Risk manager
- Marketing

In order for these teams to succeed, it helps to understand what is being protected and from whom, at the organization being assessed. For example, critical infrastructures, it is protecting facilities from acts that cause interruption to services that the public, businesses, the government, and our nation have come to rely on to sustain life and ensure everyone's well-being. Services need to be protected from terrorists, disasters, and other threats.

When a team comes together to begin the process, it is often a major period of discovery, surprises, resistance, and delays. Scheduling time to perform the effort becomes burdensome for one reason or another. There are shrinking resources. Existing resources are overextended in more than one job function. The effort loses importance and steam. It becomes overshadowed by other activities and gets tossed aside to the "We'll get to it later" pile.

When the team finally comes together and compiles a list of critical facility aspects that must be protected, they are surprised to see what shows up on their list. What usually happens in such sessions is that each business unit, for the first time, successfully articulates what is truly critical for them, and now everyone in the room is enlightened and on the same page. Sometimes this same discovery occurs when contingency or business continuity plans are being developed. The result is that the team discovers some of the items they previously considered important

Table 3.2   Threat Information Sources

Source	Data Produced
Police	Criminal trends and statistics.
Fire department	Can report vulnerabilities in response measures, and an existence of chemical or fire hazards in the vicinity or close proximity of premises.
Neighboring tenants or residents	Threats to their premises.
Employees	Might report suspicious visitors or activities observed on the premises during business or nonbusiness hours.
	Might report suspicious telephone calls, e-mails, or faxes received.
Internal reports and logs	IT personnel may provide snapshot of network probing or Web site–defacing attempts.
	Security forces may have reports of suspicious vehicles parked in the vicinity or suspicious individuals who approached the premises appearing lost or in need of directions.
Public relations	May have knowledge of strange queries or callers.
Legal	May know that at other times, someone was trying make the company "look bad" or "make the company pay" — possibly disgruntled persons.
Information technology	May know that someone was probing the network; may know of defacing attempts, hacking attempts, and anomalies on network traffic that alone mean nothing — but, in the context of all threats, put all the pieces of a threat puzzle together.
Newspaper and journals	May talk about a threat that already occurred at a competitor site.
Visitors and guests	May be imposters simply there to collect information for exploitation.
Security personnel	May see patterns in their daily logs at a particular time, which alone meant nothing to them but in the face of the threats collected indicate a serious threat.
Human resources	May have records of disgruntled employees or red flags (i.e., employees who only worked one day).
Finance	Strange activity relating to money, the movement of money, or theft of funds.
Local, state, and federal government	Local and global threat trends.
Competitors	Suspicious things that they noticed in their companies that are outside the normal scope of threats they normally face.
Company Web site	May be defaced, leaving a footprint of the attacker.
Internet	Blog sites used by terrorists to share information or by other people talking about events that have happened or things they have seen.

are now hardly worth the money spent to protect them. The threat landscape of most organizations is formed from an amalgamation of data obtained from various internal and external sources, such as the example in Table 3.2.

Step 2 involves performing data collection and analysis from some of the same threat sources and compiling a list of identified vulnerabilities. The results of the threats and vulnerabilities analysis should be protected and shared outside of the organization only on a "need-to-know basis." In the federal and defense industries, such information is generally classified, not releasable to the public, and highly safeguarded. If compromised, it could be used to wipe out an organization or cause severe damage to its financial well-being. Therefore, all documents gathered for this process need to be properly marked and controlled so they do not end up in the wrong hands.

When conducting organizational threat assessments using the intelligence and information we have gathered, it is best to create a table that provides information in a sensible format and identifies all the possible threats. Regardless of how informal the threat assessment process is, a dedicated, diverse, and experienced team should be organized to conduct a threat analysis, and perhaps a separate team should be created to come up with a risk snapshot and countermeasures. Threat assessments must be performed on a regular basis to accommodate the changing threat environment we live in. Combining this with the vulnerability assessment helps to focus the efforts and resources for risk mitigation efforts through effective countermeasures. Table 3.1 is an example of just one subjective and qualitative method of rating threats — if no other preferred method exists.[6]

WHAT THE RESULTS SUGGEST

By analyzing Table 3.1, it is evident that everything displayed in red requires several "What if?" exercises by the team to determine what steps are appropriate, required, or within the realm of reality. For example, what are the details that caused sabotage to score "high?" What corrective steps were taken when this last occurred? Has it occurred or been attempted in "like" facilities, and what did they do? Generally, this threat can be

---

[6] Elsa Lee, "Threat Assessments: Those Blind Spots Can Be Dangerous," *Risk Management Executive*, 2005.

mitigated through the use of closed-caption television (CCTV), electronic access controls, signage, changes in procedures, training employees and security guard personnel to properly detect and respond to sabotage indicators, and establishing relationships with local law enforcement and fire department personnel to obtain information on previously reported trends relating to the threat (official and unofficial). Though this is a subjective method for rating threats, it also provides a subjective criterion for determining a threat level.

Trend analysis should be performed at this stage, and it can be done by the most analytical person on the team or simply someone who emerges with analytical skills — ideally from a former law enforcement or intelligence resource. Trend analysis is the ability to view all the collected information and see if patterns of threat behavior emerge.

Terrorist Activity Indicators

- Did any information collected point to possible surveillance of the facility?
- Past examples, include people walking, pacing, taking notes, and taking photos.
- Were any suspicious vehicles observed several times in the vicinity?
- Did any employees receive suspicious calls asking "weird questions?"
- Have any uniforms from guards or others been stolen recently?
- Did any of the tenants colocated report suspicious activity?

Espionage or Insider Threats

- Are any documents or materials missing?
- Did anyone suddenly quit after being on the job for only a few days?
- Does anyone show signs of unexplained affluence — lots of money — but can't explain why?
- Any network anomalies — unexplainable remote log-ons or file downloads?

Information and Technical Threats

- Was any of the company's information found on a blog site where someone made a threat?

- Did anyone try to attack our computer systems?
- Did any viruses come through and cause excessive downtime?
- Did the Web site get defaced?

From these questions, you can see that the team or the trend analyst can come up with many more valid questions to attempt to produce a picture of realistic threats faced. One could build this model of assessment and tailor it to the facility. When this process is completed, there are two possible steps to follow: (1) move onto Step 2 and assess vulnerabilities, or (2) discover threats requiring further investigation by the organization or the police to further categorize them as imminent or "early warning" and reportable to DHS or law enforcement. This will be determined by the person in the organization who interfaces regularly with DHS under critical infrastructure protection (CIP) efforts.

Step 3 involves taking the collected information and analyzing it to see what kind of risk picture emerges. DHS expects that each one will be evaluated separately to include the consequences. We cannot possibly address all the findings that are likely to turn up in the data collection and analysis, or how long it would take to perform all the steps and sub-tasks under each step. What the risk managers should be able to do with the simple model above is to apply more comprehensive techniques if desired or necessary — by merging the steps above with other comprehensive methodologies.

HOW TO HANDLE DISCOVERIES OF THREAT AND VULNERABILITIES

Certain aspects of assessment results may need to be shared with DHS. The method for transmission can be decided when the need to share arises, but the preferred way is through face-to-face contact. It provides a contact who can sign for the information. The documents should be marked on every page with "Company Confidential" at minimum. Prior to reporting the reportable information with DHS, contact should be established with the government sector representative because DHS has certain templates that they will use for reporting information.

Other assessment methods exist through the DHS model and academic centers where formulas for measuring risk are provided and the application of formulas is more comprehensive and less subjective than the simplified model. There are more sophisticated methods and practices the public sector uses, but in the private sector, where the threat assessment process may be new, this is just one simplified way of quantifying threat to properly allocate resources to mitigate risk.

Determining Vulnerability

Once the threat picture has been captured, the next step is assessing vulnerabilities against the known threats, or simply vulnerabilities. The most common vulnerabilities found in past assessments included the following, against the correlating threats:

Threat	Vulnerability
Suspicious males photographing a metro train	CCTV was broken and not working
Suspicious male photographing a high-rise	Employees did not notice him
Suspicious person called in a bomb threat	None — an employee enacted a bomb threat response checklist
Network intrusion attempted	None — the firewall prevented access
Internal workers stole documents	No checks and balances to detect insider theft
Facility plans found in the public library	None — item discovered in vulnerability assessment phase

Figure 3.6 is one example of a critical infrastructure facility's detailed facility plans, which were found stored at a local public library as part of a published environmental study. They provided the layout of the facility and other information that could be used by terrorists to collect target intelligence. It was required to be there because it was an environmental agency document and had to be made available as public information. Since these details have to be publicized, it is important to be aware of what exploitable information is sitting "out there." The difference between this document and documents that may contain vulnerabilities and security information are the titles of the documents and the information in the documents. A security document detailing security, facility security procedures and operations, and risk and vulnerability assessments is exempt from the Freedom of Information Act (FOIA) rules and is not required to be publicized. The Critical Infrastructure Information Protection Act

Figure 3.6 Facility Plan

of 2002, in section 214 of the Homeland Security Act, exempts security-related information from being released to the public — and classifies this as Protected Critical Infrastructure Information.

Once threats and vulnerabilities are identified, an assessment team would decide what the risk level should be and the best mitigation and risk management measures to recommend as well as the consequences of every recommendation. The threat, vulnerability, and risk assessment is a continuous process. The organization needs to have a baseline report of what the threat conditions are — otherwise, it has nothing to compare to and will not know what is normal activity compared to abnormal activity. It will not have the ability to go back in time and compare threat activity to see if it is normal or increased.

Sometimes the vulnerability in an organization stems from the hiring process. The screening is not conducted at all, or the methods of screening and performing due diligence are not reliable. Some companies are transitioning to more frequent checks even after people have been employed for a year.

Figure 3.7 Border Crossing

Sometimes America opens its arms warmly to people from other countries and adds to its vulnerability. Borders are easily crossed, especially in North America between the United States, Mexico, and Canada, as depicted in Figure 3.7. Nidal Ayad was employed at the Allied Signal Corporation.[7] Nidal Ayad, a Jordanian citizen who came to the United States, was fulfilling the American dream: he had a master's degree from Rutgers University, a good job, and he was married and had a child. Despite all of this, "he became the brains behind the 'witch's brew' used in detonating the bomb at the World Trade Center in 1993."[8] Within a short time, the adopted country also became the battlefield and the target.[9]

---

[7] Judson Knight, "World Trade Center, 1993 Terrorist Attack Encyclopedia of Espionage, Intelligence, and Security," 2004, http://findarticles.com/p/articles/mi_gx5211/is_2004/ai_n19126798 (accessed March 23, 2008).

[8] Bruce Hoffman, William Rosenau, Andrew J. Curiel, and Doron Zimmermann, "The Radicalization of Diasporas and Terrorism," Rand Corporation, http://rand.org/pubs/conf_proceedings/2007/RAND_CF229.pdf.

[9] Hoffman, Rosenau, Curiel, and Zimmermann, "The Radicalization of Diasporas and Terrorism."

COUNTERMEASURE

Countermeasures usually have to do with denying the threat access to the information or materials needed to exploit the vulnerability and allow the attack. After reviewing a list of identified threats and vulnerabilities, a team needs to determine the best way to deny their threats what they seek. In many threat assessments that I have performed, we walked the employees or guards through the process of exploiting the identified vulnerability. We shot the video after discovering certain vulnerabilities so that we could use the footage as training, but the videos were controlled as security-related information. We showed them videos of their actions. Often, the vulnerability discovered involved human error, and the solution was not to buy more technology but rather to train more and build skills. Some of the ways that other teams have secured vulnerabilities included the following:

- Training guards to recognize and detect terrorist reconnaissance or terrorist intelligence gathering, and testing them through red team exercises.
- Training security managers with one-on-one Train the Trainer exercises so that they would then train the workforce on recognizing suspicious calls, suspicious probes, and suspicious persons surveilling the premises or other identified threats.
- Training the employees to recognize social engineering attempts by phone where a person calls in pretending to be the help desk but in fact is a threat trying to gain access to networks.
- Testing response personnel through simultaneous attacks at multiple access control points so that they would improve their response capabilities and the procedures for capturing and detaining a suspicious person until authorities arrived.

The U.S. military is well experienced in dealing with a variety of threats from terrorists to adversarial enemies — they simulate collecting and gather intelligence on vulnerabilities, operating like the terrorists do. To mitigate the terrorists' ability to gather accurate information, as a tactic used in conjunction with increased security and technology to deter them they also use Random Antiterrorism Measures (RAMs; not to be confused with Risk Assessment Methodologies). This tactic includes plans that are used by security and employees to change the security atmosphere surrounding a facility. RAMs alter the security "signature" to terrorists or their supporters who may be providing surveillance, thus resulting in confronting a terrorist group with a very ambiguous situation. They also provide an alternative to trying to maintain the highest posture of security at all times, which can be costly. This puts the terrorist in a position to ask, "Do they know we are here?" "Have we been compromised?" "What is the impact of these new security practices on our ability to achieve our operational goals?"

Some examples of RAM tactics include the following:

- Checking vehicles at random; the number and timing are changed on an irregular basis but are planned for by security personnel.
- Regularly changing the facility or building entry points of employees and visitors.
- Requiring different requirements for visitors proving their identification.
- Altering visitor access control procedures regularly.
- Altering guard shifts and amount of guards at different posts so there seems to be no regular schedule to an observer.
- Changing procedures for deliveries — supplies, FedEx, etc.

These procedures are only limited by the creativity of the team that develops them but a tool for RAM has been designed by a research team at USC's Academic Homeland Security Center of Excellence for just such a purpose. Keep in mind, though, that too many changes may frustrate employees and cause them to find ways to circumvent security procedures. The key is to conduct operations where patterns cannot be determined by those who aim to exploit them.

A threat assessment can be used to evaluate the likelihood of terrorist activity against a given asset or location.

REPORTING INFORMATION

If criminal information is discovered in any of the above steps, the information needs to be reported as soon as possible to authorities. Controls need to be established immediately. The organization should convene to determine how the information or discovery will be protected from other employees, from suspects, and from the media. Only one person should be designated to speak with media, and the information discovered has to be protected and controlled as it may now be evidence. A possible scenario is that evidence will be collected and the scene is released from law enforcement so normal activities can resume. Another scenario is that law enforcement will confiscate the materials and take them to their evidence room, where they will remain until no longer needed — plan for the latter. It is important not to disturb evidence as soon as it is discovered to be evidence. Be aware that the media plays a role in covering threats and methods in which companies handle them thereby publicizing them. Establish a proactive approach — call them before they call you, and have a press release expert ready to prepare a release if the need arises. If you are trying to protect information, the media may unintentionally or inadvertently compromise your security, your plans, your weaknesses, your capabilities, and your limitations to protect assets. More importantly, that information must be protected under several Homeland Security Acts, as previously mentioned.

Decide ahead of time what is reportable and required to be reported and what is not. You do not want to publicize critical details if there is no requirement to volunteer such information. All vulnerabilities and secrets about your defenses must remain secret and controlled. All documents that list your threats and vulnerabilities should be controlled, marked as "Copy of 1 of 10 assigned to __," and entered into a control log. Also include responsibility for control of information on the bottom of each page, and educate employees on the dissemination of information contained in marked documents. If you have a better way for document control, use your own methods, but make sure they enforce "need-to-know" controls and education. Companies and even lawyers from government agencies get confused about FOIA and what information is exempt from FOIA. If something does not feel right to you and you get a "gut feeling" in your stomach, pay attention to it. Sensitive information — or whatever classification label you are using relating to critical infrastructures — must be protected. If there is confusion, seek several interpretations. The last thing you will ever want to know is that your disclosure caused an attack — this is the single most important message about release of information under FOIA — this is from experience of watching. Some organizations make costly mistakes.

COST VERSUS INVESTMENT

Capital expenditures on security programs have always been viewed as a cost — not a money-making function. That paradigm has to shift to align with realistic modern practices. There is a definite risk in not taking action;

not increasing security measures will result in penalties and liability that will result in high costs, probably more than it would have cost to implement procedures and technology to protect the assets upfront. Everyone buys car insurance, home insurance, life insurance, and short-term disability policies. We pay on them for years, and there is no return on these. Some people are lucky and never have to use them. The unlucky others

Table 3.3   Safety and Security Violation Penalties

- **Other than serious violation**: A violation that has a direct relationship to job safety and health, but probably would not cause death or serious physical harm. A proposed penalty of up to $7,000 for each violation is discretionary. A penalty for an other-than-serious violation may be adjusted downward by as much as 95 percent, depending on the employer's good faith (demonstrated efforts to comply with the act) and history of previous violations, and on the size of the business. When the adjusted penalty amounts to less than $100, no penalty is proposed.
- **Serious violation**: A violation where there is substantial probability that death or serious physical harm could result and that the employer knew, or should have known, of the hazard. A mandatory penalty of up to $7,000 for each violation is proposed. A penalty for a serious violation may be adjusted downward, based on the employer's good faith and history of previous violations, the gravity of the alleged violation, and the size of the business.
- **Willful violation**: A violation that the employer knowingly commits or commits with plain indifference to the law. The employer either knows that what he or she is doing constitutes a violation, or is aware that a hazardous condition existed and made no reasonable effort to eliminate it.

  Penalties of up to $70,000 may be proposed for each willful violation, with a minimum penalty of $5,000 for each violation. A proposed penalty for a willful violation may be adjusted downward, depending on the size of the business and its history of previous violations. Usually, no credit is given for good faith.

  If an employer is convicted of a willful violation of a standard that has resulted in the death of an employee, the offense is punishable by a court-imposed fine, imprisonment for up to six months, or both. A fine of up to $250,000 for an individual, or $500,000 for a corporation, may be imposed for a criminal conviction.
- **Repeated violation**: A violation of any standard, regulation, rule, or order where, upon reinspection, a substantially similar violation can bring a fine of up to $70,000 for each such violation. To be the basis of a repeated citation, the original citation must be final; a citation under contest may not serve as the basis for a subsequent repeated citation.   *(Continued)*

Table 3.3   Safety and Security Violation Penalties (Continued)

- **Failure to abate prior violation**: Failure to abate a prior violation may bring a civil penalty of up to $7,000 for each day the violation continues beyond the prescribed abatement date.
- **De minimis violation**: De minimis violations are violations of standards that have no direct or immediate relationship to safety or health. Whenever de minimis conditions are found during an inspection, they are documented in the same way as any other violation, but are not included on the citation.

Additional Violations for Which Citations and Proposed Penalties May Be Issued upon Conviction

- Falsifying records, reports, or applications can bring a fine of $10,000, up to 6 months in jail, or both.
- Violations of posting requirements can bring a civil penalty of up to $7,000.
- Assaulting a compliance officer, or otherwise resisting, opposing, intimidating, or interfering with a compliance officer while they are engaged in the performance of their duties is a criminal offense, subject to a fine of not more than $5,000 and imprisonment for not more than three years.

who have to file insurance claims are sure glad they had a policy. It is time to view security measures as an investment — not a "cost."

Penalties

In addition to having to be compliant with Homeland Security directives and mandates, organizations also have to worry about being fined by the Occupational Safety and Health Administration (OSHA) for negligent safety and security practices. Identified in Table 3.3[10] are some of the penalties that can be imposed on corporations that are found to be negligent on safety and security: citation and penalty procedures differ from state to state.

---

[10] The U.S. Department of Labor Occupational Safety and Health Administration (OSHA) is the federal agency charged with the enforcement of safety and health legislation for employees in the workplace.

MINI CASE STUDY

At one major financial institution, a security and continuity assessment was performed along with a review of Emergency Policies and Procedures. Through these review processes, it was determined that this institution had never, in fact, exercised its plan (the plan was in existence for over 2 years), so no one knew for sure that it would even work. After the assessment and review were completed, a field exercise of the plan was put into motion and this is what it revealed:

- The plan did not identify the Executive Committee that would oversee the plan through rehearsal or execution — none of the institution's top managers had any idea that someone needed to take ownership of this plan.
- The plan listed the locations where employees would report in the event of an evacuation and emergency response due to a disaster — while exercising the plan, it was discovered that some of the locations were in hazardous areas that placed the employees in harm's way.
- Access to the locations was not properly planned and arranged — reporting to the locations was to occur in a sequential order and the keys to gain entry to the locations were in the hands of employees slated to arrive later — placing the earlier arrivees in unprotected and vulnerable positions.
- No one had interviewed the "wire transfers" employees to see what they thought about the designated areas or the plan, nor had they introduced them to the plan and the procedures.
- Many individuals who were listed as major role players within the evacuation and emergency plan were not aware of the plan or the fact that they were major role players.
- Alternate work locations within the plan were not safe and were not suitable for work activities.

If a disaster had required them to initiate the plan, and the employees reported to the alternate work locations and suffered from the potential hazards, the company could have faced fines for endangering the employees' safety. In the 2 years since the plan had been written, the areas either became unsafe — or, they were never safe to begin with. Safety and security risks lurk all around us; physically and periodically assessing safety and security in the workplace is an absolute necessity.

4

Risk Mitigation, Transference, and Elimination

It is apparent that "change" is critical to effectively manage terrorism threats and risk. Just as it requires seeing threats in a new dimension, it also requires seeing risk differently and determining the best ways to deal with it. The workforce has different strengths and capabilities. Some people are suited to assess threats, others are suited for data collection of vulnerabilities, and still others are suited to come up with countermeasures and solutions or creative ways to manage risk that we may not have thought about. It is not easy to come up with solutions because the very things that keep us busy every day prevent us from having any time to "take time" to see how we should best deal with threats. That is a problem — we do not have time "to think." So in some ways, this is not about "thinking" or finding a solution — it is about the ability of finding someone who can tell us how to do it based on expertise, experience, and a proven history of doing it for others. If we do not have time to learn and master a required skill or adapt current skills to see threats differently so that we can properly mitigate, then we should bring in people who are already good at it.

Leadership consultant Peter Drucker says that leaders need to recognize when to stop pouring resources into an effort — if something is costing too much and it has served or not served its purpose, "When do you stop pouring resources into things that have not achieved their purpose? One tries it twice. One tries it a third time. But, by then it should be obvious this will be very hard to do."[1] He calls this *creative abandonment* — a leadership principle that good leaders need to be able to exercise.

His leadership philosophy can be applied to the risk management process. Many organizations pour critical and costly resources into something that they would consider to be a solution — organizations have to make capital expenditures annually to accommodate business or secure assets. This is a necessity for them. However, often they will buy more security technology, buy the latest and greatest technology, or keep spending money to fix equipment that keeps breaking instead of replacing it. Maybe it was expensive and needs to be "made to work" because an organization is stuck with it. If it is never going to work or will take too long to fix, this creates risk because it is not going to do what it is supposed to do or intended to do. If there is a major security dependency on it, this is dangerous. Is it necessary to assume this risk? Is it smart? Does it make sense? Organizations will have to rethink how they conduct their risk decision-making process, especially if they are community partners or owners and operators of critical infrastructures (CIs). Maybe there are some organizations in existence that can afford to gamble that way, but CI owners cannot. Organizational management must ensure that at a minimum, they are at least following a risk management process similar to the one in Figure 4.1. The process is ongoing and never ends. It is a program, not a project.

RISK DECISION PRINCIPLES

The courses of action taken to manage risk require reviewing and understanding four principles:

1. Accept risk when benefits outweigh the cost.
2. Accept no unnecessary risk.
3. Anticipate and manage risk by planning.
4. Make risk decisions at the right level.

The center of risk management decisions should rely on six considerations:

---

[1] Peter Drucker, "Peter Drucker on Leadership," http://www.forbes.com/2004/11/19/cz_ rk_1119drucker.html.

Risk Management

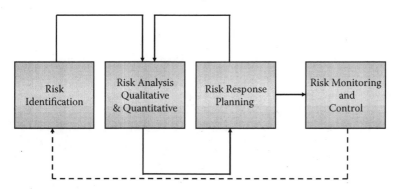

Figure 4.1 Simplified Risk Management Process

1. Identify and characterize the threat.
2. Assess the risk of the threat.
3. Assess your asset values — what is important, what is valuable, and what is critical? (Don't forget the value of human life — which should outweigh other values.)
4. Analyze the vulnerabilities.
5. Identify and cost-analyze the countermeasure being considered.
6. Implement cost-effective security measures.

One simple but important lesson comes to mind — several years ago, I received a parking ticket because the meter had expired. If I had parked farther away at a public parking lot, it would have cost $10. I decided to park at a metered slot near my meeting, and I dropped about $2 worth of coins in the meter, but when I returned the meter had expired and a parking citation was issued — it cost me $35. So to park at the metered slot — the cost of parking was $37 and 2 hours of labor afterwards to deal with the problem. If I were paid $100 or $1000 an hour for my services, then it is possible that the ticket actually cost $237 or $2,037 with labor factored into it. Was it worth the risk? Did I assess the risk of the possibility of the meeting going longer than expected or forgetting to put more money in? Was the risk acceptable? Could it have been avoided? This is just one simple exercise to illustrate how hard it is for us to take time to see risk with a strategic perspective that really takes into consideration the value of our time and the true cost. That risk could have been eliminated if I had better planned the time and parked just a block away. I could have possibly transferred the risk if one of my coworkers had driven with me and we had taken his or her car.

In the security assessments that I performed over the years, there were many similarities in how people viewed risk. Not everyone had the ability to see intangible things. Here are some common trends observed:

Example 1:

The virus software and intrusion detection hardware requires updating, but if we change over now, the current products are not compatible with other components that we have in place. To replace the other components is cost-prohibitive. The decision made was to have a "work around" for the potential viruses to be experienced even if it did make the organization vulnerable to viruses, which could mean downtime for a few hours to a couple of days. A major procurement would occur in the coming 12 months.

Example 2:

"The suspect cannot ride in our car," said a security manager in one of our Red Team exercises. In one critical infrastructure assessed, a member of the Red Team (posing as terrorists) was detected and detained inside the gate of the facility. It was a hot day, and several guards surrounded him until someone could show up to tell them what to do — others came over to help decide what to do. As controllers and knowing what else was going on, we realized they had taken their attention off of the critical duties of providing security to protect this important facility, so we asked them why not just take him to the security building. Unbeknownst to them, we already knew that other Red Team members were busy with other breaching attempts that were being missed because of this activity. "We cannot let this person ride in our vehicles; our insurance policy will not allow it," they said. So we waited and waited, and at the end of the exercise, they realized they have to be able to weigh and compare risks, or additional greater risk will be assumed if something as simple as decisions about detainment were not part of the guards' training.

Once threats and vulnerability are known, organizations have generally four options to consider in addressing risk.

1. Accept the risk: is the risk acceptable, or is the cost of managing it greater than the benefit? Management or decision makers may opt to accept the risk.
2. Transfer the risk: many risks can be transferred to other parties (often at a cost), e.g., insurance coverage or well-negotiated third-party and vendor agreements.
3. Treat the risk: take action to reduce the impact or likelihood of the risk, e.g., policies and procedures, training, disaster recovery procedures, or implementation of physical or logical controls.
4. Terminate the risk: if the risk is too great or cannot be managed, the activity may be terminated to eliminate the risk entirely.

Many business owners often feel that they can mitigate risk through insurance policies, but that may not be entirely true. Insurers have changed the way they issue insurance policies and the limits of what they cover due to cost incurred in incidents like the World Trade Center attack and the Oklahoma City bombing. In the article "One Hundred Minutes of Terror That Changed the Global Insurance Industry Forever" by Robert P. Hartwig, Senior Vice President and Chief Economist at the Insurance Information Institute,[2] in the subparagraph titled "To Pay or Not to Pay: 'Act of War' and Terrorism Exclusions" he states,

> Ability to pay is distinct from willingness to pay. While insurers made it clear that that they had sufficient resources to pay losses arising from the attacks, the question of whether the attacks themselves represented a covered cause of loss became a temporary sticking point for some companies. First, some insurers and reinsurers seem to conclude more readily than others that the attacks were compensable. A number appeared to be quietly wondering whether the attacks could be interpreted as an 'act of war.' Such an interpretation would have freed insurers from their liability to pay because *act of war* exclusions are found in virtually every commercial property and personal property insurance policy. The possibility of invoking the *act of war* clause was probably very tempting because President Bush and many other top administration officials repeatedly referred to the attacks as "acts of war." Political rhetoric and saber-rattling aside, insurers and reinsurers quickly concluded that invoking the *act of war* exclusion would probably not withstand a court challenge. This decision was reached after considering court precedent as well as observation of the fact that no formal state of war between

---

[2] R. P. Hartwig, 2002, "One Hundred Minutes of Terror That Changed the Global Insurance Industry Forever. Online: Insurance Information Institute," PDF file, http://www.iii.org/media/hottopics/insurance/sept11/sept11paper/.

the United States and any nation (including Afghanistan) existed on the morning of September 11, 2001.

Rumors that there might be terrorism exclusions in some of the affected property policies were also quickly debunked. Nevertheless, for a period of time it seemed plausible, even likely, that terrorism exclusions might have been negotiated into the terms of the property policies sold to the owners of the World Trade Center complex. After all, terrorists had already tried to blow up the buildings in 1993 by detonating a truck bomb in a parking garage under the towers. Insurers paid $510 million to cover the costs of that attack. Insurers had also paid $125 million to settle claims arising from the 1995 Oklahoma City bombing. No such exclusions were in place, however. The fact that the industry was providing coverage against terrorist attacks for little or no additional premium is a practice that Berkshire Hathaway president and investment guru Warren Buffett would later deride as "foolish" and "a huge mistake." In the wake of the attacks, however, Berkshire quickly emerged as one of the few insurers to offer coverage against terrorist acts, but in exchange for tight limits and a sizable premium.

Further studies and personnel experience have proven that conducting effective risk management and demonstrating proof of plans and procedures to mitigate risks can reduce insurance rates. My observations are that businesses have not adopted effective risk management strategies if they think their policy alone is going to cover any catastrophe and so far there is nothing that guarantees that insurance policies will provide that.

How do you know if you are investing enough to protect critical resources that we rely on to sustain all the daily activities that we seem to take for granted?

Many CI/KR owners and operators recognize the importance of securing and protecting facilities from terrorists and other threats. They make sure their systems can be upgraded or retrofitted to sustain the growing populations that were not foreseen when the infrastructures were first built. Many recognize that proper expenditures are needed to meet their objectives. They perform a good risk assessment to ensure the security expenditures support the risk. Others see it as "a cost" or "not their responsibility," "the government will take care of them," or worse, they overspend on improvements for security when the threat and risk are minimum, or they decide their risk can be mitigated through an insurance policy. Was getting an insurance policy really a risk assessment decision, or was it an easy way out that you hope is not a gamble?

A few years back, an international engineering firm contacted my company for an assessment on their decision to mitigate computer system outages due to a 9/11 type of attack. After a review of their solutions, we informed them that their solution was quite expensive because they were requiring a "zero" outage time for all their systems. Were all the systems really that critical? Did they have alternative procedures for some of the applications on other servers? Were the business units that used those applications really critical to the continued operations of the organization? After several discussions, we asked for their risk decision process analysis so we could review it. Guess what? They did not perform a risk analysis. Their Vice President of Information Technology was the one who made the decision that all systems needed to have zero tolerance for outages, none of the business managers were involved in the decision, and of course they did not complain about the solution. After an extensive education on the risk process, a new solution was identified that still provided the organization effective continuity if a disaster were to occur. The new solution saved them 50 percent in cost. That is a lot when we're talking over a million dollars. Of course, if you have the money to throw around, go for the full gambit of technology solutions and mitigate all possible threat scenarios. I don't think many organizations today have that much money just lying around.

Many risk decisions are made on assumptions: "it has never happened in our industry before," "it happened once and there is no way it will happen again" — and "what are the chances?" The sad thing is that management rides on these assumptions and risks. It's like playing craps, and as in Figure 4.2 the roll could be the lucky seven at the beginning of the game or the unlucky seven that later ends the game.

LESSONS NOT EASILY LEARNED

According to the *9/11 Commission Report*, there are many threat cues that people are just not attuned to. This lack of awareness leads to threats being bold enough to find vulnerabilities to exploit, thus causing us to face high risk. The report showed that analysis, which should have been taking place did not take place. Here are some of the highlights of lessons from the report[3]:

---

[3] 9/11 Commission, *9/11 Commission Report*, http://www.gpoaccess.gov/911/index.html.

Figure 4.2 Lucky or Unlucky Seven

1. The CIA's Counterterrorism Center (CTC) did not analyze how an aircraft, hijacked or explosive laden, might be used as a weapon. It did not perform this kind of analysis from the enemy's perspective ("red team" analysis), even though suicide terrorism had become a principal tactic of Middle Eastern terrorists. If it had done so, such an analysis would have pointed to a suicide operative and large jet aircraft alerts.

2. The CTC did not develop a set of telltale indicators for this method of attack. For example, one such indicator might be the discovery of possible terrorists pursuing flight training to fly large jet aircraft, or seeking to buy advanced flight simulators.

3. The CTC did not propose, and the intelligence community collection management process did not set, requirements to monitor such telltale indicators. Therefore, the warning system was not looking for information such as the July 2001 FBI report of potential terrorist interest in various kinds of aircraft training in Arizona, or the August 2001 arrest of Zacarias Moussaoui because of his suspicious behavior in a Minnesota flight school. In late August, the Moussaoui arrest was briefed to the Director of Central Intelligence (DCI) and other top CIA officials under the

heading "Islamic Extremist Learns to Fly,"[4] language which did not cue them to events like 9/11.

4. Neither the intelligence community nor aviation security experts analyzed systemic defenses within an aircraft or against terrorist-controlled aircraft, suicidal or otherwise. The many threat reports mentioning aircraft were passed to the Federal Aviation Administration (FAA). While that agency continued to react to specific, credible threats, it did not try to perform the broader analysis warning functions described here. No one in the government was taking on that role for domestic vulnerabilities and exploitation by terrorists.

The methods for detecting and then warning of the surprise attack that the U.S. government had so painstakingly developed in the decades after Pearl Harbor did not fail according to the 9/11 Commission; instead, they were not really tried. They were not employed to analyze the enemy that, as the twentieth century closed, was most likely to launch a surprise attack directly against the United States.

We should study the past to learn about changes that are needed in our behaviors and in our procedures to better mitigate terrorist attack risks. The following events are worthy of our own analysis to help us see attacks in a new light with this question in mind — is my organization a target? What did facility owners miss in the months or years before the attacks that could have served as cues of an impending attack?

It is 12:17 P.M. on a Friday in New York City, and a van loaded with 1,500 lbs. of urea nitrate fuel oil has just exploded in the underground garage of World Trade Center Tower 1. The explosion blasts through four sublevels of concrete, killing six people and injuring 1,000, but fortunately for us it did not have the intended domino effect. Tower 1 did not topple over, bringing Tower 2 down and killing the intended 250,000 people on February 26, 1993. How can industry better anticipate such risks to properly mitigate them? Intelligence, early warnings, and threat analysis can address this area of risk. After this incident, risk management was performed and solutions were provided to prevent it from happening again, but it seems the focus was on only this type of threat, and the expansion of other threat possibilities and risks were not considered.

At 9:50 P.M. Tuesday night on June 25, 1998, a dump truck carrying 20,000 pounds of TNT explodes outside the front barriers of the Khobar

---

[4] 9/11 Commission, *9/11 Commission Report*.

Towers in Saudi Arabia, killing 19 airmen and injuring many more. In the months prior to the attack, the unit had taken steps to implement security measures to diminish 36 of 39 vulnerabilities permitted up until that point. The other three were still being worked on. The highest ranking officer had spent most of his assignment implementing risk mitigation measures for Khobar Tower facilities, but three were not within his powers or control. Intelligence sources and an early warning, combined with a plan to act on trend analysis may have helped them in addressing the other vulnerabilities, such as is the host government stable, and can we rely on their security and early warnings?

It is 3:45 A.M. on August 7, 1998, in Washington, D.C. Any minute now, someone is going to receive a call. Two bombs have just exploded, killing 257 and injuring more than 5,000 people at the U.S. Embassies in Tanzania and Nairobi. There is blood and carnage everywhere. What could have prevented this attack? Perhaps, a timely interpretation of threats is easier to perform by people from "low-context"-communicating countries, Low-context communicators prefer to be less direct, relying on what is implied by communication.[5] The United States is a "high-context-communicating" country, where things can be taken at face value rather than as representative of layers of meaning.[6]

At 8:47 A.M., September 11, 2001, citizens of New York feel the blow of another attack at World Trade Center Twin Tower 1. If not for the fact that an airplane was used like a guided missile, we could almost call it a barbaric act from another era. How could we have mitigated this risk? We all need to read the *9/11 Commission Report* — it is surprisingly comprehensive and straightforward on what could possibly have been done to mitigate this risk.

It is 3:11 A.M. on October 12, 2000, and someone in Washington, D.C., will be getting a call in the next 2 minutes. A bomb has just exploded and created a hole on one side of a U.S. Navy destroyer, killing 17 people and injuring 39 others. Some say that sailors at the top deck had just given a friendly wave to the two men on the boat that delivered the bomb as it got closer. The two men on the boat allegedly returned the friendly sentiment. Comprehensive risk analysis on a country's political climate is helpful (for example, is the host government reliable to provide security and early warnings?).

---

[5] Michelle Lebaron, "Cultural Diversity," 2003, http://www.beyondintractability.org/essay/communication_tools/.

[6] Lebaron, "Cultural Diversity."

Along with the 1993 World Trade Center bombing, the 1996 Khobar Towers bombing in Saudi Arabia, and the 2000 attack on the USS *Cole* in Yemen, the U.S. Embassy bombing is one of the major anti-American terrorist attacks that preceded the September 11, 2001, attacks. Comprehensive risk analysis on a country's political climate and its propensity to help terrorists is helpful (for example, is the host government reliable to provide security and early warnings?) in order to develop plans that take this type of imagination into consideration.

What do all these attacks have in common? They put people in high-risk situations in places where the "best of the best" risk managers and security experts need to put their heads together to develop the best risk management solutions. People who work at critical infrastructures have to be "risk aware" and imagine all types of scenarios. Is there a dry run being conducted today for a possible terrorist attack? Are the cars or people who are seen on a regular basis on our premises but not from this company actually collecting information to determine vulnerabilities? Is your "response" being tested through devices being left for you to discover — backpacks with weapons, clay with wires made to look like explosives, or a knife or cutter left inserted into a book with a cutout in the center — as others have reported finding.

The American Society of Civil Engineers (ASCE) report on America's infrastructures and their preparedness ratings. Appendix B includes a copy of the report dated for 2005.[7] The critical infrastructure engineers monitor progress for protecting our CIs; based on the only available report for how this nation is doing on protection and risk mitigation of the 17 CIs, it is not all that great and could use improvement according to what seems to be consistent findings with other annual reporting.

---

[7] American Society of Civil Engineers, "2005 Grades," 2005, http://www.asce.org/report-card/2005/page.cfm?id=103.

5

Readiness Plans ·
Develop, Validate, and Update

A good plan today is better than a perfect plan tomorrow.

U.S. Army General George S. Patton

OVERVIEW

What would you say about the status of your organization's plan for terrorism preparedness and response? Do you have one? It might be found as a component of the organization's security plan, emergency response plan, business continuity, or continuity of operations plan. Is your organization totally prepared and ready or is your plan located on a bookshelf with a little bit of dust on it or in a storage room? Over the years of reviewing hundreds of private and public sector organization plans for terrorism response, I have found that about 75 percent of the organizations (mostly in the private sector) do not have a documented plan. Management's answers for not having a documented plan to respond to terrorism include comments like the following:

"We don't need a written plan; all of our lead personnel know what to do."

This is a common response from many organizations that are not regulated or required to have a documented plan. It is true that if plans are exercised regularly, then detection and response procedures become second nature, but without some semblance of a documented plan or checklist, in the heat of chaos during a disaster critical items will be missed. How do you train new personnel on their responsibilities or procedures? What if lead personnel are not available or do not show up due to circumstances relating to the disaster? How do their "fill-ins" know what to do? A documented plan would provide them with a place to go to obtain information on what to do or whom to contact. It needs to be physically available — not just on the network, in the event of a power outage.

Another common response is "We have a business continuity plan that addresses disaster response, and a terrorism attack is just like responding to a disaster so that the plan will do just fine."

Most business continuity plans only address natural disaster. Yes, there are some similarities between responding to a natural disaster and a terrorist attack. In natural disasters, however, warnings are issued before they hit so personnel have time to take appropriate actions. The plans that do address human threats don't take into account weapons of mass destruction (WMDs) — chemical-, biological-, nuclear-, or radiological-related terrorist events requiring a whole set of response procedures like no other.

Another common statement is "We have an emergency evacuation plan that is practiced regularly, and that is all we need. If an attack happened, we would just evacuate anyway."

That is great — however, even an evacuation plan that is practiced regularly is only one component of a terrorism preparedness plan. It should also address security reporting and response to suspicious activities or events. What if the attack was a WMD attack and you were informed that you were required to shelter in place for 3 to 6 hours or longer or a few days? Will security staff know how and when to control access to the building to prevent further contamination? Has the building been evaluated to identify the best location with the least effect from the outside environment? Will employees know where to assemble to provide them with the best chance of survival? Do you have a communications plan to receive updates from the response teams? Who will know when and how to shut off ventilation systems if facility management is not available? At one evacuation relating to a chemical hazard, firemen responded in full gear — mask and all. No one knew how to get to the heating, ventilation, and air-conditioning (HVAC) room except for the building janitor — and, eventually, someone found him and sent him in. He walked responders to the HVAC room, explained a few things, and then came back out and left. No one thought to give him protective gear, a mask, or even a set of gloves before dispatching him to the "hazard zone."

Some businesses say, "We have insurance for disasters and have a rider policy to include terrorist attacks."

There is no reliable knowledge on whether an insurance policy would cover all the damages and impact caused by a terrorist attack, as discussed in Chapter 4 — especially all the human life that might be lost. Employees would be devastated and morale would be affected if they knew the organization had not provided reasonable efforts for their safety and security to protect them from a terrorist attack and instead relied on insurance to mitigate the risk of loss. There should never be an overreliance on insurance. Insurance laws on this topic are still relatively new and not the most reliable method for mitigating terrorist risk when a plan would be the better approach. Additionally, any company that is part of the critical infrastructure (CI) community must have plans developed and implemented.

Some have stated, "Terrorists wouldn't attack us because we are a 'widget' company. Besides, there is a federal building down the street that they would attack over us."

Based on the attack history of terrorists, a "widget" company more than likely would not be a terrorist target. But, does that widget company provide products to the government or a critical infrastructure? If so, it could be identified as a possible target of opportunity or a secondary target. Terrorists' thought process is as follows: if the federal building seems to be too hard of a target and this company provides products to the government or a CI, and are an easier target, it's just as good of a target. If you do not provide products to the government or a CI, think about an attack on a federal building that may be nearby. If the attack was a large one or it included WMDs, how would that affect your organization? I am sure that businesses in the vicinity of the Twin Towers that felt they were not a target never expected to be impacted the way they were on 9/11.

Terrorism preparedness plans should be documented, well communicated, and rehearsed by everyone affected, and they must be able to guide a wide range of responses to different threat scenarios. General thoughts from planners on the purpose of a plan include the following: a plan is a tool to educate and provide instinctive response when it is exercised regularly; and another thought is that it is a checklist to provide guidance because rarely is the scenario you develop a plan for the one that happens. Both thoughts have their merit. The human body may go into shock and freeze when faced with a terrorist attack, but confident people who know what to do are likely to minimize the impact of the incident, respond rationally, and assist in recovery efforts.

Large corporations that do not seem to be classified under any of the 17 critical infrastructure sectors need to adopt their own preparedness strategies — that includes planning, as if they were part of the critical infrastructures. They can utilize the resources that the Department of Homeland Security (DHS) has assembled for private sector use and guidelines. Hopefully, your organization is well ahead of the Homeland Security requirements and plans are prepared, well communicated to employees, exercised, and efficient and effective for response.

HOW TERRORISTS PLAN

Al Qaeda dedicates extensive resources to planning and training through various means, including distribution of publications as well as planners meeting in training camps and other locations worldwide. They plan carefully and extensively and exercise their plan before carrying out their attacks. Figure 5.1 shows Al Qaeda's training manual and other publications that are used to spell out how a terrorist should put a plan together. Al Qaeda conducts hands-on planning after all the information is gathered, assessments are made, and risks are evaluated. Sound familiar? Terrorists receive extensive training to plan attacks. They have support cells that are dispersed throughout the world, and almost all are on standby to render the assistance needed to plan attacks. How would you compare your efforts against Al Qaeda's planning efforts?

| Al Qaeda's Biweekly Online Training Manual | Al Qaeda Training Manual | Magazine for Women Mujahideen | Al Qaeda's Biweekly Online Propaganda Magazine |

Figure 5.1 Al Qaeda Training Publications

Figure 5.2[1] is the work of Valdis Krebs, an expert on social network mapping who took public sources and began mapping the terrorist links after 9/11. The different shades of gray represent the event linkages. As illustrated in the map, a large amount of coordination was required to execute the mission. Obviously, this was not executed without a plan. Krebs has been mapping networks since 1988. His type of skills can be useful to protect us from such future attacks. To be able to respond effectively to an organization that puts this much effort into its attack-planning efforts, we need to put as much effort into our plans for prevention and response.

COLLABORATION WITH EXTERNAL ORGANIZATIONS

When developing plans for terrorism preparedness, external collaboration with other organizations is critical. This includes professional security and

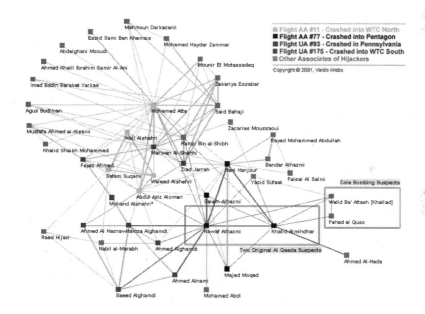

Figure 5.2 9/11 Attack Terror Network

---

[1] Valdis E. Krebs and INSNA, 2001, with the kind permission of *Connections* and the International Network for Social Network Analysis. Copyright © 2001, and http://www.firstmonday.org/Issues/issue7_4/krebs/#k1.

continuity-planning associations in your area, local industry and response organizations, city response planners, and neighboring businesses. They can provide insight on lessons learned, particularities with the local area's detection and response, and dismiss any assumptions you might have on immediate response and whom you can rely on for support.

About 4 years ago, a business occupying a high-rise building in downtown San Francisco had just finished its emergency evacuation plan and was eager to exercise and validate it. The date was set; all plans were in place and disseminated. Management, key personnel, and all the employees were trained on how to evacuate, where to go, and how to report so accountability could be performed. The alarms went off, and the planned evacuation was in progress. Unbeknownst to this company and by coincidence, about two blocks away another high-rise was exercising its evacuation. Employees began arriving at their designated assembly area — a small grassy park about four blocks away that was easily identifiable and far enough away not to impede emergency responder efforts. The assembly area began to fill quickly; in fact, people were overflowing into the streets. As managers began to get accountability, there were many people who were not on each group's list, and managers could not find some of the ones who were. Employees were reporting to someone who was doing accountability where they were located, but they did not recognize him or her. Finally, it dawned on one of the planners that this comprised more people than they had in his company — and he wondered, Was there another event going on that they did not know about? Employees were given the "all clear" to return to the building because of all the chaos. The planner went over to an employee he did not recognize to find out what was going on. He found out that two other large companies had identified the same assembly area — not a problem, since it is unlikely that both buildings would be evacuated at the same time. They agreed to precoordinate their exercises so they would not get so messy. Weeks later while attending a city facility manager emergency response seminar, the two planners were talking and laughing about the incident and were overheard by other building emergency response planners. To their amazement, several other high-rise buildings had the same assembly area. If they had coordinated through an organized effort or shared information among each other, this would not have happened — again not a problem, since it is unlikely they would all evacuate at the same time. But what if a terrorist event with WMDs, an explosion that causes structural failure, a fully engulfed high-rise fire, or an earthquake required more than the building affected to evacuate — and all did happen at the same time? In

100

several other planning meetings with the other planners involving the city fire chief, other adequate assembly areas in the city were identified and everyone agreed to incorporate changes and adjust their plans. In fact, the city plan had identified several assembly areas in case of a city-wide disaster, and now both businesses and city were on the same sheet of music.

In the northwestern United States near a small city, a consultant was asked to review a government facility's antiterrorism and response plans. The plans were not very robust: the responses to all hazardous events were to evacuate and wait for first responders and city government support or move to their continuity site if the situation dictated, and transportation routes were available. These plans were in place even though the facility had people from previous assignments trained in medical emergency response and hazardous materials due to their storage of those types of materials on-site. The consultant inquired and was informed that the city would take care of them, and if it was a terrorist event the federal government would be involved. The facility did not have the time to develop robust plans or train people, so it kept its plan simple. The consultant attended the city's monthly terrorism planning response meeting and met with some of the key planners. What he found out was contrary to the facility security and emergency planner's assumptions. He requested that the city and facility planner meet. The city plan indicated that during an event that affected the city, they would request support from the government facility since they had personnel trained in emergency response and hazardous materials. The plan also indicated that the federal facility was low on the city's response priority because the city assumed that since the facility had trained personnel, it could be self-sufficient longer than other facilities and businesses and not expect any city help for 3 to 6 hours or longer depending on the scale of the attack or other hazardous event. The key point of this actual story is that both entities developed assumptions of support or nonsupport in their plans without ever coordinating their planning efforts. The chaos would have never been known until an event occurred or they had exercised their plans with all parties involved. It is important that organizations — both corporate private and public — are involved not only in the local business and city disaster or antiterrorism response planning efforts but also in local business, city, and government terrorism prevention and detection planning efforts.

Sharing of plans, information, and experiences is vital to efforts against terrorism. Developing collaboration and mutual agreements with local businesses can expand the areas of awareness, detection, and intelligence —

like a business community watch. Of all the sites assessed over the years, only about one-fourth of the organizations of public sector critical infrastructures were taking advantage of this opportunity; none of the private organizations were known to be using this concept. There are several associations that organization planners or security directors should become involved with to obtain additional information that may be helpful in the preparedness and planning process. They include the following:

- Local Association of Contingency Planners
- Terrorism Early Warning Groups (TEWGs)
- FBI InfraGard
- Local ASIS International Chapter
- ASIS International
- Information Systems Audit and Control Association (ISACA)

My interaction with DHS and private sector entities has provided a unique look into how government and business view terrorism preparedness requirements. Both audiences must work together, and a few work together efficiently and effectively, but others do not yet know that they have to work together. The latter — consisting mostly of private sector infrastructure owners — creates many gaps in critical infrastructure preparedness. Plans that should be in place are not. Some reasons cited in a Government Accountability Office (GAO) report as to why 100 percent of the plans are not completed by mostly the private sector is that key representatives from all sectors' agencies and their private sector counterparts have not yet established communication.[2] Some had good relationships because of a history of working together to solve money-laundering crimes or because of the need to prepare for Y2K, and simply kept building on those relationships. The need to educate the private sector was cited as one solution for promoting self-governing and self-preparing in order to have effective plans. Effective plans come from learning from others and sharing with others — which require relationships and collaboration.

BEGINNING THE DEVELOPMENT PROCESS

If your plan is not yet put together, determine why. Once the threat and vulnerably assessments have been completed, risks have been identified,

---

[2] Eileen R. Larence, "GAO Report," GAO-07-626T, http://www.gao.gov/new.items/d07626t.pdf.

and measures have been taken to mitigate the risks, the next step is the development of the written plan. To begin "plan development," management must develop a strategy for its approach, or "plan to plan." One of the best ways is through "brainstorming," as illustrated in Figure 5.3. Is the plan going to be a part of an existing plan or a separate plan? What members of the organization will be members of the plan development team? How will the company or organization communicate, train, exercise, and maintain the plan?

The "human factor," among other things, is what gives companies the ability "to imagine" and plan for different disasters so that they can write good plans. The team that works on the plan — note that I do say "team" — has to be carefully selected in order to take advantage of this quality. Some forethought should go into organizing the team. As discussed in Chapter 7, some people have a better imagination than others and will be able to imagine all the possible scenarios quite easily. The plan development team or workgroup should be a diverse group of individuals who can provide different perspectives based on their experience and critical functions within the organization. External individuals such as law enforcement and emergency responders should be identified but

Figure 5.3 Brainstorming

103

only included when the discussions are planned for an area in which they have expertise that would be vital and to review response procedures to ensure the procedures are in line with how they could actually respond. When personnel are notified they are on a team like this, they usually are not highly motivated. It is seen as just another additional responsibility among the list of others they already have, or as a waste of time because in their view, it will never be implemented. Where will the plan be reviewed and worked on? If the conference room where this will happen is not well lit, smells bad, or is too hot or too cold, choose another place or make some changes to improve the room. People are already stressed with all the activities in the workplace — the last thing they need is to be distracted by the physical distractions and negative energy of the room. On the day that team members come together, perhaps make it a casual dress day so that people can be comfortable — one less distraction. Many of the people who were involved in threat assessment, vulnerability assessment, and risk management in earlier phases will end up being on this team.

The team or work group may be very large at first. After the first meeting, it is ideal to divide the effort into subgroups with expertise in specific areas to develop components of the plan. Several times during the development process, the whole group should come back together again. Some team members will be members of different work groups because of their specialty skills (e.g., security, lawyers, and facility engineers).

The first meeting is very important to set the stage for all participants. Develop meeting objectives and an agenda, and stick to it. Communicate it to all participants ahead of time. Start with the following:

- Identify a person experienced in facilitating meetings.
- Identify a recorder.
- Schedule a conference room large enough to accommodate all persons comfortably and that is scheduled to allow for going over planned time, so you will not be disrupted.
- Ensure that all those involved rearrange all appointments and turn off cell phones.
- Instruct invitees on the importance of not delegating attendance of this meeting to subordinates.
- Schedule a corporate executive to kickoff the meeting — this demonstrates organizational support — and request that the same individual occasionally check in and make an appearance at other scheduled meetings to show continued support.

One method for jump-starting the process is to make it fun. It is not what you know that makes or breaks your plan but being able to apply what you know in a way that will work. People provide valuable input when they are excited about something. Adding a few elements of creativity into the process that are different than what the participants are used to enables their brains to work differently. If people involved in developing a plan feel that it will never get management support or be exercised or used, they will not put in the effort — and will consider it a waste of time.

Find a different way to relate to this important document. Studies show that people learn or adopt practices when the following apply:

- They have to — after they have suffered a terrorist attack or survived a disaster.
- When the process is fun and interesting.
- When creating an environment where everyone feels that upper management supports the effort.
- When it is elevated to a high level of importance.

Have an icebreaker to put people at ease. Have little trinkets you can give to people every time someone comes up with a good "brainstorming" idea. Pass them a trinket in a spontaneous, unexpected way — pull it out of a sack when it warrants giving away. Do not make such a big deal about the different method in which the meeting was conducted — people will walk away from the meeting feeling as if they were a part of something important and bigger than them. They will also appreciate that there were surprises — the unexpected trinkets. The trinkets can come from a bag of trade show goodies that usually pile up somewhere in the company or anything else that is not expensive and excessive. This method of conducting the meeting is, as mentioned, just an icebreaker; in Chapter 8, there is more information for implementing change and building a strong team to tackle any task or respond to terrorism.

PLAN DEVELOPMENT

This chapter is not intended to provide all the details of plan development — that would be a separate book on "how to develop a response plan to terrorism." It is intended to provide insight, stimulate thought, and provide lessons learned to help your organization in effective preparedness against terrorism.

It is important first that we understand some flaws that make plans ineffective. There are a few common flaws consistent across industries with regard to most plans that organizations should strive to change:

- Often, employees and key personnel do not know the plan exists.
- Plans tend to exist in draft mode.
- Communication trees are often out of date.
- The procedures that people are practicing do not match the plan.
- Plans are developed in a "vacuum" by one or two persons.
- The plan is great "on paper," but it has never been exercised to be validated or to identify gaps.

Corporations with global locations and employees abroad need a plan with a preset list of procedures in the event of a terrorist attack at their location — as well as how the headquarters will respond to an attack at one of their overseas facilities. Events can quickly become volatile, requiring immediate evacuations out of the country without the possibility of getting assistance from a U.S. Embassy, the U.S. State Department, or any other government agency. Who can you rely on to assist with such a requirement? In such cases, DHS usually cannot advise those corporations on what to do. This requires extensive research and planning on the corporations' part when they are in the brainstorming stages of plan development. It is not uncommon for a large company to turn to DHS and say, Now that the train or subway has been attacked in (fill in the blank), what should we tell our people? Should we tell them to stay in their office and shelter in place? Should they stay away from public transit? There is general information available through the Department of State that can be interpreted and adjusted to assist the corporation in developing their plans for these situations, but information may not be that tactical in nature, and Web sites may not be updated in a timely manner when the information is needed.

For plans to work as intended — certain fundamentals are essential:

- Executive "buy-in" and support.
- A budget for proper plan maintenance and exercising.
- Plans must be documented in a clear, concise manner that is easily understandable by anyone who reads them.
- Training needs to be provided to employees and personnel with key responsibilities in the plan.

- The plan must be exercised to be validated and to ensure the plan is going to work.
- The plan must be kept updated.

Remember that plans are a vision of how an effort will be managed. Plans also require guidance — some will be included in the plan and other guidance is developed to support the plan, such as the following:

- *Policies*: The general rules to be followed and enforced within the plan.
- *Procedures*: The formal methods for "how to" perform tasks that comply with the policies and the plan.
- *Practices*: Enhancements to the procedures but not replacements for them.

Terrorism preparedness plans — whether they are stand-alone plans or are part of another plan such as business continuity or emergency plans — have to be in compliance with DHS standards (i.e., the National Infrastructure Protection Plan, or NIPP) in private sector critical infrastructures and key resource facilities, as listed in Table 1.1 in Chapter 1. The plans need to dovetail or comply with the NIPP, as already mentioned in earlier chapters. DHS has dedicated many of its resources in human capital and funding to developing frameworks and models for preparedness plans across many domains — for how government will work with government before, during, and after an attack or disaster, and how it will interact with the private sector (critical and noncritical organizations), citizens, and families.

Everything needed to put the preparedness plans in place resides in the DHS Web site. DHS has not done a very good job of publicizing and reminding the end users of the vast resources available, but many businesses do not know this. What private sector companies will find at the DHS site is "everything" needed to be in compliance with Homeland Security requirements — and, comprehensive or not, they are still useful.

OVERLOOKED PLAN ITEMS

One recommended document to use as a template for plans is the NIPP. It may seem that I am championing this plan — and overlooking anyone else's great plan. That is not the case, but if we are to all use similar standards for preparedness, and if critical infrastructures already use the

NIPP, then all of us need to have similar — if not the same — response measures and capabilities. Every organization is different and has different requirements, and there is not one template to use as a guide for all industries. Thus, the NIPP is not the only one to choose from among guides or templates. All plan templates I have seen or developed required customizing — but they retained the critical and basic components to meet the organization's culture and requirements.

Internal Communications Considerations

The planning process must include discussions on employee communications — how to communicate, when to communicate, and what to communicate. People need time to prepare mentally and emotionally for change or for whatever is coming. Incorporate a good communication plan that addresses communications before, during, and after an incident. The communications must meet code requirements and include details about people with special needs. Determine the different communication methods that can be utilized. Also consider how you will communicate when power is out and the "public address" system or phones are down. Do you have a backup for this, are there emergency backup generators, and is the public address system included on the grid or does it have its own backup power? This is of paramount importance because people may need very specific direction and instructions.

Your plan must also address how security will communicate with building occupants and key personnel during an attack or an emergency. Consider an alternate method of communication with key personnel within the building using two-way radios. Include a component for the communications plan for when electronic means are not available or — even more importantly — if cell phones should not be used in a bomb threat or when a bomb has been identified in your facility. Bombs can be accidentally electronically activated by cell phones and two-way radios (when you key the mike).

Internal communications between security personnel should be included in the plan. The use of two-way radios is common, with the telephone as a backup. Even though they are more expensive, encrypted radios should be used if the budget accommodates. Even with encrypted radios, a code system (similar to what the police use) should also be used to prevent intelligence-gathering efforts conducted by criminals and terrorists.

External Communications

The mechanism for communications between federal, state, and private sector responders just prior to an incident and after an incident is still not efficient today.

A major component of the preparedness plan should incorporate how industry will interact and communicate with DHS — starting with assigning the right people with "people skills." There is a good outreach effort on the terrorism prevention front between government sector councils and private sector owners of critical infrastructures and key resources. They meet annually, quarterly, or more frequently, but this is not adequate to enable integrated communications between both sectors in a recovery situation.

Crisis and Media Communications

In the planning process, discussions must occur that identify communications to the media and family members — how to communicate, when to communicate, and what to communicate.

Employees, family members of the employees, stakeholders, and the media need to be kept aware in a crisis or panic before rumors set in. If handled improperly, it could affect employee morale, destroy the organization's reputation and bottom line, and result in negative publicity. They need to know that something is being done other than what they are observing on television. In most situations, the first time we find out how this impacts recovery is after a disaster or in the conduct of realistic exercises. The solution is to prepare ahead of time through planning — identifying a team to handle crisis communication, developing a plan that identifies potential problems and solutions, training the crisis team, and exercising the plan with the team.

A crisis communications plan requires facility executive managers to be involved as soon as a crisis hits — not just any manager but management at the top level who can make a decision on behalf of the organization. This part of planning needs to include what the line of authority or chain of command will be in a response effort. What if the President and CEO are involved in the incident and are incapacitated or, worse, hospitalized — who is next in line?

When selecting the right people for the crisis communications team — note again that I do say "team" — they need to be formally trained and experienced in crisis communications and conflict resolution.

In most companies, crisis communications is the responsibility of the Public Relations Department, and in some cases I have seen it tasked to the Human Resources Department. To prevent conflicting statements and rumors and provide continuity, a single person should be selected as the spokesperson; of course, you should identify alternates in case the primary person is not available. This is often and commonly overlooked. That designated person needs to have the ability to be in direct communications with the top management decision maker who is available.

It is best to identify primary and alternate locations to set up a media communications center and equip it with the tools needed to communicate — phones, computers to prepare news releases, and fax machines or an Internet connection. All this is needed to communicate to employees as well as the media. For the media, it is best to plan on at least two news updates a day. Tell the whole story — openly, completely, and honestly. For employees and family members, a call center should be available for them to get critical updates. New technologies today allow for updates to be provided via 1-800 numbers that employees and family members call into to get the latest information. Remember, though, that these must be kept updated, and the information provided must not have any inconsistencies or conflicting guidance — none. There is nothing worse than an employee or family member calling into a number for 4 hours and hearing the same message — provide as much accurate information as possible, keep them informed, and demonstrate the company's concerns through your statements and actions. Designate one person for this effort — a detail-oriented person who can multitask.

The last thing in developing your crisis communications plan is ensuring that policies are in place for employees and education is provided on how to deal with the media. A company recovering from a disaster does not want the added pressures of having critical information breached, having to retract statements, or having rumors become like reality — especially when they are about who is to blame, how many people were injured or killed, and who they were.

Over the years, many corporations and government agencies have suffered the consequences of ineffective crisis communications plans — public blame, a lack of confidence by customers and employees, and financial losses. These were caused by representatives and employees providing speculations; pointing the finger at who was to blame; refusing to answer media inquiries — leading the media to make their own assumptions; releasing information that violates individuals' privacy; or even using a crisis to pitch products or services. You will find that by developing and training employees in an effective crisis communications plan, there will be fewer interruptions during recovery efforts and more cooperation and understanding by employees and the public.

Plan Response for Bomb Threats

Bomb threats are by far the most common method used by terrorists and others seeking to cause alarm and disruption. Generally, terrorists do not begin a campaign with bomb threats, but the potential exists that it would be used as a ploy to gather intelligence about response capabilities. However, the disruptive effects of actual terrorist bombings may be amplified subsequently with bomb threats. Bombings also inspire hoax threats. Therefore, all organizations must have well-established protocols for dealing with bomb threats. First, it is essential that the threat be relayed to the responsible persons, whether it initially is telephoned to the police, transportation company headquarters, switchboard operators, stationmasters, toll-free help lines, reservation centers, or any other number. Everyone should be trained to obtain as much information as possible from the caller and promptly forward it to the appropriate authorities. A sample bomb threat checklist can be found in Appendix C, "Bomb Threat Checklist." This checklist should be located next to anyone's phone whose number is published. Using a checklist is important in gathering valuable information for investigations. It has been proven that no matter how much training is provided for response to a bomb threat phone call, people forget under a crisis situation. Using a checklist provides them with a quick reference list of information to gather and particular sounds to be aware of in the background, especially immediately after the call.

A protocol for evaluating the threat is needed. Actions can range from watchful waiting to local searches to shutdowns and immediate evacuations. Evacuations will be rare. Authors of bomb threats are rarely bombers. Still, even when threats appear to be hoaxes, as almost all are, they cannot be ignored. A reasonable assessment must be made, and appropriate action taken. The desire to avoid needless disruptions must be balanced against the threat to public safety. Guidelines based upon actual experience (and defensible in a court of law if things go wrong) are helpful in taking the pressure off local decision makers.

During an exercise last year, a bomb threat was called into a manager's office to evaluate training requirements and procedures. Once the caller informed the manager it was a bomb threat, the manager immediately dropped the phone, stood up, and yelled out in the office, "Bomb

111

threat — everyone get the (expletive) outta here!" — and the manager proceeded to run for the exit, leading the pack.

Addressing Loading Docks and Mailrooms

Mailrooms and loading docks are vulnerable to the delivery of chemicals or bombs, especially if you are not fortunate enough to have high-tech equipment for inspecting received packages. A vulnerability of a loading dock is that it usually receives large vehicles capable of delivering explosives. Human visual inspections may not be enough to detect true threats. Appendix D, "Best Practices for Mail Center Security," provides mailroom procedure guidelines that may be helpful in developing your own.

What should you address in your security or antiterrorism plan? Your plan should address measures to deter the threat, detect the threat, and respond to the threat. To deter a threat, many organizations do not have their mailroom located in the same building as the one that the other employees work in — unlike others, where it is located in the basement. Loading docks receiving deliveries should also not be located in the same building as the critical functions of the organizations or where most of the employees work.

Access control should be limited and restricted so delivery vehicles are not allowed to veer from their course to another area. Inspections of vehicles by security must be thorough, including the undercarriage and inside. Many facilities establish procedures so vehicles do not enter unless the person expecting the package notifies security that a delivery is coming and provides them with information on the company and driver delivering. These are just some examples. During terrorist or criminal intelligence gathering and surveillance, it may be enough to deter and gives the perception that your facility is difficult to attack.

Keeping informed on the latest trends on attempts and actual attacks using mailrooms is critical in conducting your threat and risk assessments as well as in improving your ability to detect threats and developing good plans. One of the best Web sites and nationwide mail incidents alert providers is Mail Center Security (www.mailroomsafety.us). This site also provides mailroom security information and training. By registering, you can receive monthly e-mail reports on tactics and trends regarding mailroom incidents nationwide. Of course, additional information on detecting threats can be found at the United States Postal Service Web site (www.usps.gov).

PLAN VALIDATION

Plan validation and plan updates are part of your plan maintenance program. Validation (commonly known as *exercising your plan*) should be addressed in your plan. It should address at a minimum the procedures for conducting exercises and an exercise schedule. Without validating your plan, how do you know if it works? Many organizations consider their plans validated when they do an annual review. This is not a plan validation and neither are tabletop exercises, as depicted in Figure 5.4. A tabletop exercise is one of the steps that lead toward "plan" validation. A "plan" is fully validated when it is either successfully executed in a "real time crisis" or after being exercised in a scenario driven exercise. Chapter 9 provides more information on exercises.

Plan validation is performed at the completion of policy integration, program awareness, and training steps. To conduct an effective exercise, the following checklist is provided. These are items you must perform.

- Develop exercise objectives that are comprehensive, approved, and measurable.
- Exercises should be scheduled on a regular basis — determined by your industry (or, if not, at least annually).
- Exercise objectives must support your plan goals.

Figure 5.4 Tabletop Exercise

113

- Each exercise (tabletop, walk-through, or full) must have appropriate metrics to meet or exceed its objectives. Auditors are included in the validation process.
- Executives, "upper management," crisis management, and security should be included in the validation objectives approval process.
- Exercise results; any changes must be documented.
- Required plan revalidation items are captured and included in the "next scheduled exercise."
- Conduct a postexercise meeting as soon as possible upon completion of the exercise, and include all key participants, facilitators, and evaluators, as well as any role players, to identify what went well and what needs improvement.
- Develop an exercise "results" report that identifies the type of exercise and includes those activities, successes, shortcomings, and individuals and teams involved (internal and external), and how each addressed the objectives.

Plan validation, or exercising, is a key measure of the success of your security and response program.

PLAN UPDATES

Plan updates are a critical piece of any plan maintenance. All organization plans, policies, and procedures require updating. This is often overlooked, especially with security and response plans since they are not used on a regular basis. Plans must be kept updated to be effective. You should have scheduled updates at least annually, updates performed when there are major organizational changes that affect polices and procedures or key personnel, and updates after exercises and after an event has happened requiring you to implement your plan. These updates are to make improvements to procedures from gaps identified during these events. In your plan development, you should describe your update review process, change control, and update procedures.

PLAN TO SHARE INFORMATION

Information sharing between the public and private sectors is difficult. Almost across the nation, there is the question of what to share, with what frequency, and how to act on the information shared. There is one premier frustration between the two sectors: "expectations" on both sides. The private sector expects timely and actionable intelligence. Neither side can define *timely* and *actionable*. But "timely" is not capable of being measured in *hours* or *days*. This creates a definite problem because the private sector most of the time defines "timely" as tactically sufficient to put decisions into action. They expect DHS entities to provide specific information and tell them within minutes of an incident that the incident is imminent and they should now take action. The government can only provide the private sector broad-based information of strategic value. When DHS discovers a terrorist plot or monitors a plot in progress — it is usually from a distance. For example, this type of "plot" monitoring involves plots that emerged in Europe, but there is no telling when, in the future, it will hit the States — if at all. What can the private sector do with that information? Sometimes, the private sector stumbles upon information that gets submitted to the right office, and on some occasions the private sector–public sector sharing networks as envisioned by everyone.

Understanding how DHS works will help us develop better plans so that areas where the private sector has to be self-sufficient can be addressed in the plan. This is how the process works when DHS learns that a specific attack is being plotted inside U.S. borders. They cannot track it or investigate it unless there are substantial actions by the terrorists for which the terrorists can be held accountable — conspiracy is not adequate. The actions have to be specific enough to demonstrate and prove "intent." The reason that the terrorist planners of the Fort Dix 2007 attack plot were able to be brought to prosecution was that they had taken substantial actions to put the plot of killing many Army soldiers into motion, and the authorities were able to link specific actions to them. The alleged plot included conducting surveillance of the Army base and purchasing multiple firearms, including assault weapons, handguns, shotguns, and semi-automatic weapons.[3] In other words, it was more than just intent or a plan in someone's head. The private sector needs to gain an understanding of these limitations because when they come to realize that these are the rules and laws by which DHS operates, it may lessen the frustration.

DHS can provide strategic information that can be used to "prepare and protect" over the long run, but generally nothing may fall under

---

[3] A group of six radical Islamist men, allegedly plotting to stage an attack on the Fort Dix military base in New Jersey, were arrested by the FBI on May 7, 2007. They were subsequently charged with planning an attack against U.S. soldiers.

immediate actions. The private sector needs to understand that although fusion centers are in place and DHS attempts to share as much as possible, the private sector also needs to develop its own capability to do the following:

- Gather threat information and analyze threats.
- Integrate their protective approach to include a unified effort between their physical security, IT security, and emergency response teams.
- Invest in whatever they feel is appropriate to protect critical infrastructures; DHS will not direct this effort or specify how much should be budgeted for this effort.
- Train and be prepared.

The NIPP is a mandate and guideline published by the U.S. Department of Homeland Security designed to ignite a national unified approach for integrating critical infrastructure protection initiatives through partnerships between the private sector and federal, state, local, and tribal governments. Make sure your corporate plan adheres to what is required in the NIPP.

Up until June 2006, it was not clear what methods of assessments owners and operators would use and how *critical* would be defined. The method of assessing, prioritizing, ranking, securing, and protecting our nation's infrastructures at first was not clear and was finally spelled out in the final version of the NIPP in June 2006 — about 2 years after sectors voiced confusion. Those who had plans in place simply had to update them, but there were many others who had not even started, and the process can take a while if no work has been done on it. Those that did not have plans were waiting on someone to provide them with a plan template. Some of the sectors claimed that they were members of a sector that was too diverse in its composition to establish relationships (for example, the food and water sectors). Some sectors did not understand the criticality of their role — they did not know if they were small role players, major producers of the information in the plans, or consumers of the plans — meaning someone is going to prepare the plan for them, and they are still trying to figure out who that "someone" is. What does it take for organizations to realize they must take care of their own?

There is a hierarchy of role players who have to put these plans together: government agencies, private sector owners and operators, and representatives of a broad base who interact with critical infrastructures. But much confusion exists as to who is required to prepare plans and submit them, and who is expected to have plans simply because it makes sense. Why do we have to be required to develop a plan before we do it? Early chapters of this book and world headlines should motivate most readers that whether it is required or not, they should have a plan.

The relationship that exists between national-level DHS resources and the private sector is one where there are many misconceptions, many wrong expectations, and a lack of understanding of roles and responsibilities within the two groups further contributing to a lack of plans in many organizations.

WHAT DHS SAYS ABOUT PROTECTED CRITICAL INFRASTRUCTURE INFORMATION (PCII)

The PCII Program was established because of the Critical Infrastructure Information Act of 2002 (CII Act). It creates a new framework that enables members of the private sector to — for the first time — voluntarily submit confidential information regarding the nation's critical infrastructure to the DHS with the assurance that the information, if it satisfies the requirements of the CII Act, will be protected from public disclosure.

The PCII Program seeks to facilitate greater sharing of critical infrastructure information (CII) among the owners and operators of the critical infrastructures and government entities with infrastructure protection responsibilities, thereby reducing the nation's vulnerability to terrorism.

To implement and manage the program, DHS has created the PCII Program Office within the Information Analysis and Infrastructure Protection (IAIP) Directorate. The PCII Program Office will receive critical infrastructure information and evaluate it to determine whether it qualifies for protection under the CII Act.

Why was the program created? An essential element of ensuring Homeland Security is the protection of the nation's critical infrastructures by Federal, State, local, and private sector efforts. These infrastructures are the systems, assets, and industries upon which our national security, economy, and public health depend. It is estimated that over 85 percent of the critical infrastructure is owned and operated by the private sector. Recognizing that the private sector may be reluctant to share information with the Federal Government if it (information) could be publicly disclosed, Congress passed the CII Act in 2002 with its provisions for protection from public disclosure. The security and protection of the Nation's

117

critical infrastructure are of paramount importance not only to the Federal, State, and local governments but also to private utilities, businesses, and industries. There are several benefits for private sector participants in the PCII Program:

- Proprietary, confidential, or sensitive infrastructure information can now be shared with governmental entities that share the private sector's commitment to a more secure homeland.
- Information Analysis Infrastructure Protection.
- Protected Critical Infrastructure Information Program.
- Information sharing will result in better identification of risks and vulnerabilities, which will help industry partner with others in protecting their assets.
- By voluntarily submitting CII to the Federal Government, industry is helping to safeguard and prevent disruption to the American economy and way of life.
- Private industry is demonstrating good corporate citizenship that may save lives and protect communities.

PCII may be used for many purposes, focusing primarily on analyzing and securing critical infrastructure and protected systems, risk and vulnerabilities assessments, and assisting with recovery as appropriate. The IAIP Directorate plays a critical role in securing the homeland by identifying and assessing threats and mapping those threats against vulnerabilities such as critical infrastructure.

6

Prevention, Detection, and Response Factors across Sectors

Trust, but verify.

President Ronald Reagan

OVERVIEW

As the public becomes more educated about terrorism and what this nation has to do to be prepared to defend itself against terrorism, the public will be less inclined to ask what government is doing to protect us. They will arrive at the conclusion that everyone, including them, has a role in contributing to preparedness. Then there will be an expectation — from a wider audience than just the Department of Homeland Security (DHS) — that companies, organizations, and government agencies responsible for critical infrastructures are taking proactive measures to ensure preparedness and protect the infrastructures from attacks. Table 6.1 ("Worldwide Terrorism by Target") shows the number of attacks documented over the last 3 years. Trends have shown that numbers of attacks climb and drop, but not dramatically; the trend for the last 40 years has been an increase in attacks altogether. Table 6.1 also illustrates the type of targets that were attacked between 2005 and 2007.

Looking at Table 6.1, if we had more details about "Other" and "Business" — whether they fall under any of the 17 critical infrastructures

Table 6.1 Worldwide Terrorism by Target

	Incidents			Fatalities			Injuries		
	2005	2006	2007	2005	2006	2007	2005	2006	2007
Business	248	264	110	323	379	236	1,134	1,188	878
Educational institutions	188	220	102	64	120	208	103	148	404
Government	1,177	1,010	433	1,207	1,147	608	2,201	1,615	1,291
Police	1,166	2,013	988	2,714	3,309	2,037	4,701	6,091	3,844
Private citizens and property	909	1,273	396	1,872	4,681	2,408	3,489	8,184	5,216
Religious figures and institutions	178	462	136	494	561	397	1,035	1,141	799
Utilities	230	331	94	72	237	68	137	177	39
Other	899	1,086	488	1,448	1,636	965	2,462	2,447	2,158
Total	4,995	6,659	2,747	8,194	12,070	6,927	15,262	20,991	14,629

Source: MIPT Terrorism Knowledge Base. Target, region, and tactic data on terrorist incidents will be reported in sequential months. (Chart by Mike Moran.)

or not — we would get a better sense of the threat against infrastructures. Assuming that they are part of the equation, by removing "Private Citizens and Property," the numbers would then show that 82 percent of the attacks were against infrastructures worldwide.

Table 6.2 ("Worldwide Terrorism by Region") shows attacks for a 6-month period in 2007. There were only four in North America, but many others around the world. What this table seems to communicate is that many terrorist attacks are still concentrated around other world regions — not so close to our borders, and certainly not inside our borders — but for how long? The world is not large anymore, and U.S. interests are geographically dispersed throughout the world — so our people, businesses, and government can still be attacked. It would seem, then, that now is the time to relook at how we practice security and what we are building in the way of preparedness and deterrence. Deterrence can work when the stage of imminent threats is not already at our door. If threats are imminent and warning messages have been issued, it may be too late to launch a deterrent campaign. The threat is in motion, and now the targets, "whoever they are," have to be in somewhat of a disadvantage and hope they can "grasp as quickly as possible" how they are going to be attacked, and then react to it as quickly as possible and hope that the *detection* component of their preparedness program will be reliable. When you need this kind of reliability, you have to put more dependence on "human factors" — technology, as advanced as it is, does not do a good job of being intuitive, curious, and investigative.

Preparedness is the overarching umbrella of security. Preparedness is the "desired state" in which we want our national Homeland Security program. When we as a nation have effective and efficient Prevention, Detection, and Response capabilities in place across the spectrum of industry, government, and the public, we will have preparedness. If we would "humanize" preparedness and the components that come under it, it would be something like Figure 6.1.

Prevention, Detection, and Response are three broad categories of preparedness, and each has many subcomponents under them from closed-circuit television (CCTV) to virus controls to guards. I chose human, physical, and cyber because those are what DHS is using in its Homeland Security national plan — and at some point, we as a nation of contributors to homeland security all need to be on the same page, communicating in ways that we can understand one another. It is easier for us to adopt DHS language than for DHS to adopt the language of millions of companies and organizations. Although there are many configurations of security

Table 6.2 Worldwide Terrorism by Region

	Incidents			Fatalities			Injuries		
	Full Year	January–July		Full Year	January–July		Full Year	January–July	
	2006	2006	2007	2006	2006	2007	2006	2006	2007
Africa	64	42	24	104	79	56	270	205	204
Eastern Europe	141	83	15	61	41	4	112	82	12
Latin America and the Caribbean	152	124	14	149	98	16	157	114	86
Middle East and the Persian Gulf	4,540	2,846	1,212	9,603	5,556	3,697	15,814	8,798	8,128
North America	4	4	0	1	1	0	5	5	0
South Asia	1,206	813	329	1,877	1,252	466	3,899	2,491	739
East and Central Asia and Oceania	394	161	0	264	118	0	677	330	0
Western Europe	152	93	34	6	2	0	35	8	0
Total	**6,653**	**4,166**	**1,628**	**12,065**	**7,147**	**4,239**	**20,969**	**12,033**	**9,169**

Source: MIPT Terrorism Knowledge Base. Quarterly target, region, and tactic data on terrorist incidents are reported in sequential months. (Chart by Mike Moran.)

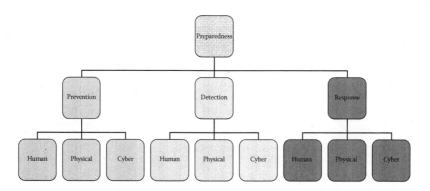

Figure 6.1 Preparedness Components

and preparedness components, Figure 6.1 is the simplest concept to grasp and includes business continuity and IT security along with physical security — and we should be able to see where they fit into this preparedness structure. Activities under prevention will generally consist of installing locks and access controls, installing CCTV, hanging up *No Parking*! and *Restricted Area* signs, installing perimeter fences, and using roving and posted security — efforts *to protect and deter.*

Detection consists of human, technical, or cyber abilities to detect and give off "warnings" that there are threats focused on our facility or that possibly others are getting ready to attack us. The detection component includes detection by means of humans, technology, animals, marine life, and insects. Regardless of how much technology you have in place for security, you should first rely on "people" for security-related actions rather than on technology. No amount of technology can replace the human factor to want to investigate further, leverage instincts, and use reasoning abilities to further investigate an event. Typical observations or inner dialogue a human would engage in to conclude or deduce what other actions may be warranted are as follows:

- I see you.
- I recognize you.
- I don't recognize you.
- I don't trust you.
- I must validate who you are.
- I need more information.
- I have a "gut feeling."
- I must ask more questions.

INNOVATIVE PREVENTION APPROACHES

"Reverse psychology" is a very economical and creative way which under certain situations could be used as deterrence measures. We can enhance existing security technology, policies, and procedures through the introduction of desired perception. It's nothing new. People do not have to be psychologists to relate to the use and meaning of this phrase.

The use of propaganda and psychological operations (PSYOP) is a similar concept having to do with tricking or influencing people. The United States has used these methods, as have many other countries. One extreme example is from a report of a military operation from earlier decades where U.S. operatives left foot-long condoms on the Ho Chi Minh Trail, presumably causing North Vietnamese Army (NVA) soldiers to hide their women as well as themselves. Other countries, however, have been less circumspect, often stumbling into embarrassing gaffes.[1]

Manipulating perceptions is a tactic used by many countries. During World War II, the Japanese leafleted American forces, trying to demoralize the enemy with the hardy perennial "Your girl is getting mounted by the strapping buck back home." To illustrate this theme, however, the Japanese used graphic pornography — a relative scarcity on the front lines. The effect of this tactic, says military historian Stanley Sandler, "did the opposite of what it was supposed to. It raised morale. Our guys loved it. They'd trade them like baseball cards — five for a bottle of whisky."[2]

One example of a large-scale deception operation occurred during WWII. *Fortitude* was the code name given to the decoy (or disinformation) mission mounted by the Allies to deceive the Germans about the date and, above all, the place of the landings in the famous D-Day invasion during World War II. The latter were convinced that the British and American attack would come in the Pas-de-Calais area, and it was important not to disillusion them. They therefore had to be made to think that a whole group of armies was present in Kent, opposite Pas-de-Calais.[3]

To deceive the German observation planes, which their antiaircraft defenses did their best to avoid, the local estuaries, creeks, and harbors

---

[1] "Dr. David Champagne, the 4th PSYOP Group's Civilian Afghanistan Expert, Who Says He Fell in Love with the Country as a Peace Corps 'Hippie,'" January 13, 2002, http://peacecorpsonline.org/messages/messages/467/2023161.html.

[2] "Dr. David Champagne."

[3] Ernest S. Tavares, Jr., Major, USAF. A Research Report Submitted to the Faculty in Partial Fulfillment of the Graduation Requirements. "Operation Fortitude: The Closed Loop D-Day Deception Plan," Maxwell Air Force Base, Alabama, April 2001, http://stinet.dtic.mil/oai/oai?verb=getRecord&metadataPrefix=html&identifier=ADA407763.

were crammed with dummy landing craft. A giant oil-pumping head made from papier-mâché was erected, while large numbers of inflatable rubber tanks (Figure 6.2) were positioned in the fields. Plywood vehicles and guns lined the roadsides. For the benefit of the Germans, a team of technicians maintained constant radio traffic between totally fictitious units.

Fortitude succeeded beyond anyone's wildest dreams. Long after June 6, Adolf Hitler remained convinced that the Normandy Landings were a diversionary tactic to induce him to move his troops away from Pas-de-Calais, so that a decisive attack could then be launched there. He therefore kept his best units prepared there, until the end of July, desperately scanning an empty horizon while the fate of the war was being decided in Normandy.[4]

Table 6.3 ("Decoy and Deception Methods") lists several concepts used by government, military, media, industry, and people to make others believe what they feel is necessary to achieve a goal or objective.

Figure 6.2   Operation Fortitude Inflatable Rubber Tank

---

[4] http://www.normandiememoire.com/NM60Anglais/2_histo2/histo2_p5_gb.htm.

Table 6.3 Decoy and Deception Methods

User	Description	Purpose
Military	Psychological operations	Used by soldiers to persuade and influence perceptions and encourage desired behavior; the truth credibly presented in a manner to convince a given audience to cease resistance or take actions favorable to friendly forces.
Military	Decoys and deception	A "trick" used to gain an advantage in the battlefield.
Government, corporations	Disinformation	Preemptive dissemination of false information deliberately and often covertly spread (through planting of rumors) in order to influence public opinion or obscure the truth.
Military, government, media	Propaganda	A concerted set of messages aimed at influencing the behavior of large numbers of people; the message can be completely truthful but manipulated in some way to downplay or highlight something to selectively produce an emotional rather than rational response to the information presented.
Private sector	Honey pots	Used often by IT personnel to determine and identify network attackers.
Ordinary people	Reverse psychology	The use of a conversation where advocacy of one course of action persuades another person to do the opposite.

Ordinarily, it is not something that could be relied on for any sustained period of time — eventually, the adversary would know he or she was being tricked. But it is an option that is thought of when there is a limited budget — it's just a matter of using the imagination — and the lawyers to make sure that the activity will not create liability.

A European counterintelligence officer once asked me a rhetorical question: if you could secure a facility with two good layers of security and add a third layer — bomb dogs, mean-looking ones — would the dogs add a comfort level? Of course, I said. Then he said, what if the dogs cost $35,000 but you only had $3,000; would you consider buying noncertified dogs even though all they could do was walk on a leash at times as though conducting a formal search? I did not answer the question because this is the type of question that if I were going to say, "Yes, I would use such dogs," I would not want to tell anyone. That information would have to be tightly — *tightly* — controlled. That would be considered *need-to-know* information only if my best approach was to use this dog.

Any decision to use deception or PSYOP should be carefully studied and discussed with lawyers. If tactics are considered or used, it should be tightly guarded and disclosed only to a small number of people who need to know because the average American has a difficult time keeping secrets. The more people who know, the stronger the chance that the use of such a method would be leaked. Then you would have to worry about the likelihood that your security weaknesses and protective measures being disclosed. Once security weaknesses are exposed, people are forced to make major expenditures to revamp security or immediately secure the vulnerabilities.

Because there are many things that can go wrong, it is important to evaluate all implications of a decision to employ these types of measures and consult with legal officers.

INNOVATIVE DETECTION TECHNOLOGY

There is much interesting research being conducted today. Government is researching the use of bees to detect explosives. By studying bee behavior and testing and improving on technologies already on the market, Los Alamos National Laboratory scientists developed methods to harness the honeybee's exceptional olfactory sense where the bees' natural reaction to nectar, a proboscis extension reflex (sticking out their tongue), could be used to record an unmistakable response to a scent. Using Pavlovian training techniques common to bee research, they trained bees to give a positive detection response, via the proboscis extension reflex, when they were exposed to vapors from TNT, C4, and triacetone triperoxide (TATP) explosives and propellants. If the bees can be trained to contribute to Homeland Security — can the workforce? Are we going to let the little ones do all the work?[5]

Today, rats can clear a minefield faster than highly trained canines. The mine-clearing process is a two-stage effort; the rats comb a grid and clear an area. Then the canines come in behind them and validate. The rats sniff out the landmines, and after detecting one they start to scratch the ground, alerting their handlers. "Basically, it's the same principle as with dogs, but because of their weight a dog could get blown away[;] rats do not have such problems and rats also do not get bored so easily."[6]

In 2007, a government agency began exploring research involving *chembots*, robots built of shape-memory materials that are capable of morphing into a new shape so that they can squeeze into openings smaller than their original form and then reconstitute themselves on the other side — making not only a detection capability but a "kill capability" as well. A robot that is a real weapons system could be useful in saving human lives in dangerous operations where explosives or hostage situations are involved.

INVESTING IN RESPONSE CAPABILITIES THROUGH PARTNERSHIP

The adoption of the National Incident Management System (NIMS) from the Homeland Security Presidential Directive (HSPD-5) Management of Domestic Incidents has found many agencies, organizations, municipalities, corporations, and businesses unprepared to address strategic implementation, coordination, and training issues affecting response to incidents.[7] The NIMS is the system by which all first responders would come together and respond to an incident. Many exercises have taken place through DHS funding and sponsorship to exercise coordination

---

[5] DOE/Los Alamos National Laboratory, "Detecting Explosives with Honeybees," November 2006, http://www.physorg.com/news83944407.html.

[6] Nikola Pavkovic, "Rats Are Called to Defuse Land Mines," http://mprofaca.cro.net/rats.html.

[7] National Incident Management System, http://www.nimsonline.com/nims_training/NIMS.

under the NIMS where local, state, and federal government and the private sector tested their ability to respond to an attack. Exercises have involved simulated network attacks, pandemic breakouts, and U.S. Port attacks.

One exercise was planned to address the concern that a poorly designed government response to the next terrorist attack could disrupt America's economy and society as much as or more than the attack itself. This concern is particularly relevant in the context of an attack that may be harmful, but not catastrophic. In the event of a future attack, government officials will be under enormous pressure to respond swiftly, more than likely with limited information about the status of the attack or what to expect next. In today's news cycle, the public — and the situation — will demand a swift and decisive response perhaps before exactly what is happening becomes clear. Confusion, indecision, or false starts at government's highest levels will be magnified and may have long-lasting ramifications. Getting it wrong will be easier than getting it right. As the Hurricane Katrina experience has demonstrated, a lack of situational awareness, a lack of understanding of current plans, and an absence of effective decision-making tools can lead to disaster.

In the summer of 2001, a group of senior-level officials participated in an executive-level simulation. The exercise simulated a U.S. National Security Council meeting at which senior officials were confronted with a smallpox attack on the United States. The exercise illustrated the issues to be addressed in the event of a bioterrorism crisis, including the challenges facing state and local governments, the role and responsiveness of the federal government, and the likely friction spots between federal- and state-level responders and responses. Coming as it did before the September 11 terrorist attacks and the subsequent anthrax attacks, the exercise generated an enormous amount of interest in both the public policy community and the media. Among those briefed were Vice President Dick Cheney; then National Security Advisor Condoleezza Rice; then Federal Emergency Management Agency (FEMA) Director Joe Allbaugh; more than 80 members of Congress; senior government officials and leaders, including approximately 20 ambassadors to the United States; and senior government officials from Asia, Latin America, and Europe. Besides raising public awareness of the bioterrorism threat, these briefings contributed to the Bush administration's decision to manufacture 300 million doses of the smallpox vaccine.[8]

---

[8] Center for Strategic and International Studies, http://www.csis.org/hs/simulations/.

The events of September 11 and additional intelligence on Al Qaeda demonstrate the potential for an attack against the infrastructure of the United States. To face this challenge, an executive-level simulation focusing on the U.S. critical energy infrastructure was designed. The exercise took place in October 2002 and employed a simulated National Security Council of senior policy makers with former U.S. Senator Sam Nunn, now chairman of the Center for Strategic and International Studies (CSIS) Board of Trustees, serving as scenario president. This exercise was designed to simulate possible U.S. reactions to a credible threat of a terrorist attack when there is not sufficient information for effective protection. The overall purpose of the exercise was to assist the administration and Congress in their attempts to improve the effectiveness of their response during the preattack phase of a major terrorist incident. This exercise challenged current and former senior government leaders to respond to increasingly credible and specific intelligence indicating the possibility of a large-scale attack against critical energy and energy-related infrastructure on the East Coast of the United States.[9]

Companies often work in their own world — most concerned about their customers and their own operations and bottom-line impacts. The companies that I have worked with in the last 4 years across industry had security programs in place and vaguely understood the requirements for Homeland Security preparedness, but something was missing. The layers of security between humans, physical and cyber, must work well together in order to contribute to Homeland Security, but they are not very well integrated in private companies, and this is an area that DHS would like to see improve — this will be crucial particularly in the response and recovery phases of an attack.

The national hierarchy plays a major role in preparedness, but there are limitations and inadequacies that impact its ability to prevent terrorist attacks. The analytical component of the intelligence community, fusion centers, and police forces is similar to private companies' independent security approaches — in that the government entities do not all talk to one another and do not have mature skills in "predictive analysis." That is the type of analysis needed in order to attempt to predict where the next attack would take place. Society is not trained on basic awareness of terrorist activities that they are likely to observe in the conduct of their everyday work routines, nor do they know the proper reporting methods or where to report information. Even if they did report information of

---

[9] Center for Strategic and International Studies.

interest about possible terrorist activities, it does not appear as though our nation has the infrastructure to handle millions of calls or reports coming in to any one entity. If that capability does exist, it is not well publicized. Many local, state, and federal agencies have their own awareness campaigns, but they are not linked across the states or across all levels of government. If there was standardization or a centralized way of doing this, we would all be able to contribute — to report information to one entity — and ideally we would all be trained to the same standard to report the basics. Through something similar to the *Play PDR!* game in Chapter 1, we could all be force multipliers — good reporting Samaritans — and we could share the responsibility of prevention and detection.

Clearly, there are many inadequacies that impact Homeland Security in government, in businesses, and within society. We collectively do not fully understand what is expected. Coordinating the preparedness effort is cumbersome and difficult for any one entity to manage. Yet, that seems to be the job of DHS.

The private sector needs to be aware of the shortcomings that exist and that have surfaced in the Homeland Security simulation exercises because in the event of an attack, the private sector will be expected to know how it fits into the overall coordinated response effort. This effort is supposed to be managed under the NIMS system — which is not yet working smoothly. One of the absolutes that will be encountered in response that will throw a wrench to compound the "unknowns," is that we will not know which agency will be in charge until we experience the event. Remember that the event does not have to be a terrorist attack; it can be a natural disaster. Also, we do not know in which jurisdiction the attack or event would occur, adding to the mystery of who we would look up to and respond to.

In the planning stages, a company may find that it has a specific liaison to interact with when things are normal and quiet. Yet, in a response effort when the incident is at hand, everyone goes into crisis mode, government representatives may be shifted around and switched out, and a company may not know who it is supposed to be dealing with during the crisis. You can expect the scene to be chaotic. Knowing that this variable will affect response coordination and reporting and using the NIMS system as if you are a pro need to be factored into your plan and procedures.

The reason that the DHS exercise lessons learned and the NIMS system are mentioned in this section instead of in a later chapter on training and exercises is because this information is a critical variable with tremendous potential to impact your response and recovery procedures.

Further, if no one in your organization has been trained on the NIMS, it will be a survival essential for someone to be trained in it. Here are the NIMS courses that are available online. A matrix guideline for which course should be taken is included in this book as Appendix E, "FY07 NIMS Training Guidelines."[10]

- IS-100 ICS-100 An Introduction to ICS
- IS-100 ICS-100 An Introduction to ICS for Federal Workers
- IS-100 ICS-100 An Introduction to ICS for Law Enforcement Personnel
- IS-100 ICS-100 An Introduction to ICS for Public Works Personnel
- IS-100 ICS-100 An Introduction to ICS for Healthcare/Hospital Personnel
- IS-100 ICS-100 An Introduction to ICS for Schools
- IS-200 ICS-200 Basic ICS for Single Resources and Initial Action Incident
- IS-200 ICS-200 Basic ICS Applying ICS to Healthcare Organizations
- IS-700 NIMS An Introduction
- IS-701 NIMS Multi-Agency Coordination System
- IS-702 NIMS Public Information System
- IS-703 NIMS Resource Management
- IS-800.A NRP An Introduction

OTHER CONTRIBUTORS TO HOMELAND SECURITY

Though DHS's focus tends to be on the private sector responsible for 85 percent of critical infrastructures, there are other categories of businesses also vulnerable to terrorist attacks. Though no one has published a total number for U.S. businesses, indirectly linked to critical infrastructures are third- or fourth-party providers to infrastructures — we know there are many. We also know that there are many businesses that are vulnerable because they are colocated with or within close proximity of critical infrastructures — also referred to as *proximity threats*. We know that there are many icon firms in the United States and abroad that are of terrorist interest to Al Qaeda networks or Jihad extremists because of their global symbolism of the United States.

---

[10] Federal Emergency Management Agency, http://www.fema.gov/emergency/nims/nims_training.shtm#3 NIMS Training.

If these businesses are not proactive, they could become targets of terrorists in future attacks or enablers to future 9/11s. For these businesses, there is no requirement to be a part of the national unified effort to put measures in place to secure and protect assets from terrorism. This category of businesses also includes thriving small businesses, which create two out of every three new jobs in America and account for nearly half of America's overall employment. They play a vital role in helping the U.S. economy thrive through the jobs they create. Since August 2003, they have created more than 5.1 million new jobs. They have helped reduce America's unemployment to rates below the average rate of the 1960s, 1970s, 1980s, and 1990s. Small businesses are also vital for supporting U.S. communities, much like the automobile industry did in Detroit before the downsizing, depopulation, disinvestment, and fate of that city. In 2004, the statistics were 24.7 million businesses, of which 99.9 percent were small businesses with fewer than 500 employees. That totals 24,675,300 small businesses.

While the concern is not that small businesses would stand out as frontrunner targets, it is that from their sheer volume they could impact the U.S. economy, and one can easily surmise that many are probably linked to critical infrastructures. If that is the case, it is unlikely that any regulatory roleplayer is overseeing what security measures they have in place to ensure that all the links of infrastructure preparedness are cohesively protected. This category of private businesses is seemingly excluded from any government effort to protect facilities from terrorism. As a result, such businesses must rely on themselves and hold themselves accountable for preparedness. The federal government concentrates its funding and assistance to prioritize the risk assessment and securing of critical facilities most vulnerable and of high target interest, and provides for equipment and training of first responders. The level of assistance afforded to private sector critical infrastructure owners and operators tends to be limited to relationship building, information sharing, and providing guidelines on security programs related to Homeland Security.

RESPONSE CONSIDERATIONS

Information is one source of many problems and challenges to Homeland Security. Everyone will be seeking information in a response stage, and it will not be forthcoming. People need to know how first responders work, that it may take firefighters 2 to 3 hours to get to the top floor of a high-rise, or that traffic gridlock may delay first responders and people may have to self-treat or shelter in place longer that planned for. The decision to shelter will need to be determined by the people in the event. Only they will know what the variables are — whether to leave right away or go to high ground or to go upwind or run perpendicular, it will depend on many other factors that perhaps a firefighter can go over during a fire drill. Hopefully, by now you have met your local fire department and they have reviewed some of your emergency procedures.

As this nation strives to form, norm, storm, and perform as if we had all been partners for years in responding to terrorism, the media can play a contributing role as everyone's communications partner. There are certain roles that media may have to take on because all responders will be engaged in the event. Media may need to assume a first responder role — in which case, there may need to be an extra person on the crew. By educating journalists on the profile of an attack, depending on the time the media arrive, the timing could be such that secondary explosions have not gone off yet. Most attacks have multiple explosions. They may be in a position to see other terrorists before they execute their attacks. A second bomber will not have the look of other citizens in the area: ordinary citizens will look shocked and disoriented, whereas the suicide bomber may appear nervous and heavily layered — but not likely to be in shock. In other words, the media may have to be vigilant and watch for other acts that have not yet come to fruition.

Another role that media may have is one of enabling communications. If they have a satellite feed into their network stations and first responders have no communication, media may have to be prepared to offer a hand to ease the response or recovery efforts. Prethinking this as part of their response effort may be a contribution to the overall effort.

The media will have some influence on how much shock the people in the event will experience. As such, they should prerehearse scenarios and how they would cover them to not promote panic, and they may want to prethink what headlines they would come up with for their next printing. What if they report that it was a "dirty bomb," but in fact it was not? What if it turns out that the attack involved a TATP bomb?[11] Would the media know the difference? Having this basic education will be essential to dissuade panic and an aftereffect of people abandoning the area and not wanting to come back to work because they "erroneously" fear that radiation was

---

[11] Officer.com, http://www.officer.com/web/online/Investigation/TATP--The-Terrorists-Choice/18$30796.

dispersed in a dirty bomb — when in fact it was a TATP bomb. If we can educate people on basic terrorism methodology and terminology, they are likely to act in a less panicked and more proactive way in response measures. Appendix F is a "Fact Sheet on Dirty Bombs" from the U.S. Nuclear Regulatory Commission (NRC) that includes protective measures.

PREPAREDNESS SNAPSHOT

Ultimately, preparedness will produce three components of activities, tasks, or focus for the purpose of achieving Homeland Security objectives. Incidents or threats will prompt workforces to take actions at every stage. If *prevention* measures fail, *detection* measures need to be relied on to prevent experiencing the attack or threat. If detection fails, one will be forced to go into *response* mode. That is what we want to avoid at all costs. There is much crossover between the three categories.

Figure 6.3 illustrates three pillars of preparedness with some of the measures that take place under each category. Each pillar builds on the next: if one pillar falls, the second and third should still serve their roles. But if one and two fall, three will have to be initiated, and there will be no reserves — it will be at full capacity containing, responding, and recovering.

All phases of preparedness consist of continuously gathering, analyzing, and assessing information — attending local TEWGs,[12] the FBI's InfraGard,[13] Homeland Security Advisory Council meetings, and security events. These efforts are part of a continuous process needed for developing and updating plans, policies, procedures, and practices for preparedness across industries and government and staying aware of threats.

Since the process of risk management is continuous — through periodic assessments and updates, and procedural improvements — monitoring for new laws and mandates that affect the organization is critical, and someone needs to be assigned that responsibility. Every month, the *Security Management*[14] journal publishes the latest laws, upcoming laws, and court rulings that affect the security industry, critical infrastructures, and workforces around the world as well as what mandates must be complied with.

---

[12] Terrorism Early Warning Groups (TEWGs) constitute a multilateral, multidisciplinary, networked effort; see http://www.markletaskforce.org/documents/TEW.pdf.

[13] InfraGard is an information-sharing and analysis effort serving the interests and combining the knowledge base of a wide range of members. At its most basic level, InfraGard is a partnership between the FBI and the private sector. See http://www.infragard.net.

[14] ASIS, *Security Management*, http://www.securitymanagement.com.

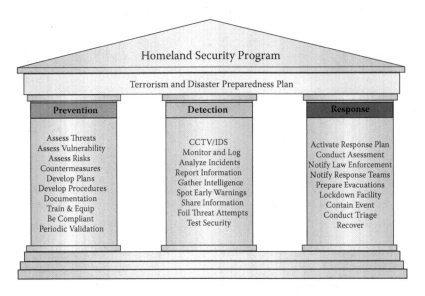

Figure 6.3 Three Pillars of Preparedness (Graphic by Jessica Farias. With permission.)

ASIS is an international organization with thousands of resources to create the most robust library ever on security and related topics.

CASE STUDY

In the Khobar Towers attack of 1996 in Saudi Arabia, the leaders reviewed threat reports and put in place 36 of 39 protective measures after they had conducted threat and vulnerability assessments. Everything that could be physically done given the money and people resources and creative solutions was done. The number of fixes is mentioned not to show that one or two of the unfixed protective measures were responsible for the attack, because I do not think that they were. What this number shows is that people were proactively doing everything within their power and humanly possible to prevent, to detect, and to respond to a potential attack. Their facility was not really theirs to totally revamp to their satisfaction of preparedness. They could not move the front perimeter to increase the buffer zone (they did not own it and were not free to do so) or add Mylar film on the windows that cost millions of dollars because it was on a future schedule of procurements. They were living in a country where they had to depend on the host country's security and law enforcement to some degree. To mitigate the possibility of being attacked or being surprised, two sentries were posted on the roof of the building at all times 2 months before the attack; their job was to alert the others if there was any appearance of an impending attack.

On June 25, 1996, at 9 P.M., many of the residents of Khobar Towers were in their rooms. The outgoing commander was writing promotion recommendations in Building 133. Members of the 58th FS (unit in the attack) were packing in Building 127 and Building 131. The commander sat at the desk in his room, writing a note to the incoming commander who was to replace him. Beyond Khobar Towers, the final Muslim prayer call of the day was just ending.[15]

Staff Sergeant Alfredo R. Guerrero, a security policeman and shift supervisor, went up to the top of Building 131 to check in with two sentries posted there. Once on the roof, Guerrero and the other policemen observed a sewage tanker truck and a white car enter the parking lot. They watched the truck drive to the second to the last row, turn left as if leaving the lot, slow down, stop, and then back up toward the fence line. It stopped directly in front of the center of the north façade of Building 131. The truck's driver and a passenger jumped out and hurried to the waiting car, which sped out of the parking lot.[16]

> The three security policemen were already in motion. They radioed in the alert and started the evacuation plan to notify each floor of Building 131 in waterfall fashion. A roving security police vehicle heard the alert from the rooftop sentries and rushed to wave people away from the building. They had managed to notify only those residents on the top three floors before they were shaken by an enormous blast. Before the wing operations center could activate Giant Voice (the sirens), the bomb went off.
>
> The bomb that did the damage was not like the package bombs in Bahrain or the Riyadh car bomb, containing only a few hundred pounds of explosives. It exploded with the force of 20,000 to 30,000 pounds of TNT. The sewage truck shaped the charge, and the high clearance between the ground and the truck gave it the more lethal characteristics of an air burst.

---

[15] Rebecca Grant, "Khobar Towers," *Air Force Magazine Online* 81, no. 6 (June 1998): http://www.afa.org/magazine/june1998/0698khobar.asp (accessed February 2008).
[16] Rebecca Grant, "Khobar Towers."

As the blast waves hit Building 131, they propelled pieces of the Jersey wall barriers into the first four floors. The outer walls of the bottom floors were blown into rooms. With no structural support below, the facades of the top three floors sheered off and fell into a pile of rubble. Walls on the east and west ends were blasted four feet from their original positions, causing floors in several bedrooms to collapse. Building 131 did not collapse because it was made of prefabricated cubicles that were bolted together. Had it been built in a more traditional manner, it might have caved in from the blast.[17]

In the assessment and risk management scenarios, leaders had thought that the size of a bomb that could be used in an attack would be about 200 lbs. — this was a huge miscalculation.

In May, just a month before the attack, the residents reported a suspicious act:

One particularly serious incident did occur in May. A car proceeding on the street along the eastern side of the compound did something unusual. The driver crossed the dusty median and banged the car against the solid concrete of the Jersey wall barrier. Then the driver backed up the car, nudged it against the barriers again, and drove away. Residents of Building 127 in Khobar Towers spotted the activity and reported it to wing security police. In response, the wing staked down the barriers along the perimeter.[18]

This appears to be a classic — *classic* — example of a "dry run" on the part of the attackers: to test the attack steps and see if the attack plan will work. A dry run!

In this attack, warnings and signals were indicating that prevention measures were not going to stop an attack. Detection measures are where the efforts were most needed — perhaps asking the Saudis to provide more random police patrols or moving all residents to the back rooms of the building, if possible. No one can think of all the possibilities, but this is one area where every perspective needs to be provided and brainstormed. By reviewing past attacks, we can see what human factors are at play and leverage those planners with natural abilities for "attention to details" to help out. Generally, ESTJs (those possessing extroversion, sensing, thinking, judging) and ISTJs (those possessing introversion, sensing, thinking, judging) are needed for this part of planning — two of the personality profiles from the Myers-Briggs Type Indicator. The Myers-Briggs

---

[17] Grant, "Khobar Towers."
[18] Grant, "Khobar Towers."

personality type indicator may be critiqued as good or bad, but this is one area where we may apply the concept or use of the Myers-Briggs test.[19] ISTJs (thinking introverts) function well in jobs requiring accurate record keeping of facts. ISTJs are quiet and reserved individuals who are interested in security.

---

[19] MBTI.com, "Myers-Briggs Personality Type Indicator," http://www.e-mbti.com/istj.php.

7

Human Factors and Team Dynamics

Bin Ladenism will never enjoy the mass appeal of other destructive ideologies but it certainly enjoys wider support than the secular Arab socialism that gripped much of the Middle East in past decades.... [T] his means we have barely begun the war with al Qaeda and its affiliated groups because many thousands of underemployed disaffected men in the Muslim world will continue to embrace bin Laden's doctrine of violent anti-Westernism.

Peter L. Bergen

THE HUMAN FACTOR

Today, relationship building is an important skill in the workplace. It is necessary to effectively interact, communicate, manage, and lead others. This skill becomes even more critical in the Homeland Security arena, in particular within the information-sharing component of preparedness between the private and public sectors. Among the many challenges confronting this nation's preparedness program is the private and public sectors' inability to establish and leverage information-sharing networks so that timely responses in any situation can be carried out. In protection and response efforts, responders need a timely flow of information —

that is, the movement of information internally, externally, up, down, and between public and private sector partners.

When it comes to security, most organizations often overlook the "human factor" — people. All security measures begin and end with the people. People develop the plans and strategies. People enforce and implement the plans and strategies. Yet, companies often have a misconception that they are "secure and prepared" simply because they have a fence around their building, a functioning high-tech closed-circuit television (CCTV) system in place, security guards in place and on patrol, and a written response plan. None of the fancy "bells and whistles" will mean anything, though — if the "people-employees" are not factored into the preparedness plan. Instead of feeling comfortable or complacent with the measures implemented, management needs to explore these types of questions:

- Is our new system simple enough to preclude disruptions to operations or hindrances? If it is too complex, the human factor will take over — people will turn it off. They will leave the doors propped open, and take shortcuts that defeat the purpose of the security system.
- Did the employees get properly trained on this system? What if there is no power and no backup power — can employees revert to human procedures and still respond effectively?
- What if the incident requires human decision-making skills or people skills — does the technology in place have the ability to use judgment and make decisions? If not, do the people have sufficient knowledge to make critical decisions? How will they respond if a variable that had not been planned for suddenly surfaces?

HUMANITY IN CRISIS AND HERO MODE

Israeli citizens, military, and police are trained to deal with crisis "by the numbers" — it's automatic. To illustrate further, a terrorist went on a killing rampage, shooting, wounding, and killing teenage students at a school in Israel. Police were on the scene, but took 20 minutes to intervene. An off-duty soldier putting his children to sleep in a nearby neighborhood heard the shots and ran to help. He ran past police, but not before demanding and getting a police cap so he would not be mistaken for a terrorist — then he entered the building and neutralized the terrorist with two shots. The human factor is best illustrated in this story and worthy of admiration

— that a person would have the presence of mind to think strategically and tactically in the heat of a massacre, respond "by the numbers," save students (and police), clear the building, attend to the wounded, and then say that he was not a hero and was just performing his duty is beyond words.[1]

The human factor also demonstrates to us that law enforcement and first responders — regardless of how well trained they are — may still freeze in the face of a crisis. Invariably, a leader will emerge, and that is what happened when a bomb threat at a public school in the United States brought everything to a halt. Students were evacuated and being held in an unprotected, wide-open area. The sun was hot, and temperatures were rising. First responders trickled in and out, but no one seemed to be charge, nor did they seem to know what to do. Finally, after a few hours of standing around, an elderly woman who worked in the cafeteria took charge of the situation and rallied the first responders: "Here's what we're going to do. Let's move the children away from here. Call in the buses, and let's move them to protective ground in the shade. Someone is going to go in and clear the building and bring back water"; she feared the children were reaching dehydration levels. Once the building was cleared, she handed control back over to first responders and went in and prepared meals.

FEMALE TERRORISTS: THE HUMAN FACTOR GONE WRONG

The givers of life are not expected to walk into a building strapped with a suicide vest under their garb with the intention of blowing up themselves and everyone else in a selected location. The human factor is most visibly in action in these situations. Security forces are really uncomfortable and unsure of what actions to take when dealing with activities that involve women drawing suspicion. In 28 years of performing red team and simulation exercises posing as a female terrorist, there was only one instance in my career where a male was not affected by gender dynamics and took the proper immediate action — denied entry to me, and handled the situation perfectly — with treatment that was professional but assertive. I later learned that he treated males the same way. Male and sometimes female security personnel show hesitancy, delays, and discomfort in dealing with

---

[1] David Shapira, http://web.israelinsider.com/Articles/Security/12702.htm.

143

women — this human factor must change, or our vulnerability to terrorism will increase as women become increasingly engaged in threat activities.

Recognizing the human factors in teams, working committees, joint groups, and security and emergency response teams is something that everyone must do to properly work within this dynamic. New information continues to emerge on dimensions of human interaction and behaviors. The research and theoretical models offered by social scientists, organizational behavior consultants, and management experts point to a compelling need to incorporate new ways of thinking and interacting in this ever changing work environment. Today's work environments are structured very differently than they were in earlier decades, requiring different methods for communicating more effectively. In these potentially remote, virtual, or global offices, the staff is likely to be culturally diverse, adding yet another dimension to human interaction — adding more human factor concerns.

HUMANS IN CONFLICT

Having a sense of a team's personalities and leadership styles helps predetermine what the team's crisis management abilities will be when it is faced with a crisis. While at one time, personality and leadership tests were more developed and were used only for research studies, there is tremendous value in applying their concepts to private and public sector teams. It will provide team members a framework to work with in organizing and assigning roles based on natural and predisposed dominant traits. The results will produce a map of strengths that are often missed and not utilized when they are necessary. There are functional and dysfunctional roles that emerge in a crisis and in normal operations. By buying into the concept of personality assessment testing on a peripheral level, a team can begin to apply human factor models that can be perhaps more rewarding than other training. It is not only fun but also revealing. The language that people use says a lot about them, how they sense the environment around them, as well as how they learn. What type of language do you use? Does your language reflect a collaborative tone — do you say "those people" or "our friends" over on the other side of the table (or river, ocean, etc.)? Do you create settings that foster trust and collaboration by your choice of words, or do you send the wrong message and put people on the defensive even before you have had a chance to introduce your message? Many leaders, managers, and supervisors are disliked by their subordinates, and often it is because these top-level executives have not had proper training or coaching. Do you have a mean look on your face? Or do you have a look that conveys, "I don't know how to handle this situation — I'm uncomfortable — I am at the verge of reacting in the only way I know how — that is, to throw a tantrum?" In the end, people who react this way tend to do it because they have not learned "coping skills," giving off displays of immaturity that shut people off or make them uncomfortable — and closing the door to any dialogue, even though dialogue is important if we are to find solutions to our problems.

Another human factor that needs to be monitored in the workplace is "conflict." Conflict does have a way of positively being addressed and can be viewed as an opportunity to make something better. Sometimes it can be sparked by emotions — or by stress, fatigue, hunger, low blood sugar, sleep deprivation, and alcohol- or drug-altered states. At other times, it is caused by personality differences, competition, and challenging beliefs and values. The model in Figure 7.1, developed by Kenneth Crow of DRM Associates,[2] is useful in understanding how conflict (if not managed properly) will impede progress or (if managed properly) can lead to collaboration.

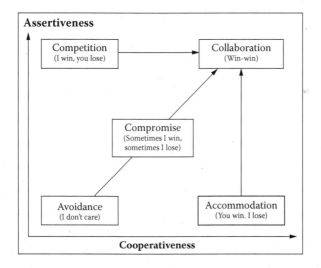

Figure 7.1 Collaboration Model

---

[2] Kenneth Crow, DRM Associates, 2002, http://www.npd-solutions.com/collaboration (accessed January 2008).

145

In Figure 7.1, there are two axes: the horizontal axis of *Cooperativeness* and the vertical axis of *Assertiveness* represent different approaches for dealing with conflict. A low degree of assertiveness and cooperativeness represents avoidance of an issue, or the approach of "I don't care." If both opponents (teams or individuals) feel the same way, they are communicating a mutual feeling of Avoidance. A high degree of cooperativeness and a low degree of assertiveness represent *Accommodation,* or the approach of "You win, I lose." A high degree of assertiveness and a low degree of cooperativeness represent *Competition,* or the approach of "I win, you lose." People generally believe that compromise is the ideal method of resolution. It represents a moderate degree of both assertiveness and cooperativeness, and says, "Sometimes I win, and sometimes I lose." This, however, is not the ideal solution to conflict. *Collaboration* represents the basis for a mutually beneficial approach or a "win-win" outcome where everyone walks away a winner and feeling good. The key to the "win-win" approach is to arrive at solutions that can mutually satisfy the needs of all sides rather than focusing on competing solutions that involve trade-offs or are mutually exclusive to one side.

Once people understand that they just need to explore the options, they will find that arriving at collaboration simply takes practice, and in time it becomes easier to adopt a collaborative effort. Collaboration is what is needed to manage risk in the workplace. This would be especially helpful in settings where the Department of Homeland Security (DHS) is trying to build relationships and partnerships internally, with external government entities, or with the private sector, or in accordance with a timeline.

HUMAN OVERCONFIDENCE

In 2005, a call came into a security consulting firm from a member of the media looking to interview a security expert. The representative engaged the administrative assistant in casual conversation while the company looked to accommodate the request. During the casual conversation, the representative remarked that he had just interviewed the manager of a major mall — one of the largest shopping malls around. The media representative related that the manager of the mall felt his mall was safe and everyone was prepared to properly respond to a terrorist attack if one were to happen. The assistant asked the media representative if that manager knew what the hundreds of thousands of daily visitors to the mall would do in the event of an attack. She asked if that manager would know that people, in general, react one of four ways to stressful situations (which a terrorist attack would definitely qualify as). Some people will take a leading role, formulate a plan, and tell others what to do; the second group will follow the leader and do what they are told to do; the third group will be catatonic and not be able to function at all; while the fourth group will respond with radical, uncontrollable behavior that will disrupt everyone and create more chaos than already existed. The media representative was surprised by the question and the concise explanation of what might ensue, and realized that he had asked the mall manager the wrong questions. If he had asked the correct questions, he felt certain that his answer would be that the mall might not really be as safe and prepared as he thought because they had not considered the "human factor" in the security equation. They had only really considered the physical security issues — what the security guards would do.

The "human factor" of security can also be seen in the aftermath of many recent U.S. disasters. The fire that razed The Station nightclub in West Warwick, Rhode Island, on February 21, 2003,[3] killing 96 people, would not have had nearly the fatalities if a few basic awareness principles had been practiced. The evacuation plan for the building was inaccurate and not posted in full view of the crowd. If the people who were at the nightclub had been aware of the evacuation plan, and knew where the exits to the building were, they may have been able to get out of the building before they were overcome by the fire. As it was, there was merely chaos resulting in a catastrophic outcome.

When the initial events of Hurricane Katrina were captured and televised, one could never have guessed that such behaviors were being displayed by Americans inside of U.S. borders. The scene looked as if it had been videotaped in a third world country. The catastrophic losses from this hurricane might have been tempered if there had been more basic education and training given to the residents who lived in the area and more businesses had continuity plans. This was possibly the most defining event in our history that revealed what humans are capable of doing when desperate. One of the most noteworthy observations was that we cannot predict how people will react in such a catastrophe and how deeply they will fall into "a state of shock" where all rational abilities go out the window and they are no longer able to use reason or make critical decisions for survival — much like the Twin Tower evacuees who

---

[3] www.cnn.com/2003/US/Northeast/02/21/deadly.nightclub.fire/.

deferred their evacuation decision to the group they were in. We all need to remember this phenomenon because we will not be able to count on certain people in a response or recovery event. On one hand, we will have citizens who will be told to evacuate now! Or, on the other hand, some will be told to stay and shelter in place — *Do not get in your cars and drive to* ... (fill in the blank).

In the anthrax scares that followed 9/11, some of our nation's emergency rooms received tens of thousands of calls from panicked citizens. This flurry of activity overwhelmed medical responders and severely disrupted emergency care operations.[4] One can only imagine the scene at hospitals if the callers had simply shown up at these emergency rooms instead of calling in. If they had, could our hospitals handle this volume or would they know how to manage such a crisis? According to some first responders, in the event of a disaster or broadcast of a code red alert prompted by a terrorist attack, the populations affected would be expected to know whether or not to shelter in place and possibly self-treat until help could arrive, which could be more than 3 days later.

It is vital that companies, both large and small, create a security program that includes education and training for their employees — bringing the "human factor" into the security environment. Employees are the windows to the company and can be of significant help in detecting and deterring risks if they receive proper education and training. The education process should include the participation of all employees from the top down; it should also include getting input from each employee on how the plan or program can be improved and what they see as their role in security. Employees need to feel that they are a part of the overall plan or program in order for them to invest themselves in the process and be a viable part of their own security, as well as an important part of the organization's security. Second, all employees must be trained — they must know the possible threats that they may face, and how they need to respond to the different threats. By educating and training all employees, companies are taking an active role in creating a "team" approach when it comes to security. This will increase awareness and, therefore, increase detection of threats; allow employees to deter threats; and limit the need to respond to threats — all of which reduce the overall cost of security. The more a company educates and trains its employees, the greater chance they will have of responding to and surviving a threat. An added benefit is that

---

[4] Elsa Lee, 2002, notes from attendance at UCLA International Institute seminar on "dangerous exotic bugs."

employees who are trained to be prepared value their companies for having their employees' interest at heart — thus making these employees more confident and focused on productivity, and helping them to possess peace of mind. This attitude would promote human behaviors consistent with an alert and concerned workforce.

HUMAN TECHNOLOGY

Another aspect of the "human factor" in security is situational awareness. People in general tend to move from one place to another without noticing what comes in between. Most of the time, they are not aware of their surroundings, nor are they aware of what the people around them are doing. Through education and training, people must learn that they need to be more aware of their surroundings. They need to heighten their awareness and make sure that they know what the people around them are doing. They need to walk out of their house, or go to their car in a parking lot; survey the area around their house or their car; and take notice of strange behavior, people out of place, and things that just do not belong there. They need to make conscious decisions about how to proceed if, in fact, they do see something strange. People can make decisions and react — fancy bells and whistles can only notify us that something is happening, but only people can take it to the next level and actually respond to the situation. It is important to remember that security is everyone's job — it does not just happen. It requires "living aware" and being super-observant.

In the evacuation of the Twin Towers, there were 15 minutes between the two attacks. This attack required people to use their powers of observation and perception to make survival decisions quickly. It was reported in a National Institute of Standards and Technology (NIST) report of human behavior in the egress of the Twin Towers on 9/11 that some deaths were attributed to the delaying of the decision to evacuate. The debriefings of survivors revealed that some deferred to group decisions instead of deciding on their own whether to stay in place or evacuate.[5] Many who were present during the 1993 World Trade Center attack relied on memory — it was safe back then to stay in place, so therefore it would be safe to stay in place again this time. Some people were not allowed to evacuate; they were told to go back to their offices. Some ignored the instruction and moved through thick smoke as quickly as possible, even though it seemed

---

[5] http://wtc.nist.gov/pubs/NISTNCSTAR1-7ExecutiveSummary.pdf.

to them they were heading to the fire, but over three-quarters of those who were moving through smoke turned back instead of evacuating. The way people made decisions to evacuate varied. Some acted and evacuated immediately because the building shook. Others waited for information. Seeing the explosion triggered a decision to evacuate in others. Some evacuated based on "something I felt" — a survival instinct prompted the decision. Situational awareness seemed to be a key determinant as to who lived and who died.

Studies have shown that people will not move through smoke, but the Twin Towers evacuation demonstrated that people will keep moving, even as conditions worsen. This incident also demonstrated that, in an emergency, floor wardens need enough information to be able to make safe decisions when the power shuts down and authorities are not able to communicate with them.[6] The floor wardens should not be "just anybody" or the lowest person on the corporate food chain, either; they should be people who have the ability to make rational decisions under stress when direction is not available or when things are not going according to the plan.[7]

The final report of the evacuation of the Twin Towers on 9/11 is a compelling study demonstrating that the "human factor" is often overlooked and underappreciated — yet it may be the only factor that we can each rely on to survive in the face of adversity. Understanding what people do in fires and why and how their actions may conform to or differ from the assumptions used in designing and planning for life safety in such a large building will help future plans and increase the survival rate in future attacks. The most frequent reason given for turning back by those who did so was the smoke; others said because of crowdedness, locked doors, difficulty breathing, not being able to see, and being afraid. It took people 2 to 30 minutes to become aware that something required them to leave Tower 1, and 10 minutes to 4 hours and 14 minutes in Tower 2. Another disturbing element about this human factor is that people will consider this behavior as "I'm just minding my own business," but if a situation arises requiring them to intervene or report details about the incident — 90 percent of the people will report faulty information.

---

[6] http://wtc.nist.gov/pubs/NISTNCSTAR1-7ExecutiveSummary.pdf.
[7] http://wtc.nist.gov/pubs/NISTNCSTAR1-7ExecutiveSummary.pdf.

SUPERDIVERSITY

It is important to understand a little bit about relationships to realize that not everyone has the skills, knowledge, or abilities to foster, build, and expand on relationships. People come in all shapes and sizes — and their personalities, skills, abilities, experiences, and capacity to work and interact with others successfully and effectively are shaped by many factors. These include where they come from, where they were educated, how much education they have, what technical skills they possess, and many other factors that we take for granted but that, when discerned as diversity strengths, can help solve problems quicker than if there was no diversity in the group. These simple dimensions of the human race are generally not of importance unless the person is going to work in a critical position of trust and responsibility. These personal attributes or traits are of high importance in law enforcement, in military special operations, and in the intelligence community where people will be faced with a lot of responsibility and authority. Applicants are tested in various ways to ensure that they are suited for the profession — have the cognitive or psychological and emotional abilities to "carry a gun," or "hold the keys to the kingdom."

Tests are not reliable predictors of employees' abilities, behaviors, or performance; however, much research indicates that under certain circumstances, these tests are helpful tools. In such cases, they can reveal which personalities are suited for certain tasks. For example, we already know that people are either introverts or extroverts, they are left-brained or right-brained, they are creative or scientific, and they are highly technical or highly artistic. Opposites tend to attract each other — until they get to know each other so well that the things they liked about each other at first, such as spontaneity and liveliness, later become the very things that are disliked most about the person. Suddenly, they are loud and obnoxious or poor planners.

What is helpful about such personality attributes is that if we know who in our group is the technical introvert, maybe we could leverage that person's natural propensity for technical details and other strengths to write the important procedures for an emergency plan. Often, teams are not skilled to think in this manner, and the person assigned to such a task ends up being someone whose brain is not inclined to spell out details, follow a methodical approach, or project-manage the effort — and it ends up taking this person perhaps 2 months longer than it would have if the better resource suited for this task had performed it. There are active listeners, rational listeners, and multitaskers who are creative and "go-getters" but whose brains are overloaded with many (sometimes too many) tasks being worked on to provide full attention to an important project. There are also the creatively inclined and technically inclined types all around us. Guess which one will pay attention when you explain that he or she is responsible for meeting a DHS compliance requirement deadline or some other important task?

DIVERSITY AS A PROBLEM SOLVER

The value of diversity is often undervalued in the workplace. Diverse teams will always outperform nondiverse teams in problem solving and in dealing with the unknown because of the uniqueness of their ideas, skills, and abilities.

Becoming skilled in the art of team selection would enable management and organizations to put together teams of relatively similar or dissimilar team members who together accomplish things that amaze themselves as well as others.

The joint efforts by members of differing talents will advance the solution of a single, undivided, perhaps indivisible problem — with one picking up where another got stuck by offering a new approach based on new heuristics for this stage of the problem reached thus far by the approaches and heuristics of others. A group with weak but diverse heuristics could accomplish things beyond the capabilities of even groups with strong but similar heuristics.[8] *Heuristic* means of or relating to exploratory problem-solving techniques that utilize self-educating techniques (such as the evaluation of feedback) to improve performance or improve what another individual or group has produced or solved.

A University of Michigan study[9] found that diverse individuals chosen randomly offer different perspectives that could result in better solutions than nondiverse individuals in a group. A group comprising the best problem solvers is likely to take similar approaches. "If the best problem solvers tend to think about a problem exactly alike, then it stands to reason that as a group, they may not be very effective at coming up with the best solution."

---

[8] http://www.garyjones.org/mt/archives/000165.html.
[9] University of Michigan, 2004, http://www.ur.umich.edu/0405/Nov22_04/23.shtml.

In the October 2004 study, diversity wasn't necessarily meant to indicate identity diversity — differences in race, gender, age, or life experiences — but differences in how problem solvers encode problems and attempt to solve them. A person's value to solving problems depends on his or her ability to improve the collective decision, the researchers say.

"In an environment where competition depends on continuous innovation and introduction of new products, firms that take advantage of the power of functional diversity should perform well."[10] The study of diversity clearly illustrates the importance of diversity in teams. By applying the concepts in this study, teamwork dynamics would be shifted into the realm of private and public sector collaboration and would also enable the private sector to build a more comprehensive response program.

THE "HUMAN FACTOR" AS A TOOL

No one can predict when the next terrorist attack will occur. No one has access to limitless budgets to buy all the security technologies on our dream sheet, so what do we do? Does all the security technology in existence really work? It seems that the more technology became prevalent, the less we relied on our human abilities. With the advent of CCTV, intrusion detection systems, computers, and the Internet, we have completely abandoned the importance and advantages of employee's abilities. Why? What does it cost to employ the human factor as a weapon? There are many people in the work pool with natural abilities for security.

The human factor can help implement better security programs without breaking the bank or contributing to this country's — or an organization's — deficit. The danger of completely losing the ability to employ the human factor as a defense technology has resulted in the worst attacks to the American people by "the enemy" — terrorists have used the "human factor" to their advantage and our detriment. They have attacked destroyers armed with missiles. They have attacked the mightiest symbol of America's defense — the Pentagon! What does Osama bin Laden really mean when he issues his fatwas? Who can translate? Maybe someone who really understands what the fatwa might mean — a good Muslim perhaps? Is there a Muslim who will help us, and if so, where should he or she

---

[10] University of Michigan.

153

go to safely provide useful information to help protect us against future attacks? How do we overcome intelligence failures and prepare for the next attack? If someone has the mental and emotional intelligence and the ability to identify the possible location and methods that could be used by future threats, shouldn't we seek him or her out? We cannot rely simply on our own counterterrorism abilities.

Some professions already recognize the value of the "human factor" and use it to their advantage. The recruitment, selection, testing, and training of certain intelligence professions are unique and different than anything the average employee in a corporation goes through. Applicants to jobs in these professions are tested to see what their limits to stress and fear will be. Factors like reliability, dependability, and trustworthiness must be known as accurately as possible if the persons are going to be entrusted with the nation's top secrets. How they handle stress must be known before they get hired. Will they cave in under pressure if captured by an enemy? In the counterintelligence profession, the training received coupled with constant round-the-clock monitoring of threats produce individuals who are very adept at seeing threats, and even sensing them. This becomes second nature to them. Counterintelligence and Human Intelligence (HUMINT) personnel operate in the field independently — often alone. They need to be able to make decisions quickly at all times. These people have an appreciation for the human factor — they know it is what will keep them alive every day they're on the job. Understanding other cultures and customs and learning to work completely immersed in these cultures are requirements. That means they have to be flexible and adaptable, with personalities that can stretch across a broad range of activities pretty much like "Oscar-winning" actors. This is a valuable attribute because they can switch gears quickly without hesitation. One day, they are out on a high-speed chase driving 140 miles per hour, thinking about every turn to be made before they get to it and all the while hoping that they will stay in control of the deadly weapon at their fingertips. The next day, they might be in a fusion center rendering assistance with special analysis and reporting. Being able to move these resources across functions relating to threats creates resiliency and redundancy in skills. This cross-functionality is something the security and intelligence planners in the public and private sectors should make better use of; they would benefit from it.

Not everyone adapts easily. Understanding a team's strengths and weaknesses is essential to all aspects of incident response. This allows for a team to leverage strengths and work smarter to be compliant and prepared without unnecessarily burdening a particular member of the team. Knowing what the leadership and team styles are helps determine what role each should be assigned in emergency planning. Are there diversity strengths? Has the team worked together before or is it just meeting? Being introduced for the first time in a crisis puts a team at a disadvantage, but getting through the crisis is possible if the right people came together — those comfortable with change, high stress, the unknown, unpredictable danger, and chaos. Those are the people who should be preselected to handle evacuations, serve as floor wardens, help first responders, and help with recovery efforts.

I have studied the behavior of humans for quite some time and now have taken an informal interest in animal behavior. This is not good because I find myself comparing the intelligence and instinct of humans to those of animals. It disturbs me to no end to discover that some animals have far superior intelligence and instinct than some humans. Their quick thinking and instinct determine if they will live or die, whether in the wild of Africa or on the loose in American cities. They do not have a lot of time to calculate risks, but their innate sense of danger is keen. That sense just kicks in, and they act accordingly. They do not waste a lot of time nor do they hesitate. They just move like they have a purpose — which tells me that perhaps they are wired to act this way, and evolution and technology simply have not tampered with their wiring — even in monkeys that communicate with humans through the use of computer technology, has not affected them.

Some animals, elephants in particular, are like duplicates of humans in nearly every respect, with the same capacity for mental and emotional intelligence as we have, only I have noticed that not all humans have that capacity — some lack mental and emotional intelligence. What is interesting about elephants' behavior is that the herds maintain order and follow a certain social order: there is a hierarchy, there are various role players, and there are babies, adolescents, and matriarchs. If one of the teenagers or one of the babies shows any signs of rebellion or resistance to group norms or any attempt to deviate from socially acceptable behaviors, the herd will not allow it. In a study that I performed 10 years ago about prisoner behavior, there was an emerging theme that resonated with the elephant behavior. In the prison study, the one memorable aspect of this paper that has stayed with me all these years was that these prisoners' behaviors were responsible for their prison sentences — society did not tolerate their behaviors. The prisoners were imprisoned because they could not conform to socially acceptable behaviors. Once in prison, there were also social norms. Even within the prison, some prisoners could not adapt to "prison acceptable behaviors." For those that could not conform within the prison, the prisoners had a way of policing their own and found ways to control unacceptable behaviors. If animals and prisoners do not tolerate unacceptable behaviors, should we as a society accept terrorism as a social norm in our country?

DYSFUNCTIONAL GROUP DYNAMICS

There are countless work behaviors that hinder employees' ability to operate efficiently in the workplace and if not recognized, these instances of dysfunctional work practices will also hinder efforts to assess threats and secure assets against them. The following are two examples that demonstrate how people often influence one another down the path of dysfunction without being seemingly aware of it.

"The Road to Abilene | Groupthink," is a story by Jerry Harvey, as told by the Reverend John H. Nichols.[11] In this story, a family is sitting around on their porch in Coleman, Texas. The temperature in Coleman is 104 degrees, and it is very muggy, but the porch is shaded, and everyone is comfortable. Then, Jerry Harvey's father-in-law says, "Let's get in the car and go to Abilene and have dinner at the cafeteria." In the back of Jerry's mind, a little voice said, "This is nuts. I don't want to travel 53 miles in the heat of summer in a 1958 Buick to have dinner in a lousy cafeteria." But Jerry's wife said, "It sounds like a great idea." And Jerry heard himself saying, "Sounds good to me. I hope your mother wants to go." And Jerry's mother-in-law said, "Of course I want to go." Four hours and 106 miles later, they returned. The heat had been brutal. Perspiration and dust stuck to their clothing and bodies. The food, as Jerry guessed, had been awful. Later that evening Jerry said, quite dishonestly, "It was a great trip, wasn't it?" Nobody spoke. Finally, his mother-in-law said, "To tell the truth, I really didn't enjoy it much. I would rather have stayed home, and I wouldn't have gone at all if you hadn't pressured me into it." To which Jerry responded, "I didn't pressure you. I was happy here. I only went to make the rest of you happy." His wife said, "You and Dad and Mamma were the ones who wanted to go. I just wanted to make you happy." And his father-in-law said, "I never wanted to go to Abilene. I just thought you

---

[11] Jerry Harvey, "The Road to Abilene | Groupthink," PDF, http://www.boisestate.edu/bsuaop/The%20road%20to%20abilene.pdf.

might be bored sitting at home with the rest of us." So, they all made a 106-mile round trip in the God-forsaken desert under furnace-like conditions to eat unpalatable food in a dingy cafeteria, a trip nobody had been looking forward to and nobody wanted to take.

"Challenger | Groupthink": 73 seconds into its mission, the Challenger Shuttle Mission STS-5 exploded, killing the entire crew. This disaster has been studied extensively to determine what went wrong and what were the immediate and the underlying causes of the disaster. The finding was that the fixture was sawed off and an attaching bolt was drilled out before closeout was completed. During this delay, the crosswinds exceeded limits at the Kennedy Space Center's Shuttle Landing Facility in Florida. There was a final delay of 2 hours when a hardware interface module in the launch-processing system, which monitors the fire detection system, failed during liquid hydrogen tanking procedures. The Challenger finally lifted off at 11:38:00 a.m. EST. The decision-making process on the day of the incident was cited as an example or fault of *groupthink*, where the groups had convinced each other to think the same way — with no one emerging to challenge even things that stood out as going counter to the group's decision. While groupthink was clearly at play, that was not what caused the accident — the accident was caused by poor leadership.

According to the Rogers Presidential Commission's *Report on the Space Shuttle Challenger Accident*,[12] the direct cause of the accident was the failure of the O-rings. They didn't fail because of groupthink; they failed because of the piss-poor engineering specs they were designed to, the lack of concern for mission failure under which the specs were created, and the launch decision being made despite all this. That's poor leadership, *not* groupthink.

Groupthink only comes into play as a contributing cause of failure on the day of the launch, in the meeting of managers of one of the contractors. Their decision to ignore their engineer's recommendations is talked about in the report, but they also talk about why there should have been other systems at work to question that decision, to ensure it was correct, and to ensure it was safe. The absence of that checks and balances process has nothing to do with groupthink, either.

The unrelenting pressure to meet the demands of an accelerating flight schedule might have been adequately handled by NASA if it had insisted upon the exactingly thorough procedures that were its hallmark during

---

[12] Presidential Commission, *Report on the Space Shuttle Challenger Accident*, 1986, http://history.nasa.gov/rogersrep/genindex.htm.

the Apollo program. An extensive and redundant safety program comprising interdependent safety, reliability and quality assurance functions existed during and after the lunar program to discover any potential safety problems. Between that period and 1986, however, the program became ineffective. This loss of effectiveness seriously degraded the checks and balances essential for maintaining flight safety.[13]

What these findings seem to suggest is that teams that could end up making disastrous decisions should perhaps have a second team or member behind them — whose sole purpose is making sure the team does not fall into groupthink.

DISCUSSION VERSUS DIALOGUE

It is important to understand dialogue — not stage actors, but in the context of task accomplishment. Meetings are usually held to make decisions. The outcome that most people would want from a meeting is that the *best* decision is made, not that just any decision is made, or another subcommittee is formed; but that a decision that delivers results is made — and then the group can move on. People hustle from meeting to meeting being very busy, and often achieving nothing in the way of measurable results, except to end up with yet another subcommittee all because they have lost the art of dialogue. So the question is, What is the difference between dialogue and discussion?

Discussion is the way that most people communicate. During discussion, we present our ideas and everyone analyzes and dissects them from their different points of view. The purpose of discussion, though, is to make sure you win, or that your point of view is the one that is accepted. During the discussion, you will support your idea and give your points more strongly until, eventually, others agree with you. You want to prove that you are right and the most knowledgeable, as does everyone else in the discussion. Great! With everyone trying to win the argument, no decision is ever made, and we eventually need to form a subcommittee to decide. Or the CEO or team leader uses his or her divine autocratic right and decides for the team.

Dialogue, on the other hand, is an exploration of ideas. It is not a new form of communication, but is the way the ancient Greeks and many so-called primitive societies are seen to explore ideas. During dialogue,

---

[13] Presidential Commission, *Report on the Space Shuttle Challenger Accident.*

everyone works together, contributing toward the idea. Remember that the team is greater than the sum of the parts; therefore, more is achieved from the dialogue as each person's ideas add to the last. In a dialogue, no one is trying to win. They are trying to learn and create. They suspend their individual assumptions and explore ideas and issues. It is a free flow of ideas where participants continue to think, watch, and teach each other to think. The great physicists Werner Heisenberg, Wolfgang Pauli, Albert Einstein, and Niels Bohr had a lot of discussions among themselves on their individual theories and findings. As we know from history, their conversations (dialogue) changed traditional physics because what they could achieve as a group exceeded what each could do as individuals.

HOW TO GET YOUR TEAM TO DIALOGUE

One of the leading experts on management communications is Graeme Nichol of Arcturus Advisors who has successfully provided management consulting across industries and who shares the following observations[14]:

1. *Everyone suspended their assumptions.* Dialogue came to a halt when someone demanded, "It will be done my way." They needed to suspend their assumptions to really see the reality at hand. Suspending one's assumptions is not easy, as often they are so deep-seated that we don't even know that they are assumptions! Instead, we take them for being the truth.
2. *Team members were thought of as colleagues and equals.* If people see each other as colleagues, they will interact as colleagues. Team members will feel less vulnerable and less likely to either want to dominate the discussion or not say anything at all. Thinking of everyone as colleagues can be difficult in a hierarchical workplace environment. If individuals who are in authority come down from their lofty positions and talk to everyone else as equals, it facilitates dialogue; but if they like being in their elevated position and pontificate wildly, no dialogue will be possible while they are in charge.

---

[14] Graeme Nichol, "Dialogue vs. Discussion," Ezine Articles, June 2005, http://ezinearticles. com/?Dialogue-vs.-Discussion&id=43241.

3. *There was often a facilitator.* Note that a facilitator can help ensure that *all* assumptions are suspended. This means questioning statements and beliefs as they are mentioned. Facilitators are also important in keeping the dialogue moving. As a team gets better at dialogue, the need for a facilitator is reduced.

People are closer to achieving dialogue when team meetings are filled with questions. Questions indicate an attempt at understanding. Next time you attend a meeting, see how often a question is asked. No questions signal no dialogue. Teams can effectively use dialogue if everyone knows what is expected of them in advance, and if everyone has bought into it and they truly want the results created through dialogue. Dialogue is a more effective way of communicating, and everyone must be willing to practice using it. Learning to use dialogue can allow for better "two-way" communication.

LEADERSHIP VERSUS MANAGEMENT

Management consultant David Straker of Syque and author of Changing-minds.org Web site offers much academic and practitioner advice on leadership and management principles for positive influence and persuasion of individuals.[15]

What is the difference between management and leadership? It is a question that has been asked more than once and also answered in so many ways. The biggest difference between managers and leaders is the way they motivate the people who work for them or follow them, and this sets the tone for most other aspects of what they do. Many people, by the way, try to be a little of both but are not very successful because the ability to be both is very difficult. You are either a leader or a manager with a birdseye view or in the trenches. Some people are great managers but ineffective as leaders, and visa versa.

Managers have subordinates. By definition, managers have subordinates — unless their title is honorary and given as a mark of seniority, in which case the title is a misnomer and their power over others is minimal to nonexistant. The two styles of manager and leader are as follows:

---

[15] David Straker, "Leadership vs. Management," Changingminds.org, March 2008, http://changingminds.org/disciplines/leadership/articles/manager_leader.htm.

Authoritarian, transactional style: Managers have a position of authority vested in them by the company, and their subordinates work for them and largely do as they are told. Management style is transactional, in that the manager tells the subordinate what to do, and the subordinate does this not because he or she is a blind robot or a puppet, but in essence, because he or she has been promised a reward (at minimum, a salary) for doing so.

Work focus: Managers are paid to get things done (they are subordinates too), often within tight constraints of time and money. Thus they naturally pass their pressures downward to their subordinates.

Seek comfort: An interesting research finding about managers is that they tend to come from stable home backgrounds and led relatively normal and comfortable lives. This leads them to be relatively risk-averse, and they will seek to avoid conflict where possible. In terms of people, they generally like to run a "happy ship."

Leaders have followers: Leaders do not have subordinates — at least not when they are leading. Many organizational leaders do have subordinates, but only because they are also managers. But when they want to lead, they have to give up formal authoritarian control, because to lead is to have followers, and following is always a voluntary activity.

Charismatic, transformational style: Telling people what to do does not inspire people to follow. One has to appeal to them, showing how following will lead to their hearts' desire. They must want to follow enough to stop what they are doing and perhaps walk into danger and situations that they would not normally consider. Leaders with a stronger charisma find it easier to attract people to their cause. As a part of their persuasion, they typically promise transformational benefits, such that their followers will not just receive extrinsic rewards but also somehow become better people.

People focus: Although many leaders have a charismatic style to some extent, this does not require a loud personality. They are always good with people. Their quiet style gives credit to others (and takes blame). They are very effective at creating the loyalty that great leaders instill. Although leaders are good with people, however, this does not mean they are friendly with them. In order to keep the mystique of leadership, they often retain a degree of separation and aloofness. This does not mean that leaders do not pay attention to tasks — in fact, they are often very achievement-oriented. What they do realize, however, is the importance of motivating others to work toward a vision.

Seek risk: In the same study that showed managers as risk-averse, leaders appeared as risk seeking, although they are not blind thrill seekers. When pursuing their vision, they consider it natural to encounter problems and hurdles that must be overcome along the way. They are comfortable with risk, will see routes that others avoid as potential opportunities for advantage, and will happily break rules in order to get things done. A surprising number of these leaders had some form of handicap in their lives that they had to overcome. Some had traumatic childhoods, some had problems such as dyslexia, and others were shorter than average. This perhaps taught them the independence of mind that is needed to go out on a limb and not worry about what others are thinking about you.

The difference between leaders and managers is best captured in Table 7.1, which illustrates their differences. This is, of course, an illustrative characterization, and there is a whole spectrum between either ends of these scales along which each role can range. Some people (very few) can lead and manage at the same time, so they would display a combination of behaviors.

ROADBLOCKS TO EFFECTIVE TEAMWORK

As reported in a study by Kate McLeod, Project Management Professional (PMP), of Algonquin College, in "Communication in the Workplace,"[16] there are barriers that impede effective communications in any operating environment. By breaking down and categorizing the issues, we find that there are three major roadblocks. These resonate with problems that DHS and industry face today as well as other organizations not linked to Homeland Security. The problems in understanding each other impact the ability to share information or communicate information effectively.

---

[16] Kate McLeod, "Communication in the Workplace," http://www.allpm.com/modules.php ?op=modload&name=News&file=article&sid=986&mode=thread&order=0&thold=0.

Table 7.1 Leaders versus Managers

Subject	Leader	Manager
Essence	Change	Stability
Focus	Leading people	Managing work
Have	Followers	Subordinates
Horizon	Long-term	Short-term
Seeks	Vision	Objectives
Approach	Sets direction	Plans detail
Decision	Facilitates	Makes
Power	Personal charisma	Formal authority
Appeal to	Heart	Head
Energy	Passion	Control
Dynamic	Proactive	Reactive
Persuasion	Sell	Tell
Style	Transformational	Transactional
Exchange	Excitement for work	Money for work
Likes	Striving	Action
Wants	Achievement	Results
Risk	Takes	Minimizes
Rules	Breaks	Makes
Conflict	Uses	Avoids
Direction	New roads	Existing roads
Truth	Seeks	Establishes
Concern	What is right	Being right
Credit	Gives	Takes
Blame	Takes	Blames

One of the most annoying examples of easily misunderstood communications comes from the various numerical formats used to represent dates. One of the many examples is the following:

02/04/03 could mean any one of the following:
April 3, 2002
April 2, 2003
February 4, 2003
March 4, 2002

It all depends on where you have worked as to how the information will be discerned at the receiving end. Nevertheless, it is wise to set up some ground rules or common language that the end users can rely on.

Roadblock 1: Lack of Proper Foundation

The first roadblock to assembling and maintaining a high-performing team is the failure to establish a firm foundation. Diverse teams need a foundation upon which a working relationship is built. Ideally, a team establishes this foundation from the beginning, and continues to periodically discuss and modify elements of the team foundation throughout the duration of its efforts. A team's foundation consists of several components: mission clarity, stated values, empowerment limitations, and defined processes. Some experts in the field of team dynamics point to an unclear team mission as the single largest reason for a team's failure to perform at optimal levels. A team's mission may seem obvious, but it is vital that each member understands the team's purpose, vision, and goals in the same way. To achieve this common understanding, the team's project manager or leader must provide a shared purpose; short-term, long-term, and endgame goals; measures for goal achievement; and a timeline for goal achievement.

Next, team members must generate and believe in a shared value system of team interaction. Clear ground rules must be formulated by the team and accepted by each team member. These ground rules form the rules of engagement, a framework for team conduct when interacting with one another and externally beyond the team. Behaviors to be included under the rules of engagement are those that are important to team members such as conduct for meetings, keeping promises, timely communication of information, mutual respect, conduct for customer interaction, and speaking with one voice on settled issues. The rules of engagement should be established and then periodically reviewed. They should be modified anytime the team believes it is necessary, and the rules can be used as a compass to help find common ground when team conflict arises.

The term *empowerment* seems to be overused and misunderstood in segments of today's workforce. Empowerment is not a ticket for management to exclude themselves from the working level and then point a finger of accountability should things go awry. Nor does it provide the working level with unlimited authority. Instead, when managed appropriately, empowerment is documented with well-defined limits that are understood by team leaders, individual team members, and functional area managers outside the program. For instance, to help clarify roles and ease any issues between program office and functional managers, drafting a memorandum of understanding defining limits of the team has been very effective. This is particularly important to ensure that members have authority to make most decisions regarding their functional area without having to constantly check with superiors. In addition, by assigning team and individual responsibilities, problems can be avoided that might otherwise arise when authority is perceived or unduly assumed. The delegation of authority must be visible to the entire team and can be shown via letters of authority or introductions at staff meetings. Team empowerment, when appropriately applied, provides a sense of mutual accountability, and is vital to the long-term health of the team. Equally important is the manager or project manager's support of decisions that are delegated.

Roadblock 2: Linguistic Differences

Men and women often use different methods of interruption during group interactions. A typical male behavior is to jump in and interrupt the speaker, while on the other hand females frequently wait for a pause in the discussion. These differences can lead men to mistakenly believe a woman is not participating. Women can misinterpret the situation as well, believing that men are 'bulldozing" them and stifling their inputs.

Men and women also have different linguistic styles. Linguistic differences can lead men to not always recognize women's ideas or to fail to give women credit for ideas generated in a team discussion. For example, women often include the use of an add-on question in their speech. The comment, "Normalizing the data shows a trend, doesn't it?" can make men think a woman is unsure of her conclusion when in reality the add-on question is simply a speech mannerism. Another example of linguistic differences is that men will often use the pronoun *I*, while women will often use the term *we*. This, too, can lead men to misinterpret a woman's statements and vice versa.

A final example of linguistic differences that can lead to miscommunication is the common use of qualifiers in women's speech. Men are not as prone to tag qualifiers such as *probably* onto the ends of sentences, and this stylistic difference can add to confusion and misinterpretation. One method of turning team conflict into synergy is to teach team members to recognize conflict and then reinforce self-resolution. Team members need to be trained in conflict resolution methods to enable problem solving without finger pointing. The lack of training can result in a failure to understand differences and may increase the conflict level. Once trained, team members in conflict must first agree that there is a problem, agree on just exactly what the problem is, search for a solution, agree on what each must do to mitigate the issue, and then follow up. Individuals learn to resolve differences by acting early to acknowledge conflict, directly engaging the other party with whom the conflict exists, responding rationally and without emotion, and dealing with each other honestly and directly.

At times, management needs to recognize when self-resolution approaches are not effective and intervene in the situation. In such cases, the manager or project manager (PM) should resolve the conflict with all parties present. The first step is to hold a meeting for the sole purpose of resolving the conflict. The PM needs to get those in conflict to recognize a problem exists and allow them to define the problem. Technology should not be used to avoid uncomfortable issues; face-to-face meetings work best. Initially the PM should strive to mediate, not judge. This is best achieved by being open-minded and actively listening. Active listening fosters feelings of acceptance and appreciation, saves time, keeps team members responsible for the issue, and builds relationships. The goal is to create an environment of healthy discussion of viewpoints and to foster candor. As such, the person at the top should withhold judgment until the situation is fully understood.

Roadblock 3: Conflicts

The third roadblock to effective teaming is the inability to resolve conflicts. Conflict in any team is inevitable, and many successful managers agree that team conflict is healthy — even vital. However, conflict becomes unhealthy if not managed appropriately. Typical reasons for conflict include role ambiguity and disagreements over methods, goals, procedures, responsibilities, values, or facts. Team facilitators and project managers can ensure the most prevalent sources of conflict are avoided by addressing the roadblocks identified. Yet, even those who carefully plan to avoid the principal roadblocks must still actively manage conflict. It is best to manage conflict by providing team members the tools to resolve conflicts themselves and by quickly addressing issues when self-resolution approaches are not successful.

Another challenge in making teams function efficiently is when they are composed of civilians and military members or industry-mixed people. While this situation is often not a significant issue, it sometimes can hinder team capability. Issues can stem from perceptions, biases of the other group or differences in organizational backgrounds, cultural backgrounds, and power interests.

For instance, due to their job assignment rate, the military tend to hold a shorter-term focus while civilians often have a longer-term focus. This

166

difference can result in differing priorities and conflict. When conflict exists, civilians tend to think military personnel treat civilians as second-class citizens; however, the military team members are often unaware of the perception. Military members also sometimes perceive that civilians are less motivated and are driven more by money than by doing the right thing for the effort, organization, or team. Furthermore, civilians are sometimes perceived as clock watchers (implying a lack of commitment to a cause), so it is a good idea to set guidelines for schedule adherence.

In general, military participants are considered better leaders because they are good at caring and coaching, but they can often overlook coaching of civilians and apply these skills only to military subordinates. Should this type of conflict creep its way into a planning environment, a leader would be well advised to take time to train both groups about the other's culture. "Dictate and take-charge types" will be most effective when they recognize and alter their leadership style from the field to the corporate setting. Each group needs to recognize the benefit of both functional expertise and operational experience.

CHAPTER EXERCISE

Diversity is great and often people learn from the differences of other members, but it is important to keep one factor in mind — the differences should be sufficient that they lend helpful ideas to the group effort, but not so different that group members cannot relate to one another, understand one another, or communicate with one another.

An owner has a dog and a cat; the dog and cat get along. They have lived together since they were a kitten and a puppy. They tolerate each other, and sometimes the cat will even groom the dog, and occasionally you will find them sleeping together. They are slightly different, but they relate to each other and get along. If we had tried to pair the dog with a small water turtle, however, the teaming effort might not have worked for them because they are too dissimilar. The dog might have tried to put the turtle in his mouth, thinking that the turtle was a toy. The turtle obviously wants to run away and not have anything to do with the dog.

A team needs to come together to solve a problem — the company is going to bring all the business unit managers together so that they can report on the progress of the DHS National Infrastructure Protection Plan (NIPP) preparedness plan and make decisions on what information is needed and how to submit the pertinent information to DHS that the company has braved to share.

The manager from Human Resources is present; others include the Manager of Finance and the Manager of Marketing. The Manager of the IT department has sent a level-2 help desk support member in his place. The Risk Manager is being represented by a temp hired for the week. Is this a good diverse group? Was this proper delegation on the part of the IT Manager and Risk Manager? The President has also showed up in place of the Manager of Operations. Will every member be able to provide the critical information and make the decisions required that achieve the objective? Why or why not? This is not an uncommon practice among companies in both the private and public sectors, and it is a problem that must not continue if we are to effectively plan for preparedness and develop solutions against terrorism.

8

Toolkits and Innovative Ideas for Change

Whatever your mind can conceive and can believe, it can achieve.

                                                    Napoleon Hill

OVERVIEW

In dealing with the gravest threats today, workforces have to be creative. A few things that all workforces share in common today are shrinking resources, untrained people, small budgets, limited technology, and an amalgamation of threats zeroing in on them every minute of every day. But resourceful people always will find ways to work around problems and navigate the environment so that they get to where they want and achieve their objectives. Sometimes we look at them with a bit of envy — for they do shine and impress everyone around them. They meet deadlines. They look organized. They are organized. Sometimes their shoes are even highly polished so that you can almost see your reflection in them. There is nothing wrong with that — we should all be so lucky, and it would be nice. Simply stated, they get things done and they are successful. We need people like this — more than likely they are Extraverted, Sensing, Thinking, Judging (ESTJs), which are explained later in the chapter. In this chapter, the focus is on "change": looking for ways that the workforce can change toxic and inefficient work practices that impede productivity and operational effectiveness, and protecting against threats that cause many employees to "burn out" — how will these people affect homeland security response?

Not only do we have to worry about national security, homeland security, and corporate security, but if we can't cut it at work, we could be replaced. No one can afford to just get by today. There is always someone around the corner who is better, faster, and smarter, just inching to take your job or move in on your territory. By recognizing that our dysfunctional behaviors and lacking skills can hurt us, we begin the first step toward improvement that can only improve our lives. Clearly, people need to change and organizations need to change. Both resist change because they get used to a routine or like the status quo, and change requires learning something new and that takes time — and who has time?

If people recognize that change is needed and they implement it — and it sticks — people and organizations would have the tools needed to do battle, achieve high productivity, move product in record numbers, attract new customers by the droves, and … you fill in the blank. Your security plan is going to require more than just the "nuts and bolts" of physical security and or an emergency plan. An effective plan also requires applying management and leadership principles, problem solving techniques, communications techniques, recognizing how to avoid dysfunctional behaviors, and most certainly terrorism basics. The best way to expand the necessary skills to put a great comprehensive plan together is to increase your knowledge in these areas and learn from other experts.

ORGANIZATIONAL LEADERSHIP

Organizational leadership (OL) is the study of efficiency and effectiveness in the workplace through inputs that maximize outputs in an efficient and effective way. It includes the study of leadership and management dimensions, the effective and efficient use of teams, and successful team dynamics, among many other things. Both elements — efficiency and effectiveness — are important. We know that workforces can be efficient but not effective and effective but not efficient. Here is the best example I can offer to demonstrate this concept: a dancer just completed rehearsing the steps to a Broadway show. The steps involved 60 minutes of 100 moves. The 100 moves were carried out smoothly — which was effective — but they took 75 minutes to perform, which was not efficient.

By understanding the many dimensions of people, it is possible to have a high-performing organization composed of people who understand their strengths and weaknesses, capitalizing on the collective strengths of the organization to achieve high-performance teams in the workplace, in the battlefield, at client sites, and in Homeland Security crises. Once we recognize that we have to implement change, how do we do that? We can change by doing the following:

- Watching others
- Repetition of a newly learned behavior or skills
- Using "mavericks" to influence groups
- From the top and bottom both simultaneously pushing the change to a meeting point

All organizations need a library. In your library, you should have security, intelligence, and terrorism knowledge materials and management tools to self-manage, project-manage, and manage time and resources. Tools can consist of anything that equips your organization with a better way of conducting business — from new methods, models, theories, books, videos, games, exercises, templates, and checklists to case studies. There is no particular ranking or listing of which tools to obtain first or which ones to apply first. This is a subjective process but one that can stimulate action and achieve the mutual goals of having preparedness plans in place for Prevention, Detection, and Response to terrorism and other disasters at work and at home — and being a valued employee or team member to the organization.

The goal of this chapter is to provide a solution for increasing knowledge and skills that are necessary to enable preparedness. It cannot present you with an all-encompassing set of solutions, but if you walk away with two or three ideas that help you or your organization to train, operate, and communicate more effectively and efficiently — that is a major achievement. Ultimately, people need to do what they can to build skills that contribute to the protection of critical infrastructures.

FUNDAMENTAL MANAGEMENT KNOWLEDGE

Stephen Covey

To get take control of the information overload factor, noted management consultant Dr. Stephen Covey offers principles for being effective at work and at home. In his book *The 7 Habits of Highly Effective People,* he offers a framework for prioritizing tasks so that unimportant tasks are not performed at the expense of important and urgent ones. Nearly 20 years after this advice appeared in his book, this sage advice is perhaps more applicable today than ever before.

Dr. Covey says that highly effective people share common traits of success. They know how to manage time. They know how to manage people and relationships, and are highly organized and streamlined in everything that they do so that they succeed in whatever they do. Among the many things that we can learn from Dr. Covey is to understand ourselves as best as possible and manage our time and resources to be effective. Effectiveness is highly needed in all efforts pertaining to Homeland Security preparedness.

If we do not have the skills, discipline, personalities, and leadership to perform in the ways that we need to, then we cannot possibly expect to have workforces that will handle Homeland Security matters efficiently and effectively. In Table 8.1, we spend our time in one of four ways. The two factors that define an activity are urgency and importance. Although Covey has written many great books, there is one model that would be helpful in managing daily tasks so that security does not fall on the back burner. Table 8.1 ("Covey's Time Management Matrix") has four quadrants.

Table 8.1 Covey's Time Management Matrix

	Urgent	Not Urgent
	Quadrant I	**Quadrant II**
Important	Time spent in: fire drills, crisis, deadline-driven projects	Time spent in: self-development, relationship building, envisioning your future, exercise/recreation
	Results: stress, burnout, always putting out fires	Results: happiness :)
	Quadrant III	**Quadrant IV**
Not Important	Time spent in: interruptions, unscheduled phone calls, pressing stuff	Time spent in: distractions, wasting time, busy work, pleasant activities
	Results: short-term focus, thinking goals and plans are worthless	Results: getting fired, total irresponsibility

172

Covey himself admits that this is just common sense — but it sure helps to have it laid out logically. If we classify what we have to do in terms of both urgency (*x*-axis) and importance (*y*-axis), then we get four quadrants:

1. Important and urgent
2. Important and not urgent
3. Urgent and not important
4. Not urgent and not important

If you are feeling overwhelmed, he says it means you are spending a lot of time in Quad 1. What Covey shows us is if we allow ourselves to be driven unconsciously by the "tyranny" of the urgent but (mostly) unimportant (Quad 3), then we are condemning ourselves to more of Quad 1. The more time we spend in Quad 2, the less we will spend later in Quad 1. I believe that many e-mails fall under Quad IV — distracting.

PROBLEM-SOLVING EXERCISES

These tools help you understand complicated, difficult situations. Without tools, problems might seem huge, overwhelming, and excessively complex, or quite simply people are working with "sensory overload" and simply need a checklist or quick reference guide to get through a problem.

The following techniques come from MindTools.com, a Web site offering many management tools for today's problems.[1] The exercises below help people conduct a rigorous analysis of the problems faced. They help people look at as many factors as possible in a structured and methodical way. They give you a starting point in business problem solving (and other problem-solving situations) where other people would just feel helpless and intimidated by the situation. In the area of Homeland Security, there are many problems that we need to solve to be effective.

Appreciation Exercises: Extracting
Maximum Information from Facts

Appreciation is a very simple but powerful technique for extracting the maximum amount of information from a simple fact.[2]

---

[1] http://www.mindtools.com/pages/article/newTMC_01.htm.
[2] http://www.mindtools.com/pages/article/newTMC_01.htm.

How to Use the Tool

Starting with a fact, ask the question, "So what?" (that is, what are the implications of that fact?). Keep on asking that question until you have drawn all possible inferences.

Example

Appreciation is a technique used by military planners, so we will take a military example:

Fact: It rained heavily last night.
So what?
The ground will be wet.
So what?
It will turn into mud quickly.
So what?
If many troops and vehicles pass over the same ground, movement will be progressively slower and more difficult as the ground gets muddier and more difficult.
So what?
Where possible, stick to paved roads. Otherwise, expect movement to be much slower than normal.

While it would be possible to reach this conclusion without the use of a formal technique, Appreciation provides a framework within which you can extract information quickly, effectively, and reliably.

Key Points

Asking "So what?" repeatedly helps you to extract all important information implied by a fact.

5 Whys: Quickly Getting to the Root of a Problem

The 5 *Whys* technique is a simple technique that can help you quickly get to the root of a problem. But that is all it is, and the more complex things get, the more likely it is to lead you down a false trail.

Why Use the Tool?

The 5 *Whys* is a simple problem-solving technique that helps users to get to the root of the problem quickly. Made popular in the 1970s by the Toyota Production System, the 5 *Whys* strategy involves looking at any problem and asking, "Why?" and "What caused this problem?"

Very often, the answer to the first "why" will prompt another "why," and the answer to the second "why" will prompt another, and so on, hence the name "5 *Whys* strategy."

It helps to quickly determine the root cause of a problem.

It is easy to learn and apply.

How to Use the Tool

When looking to solve a problem, start at the end result and work backward (toward the root cause), continually asking, "Why?" This will need to be repeated over and over until the root cause of the problem becomes apparent.

Example

Following is an example of the 5 *Whys* analysis as an effective problem-solving technique:

Why is our client, Hinson Corp., unhappy? Because we did not deliver our services when we said we would.

Why were we unable to meet the agreed-upon timeline or schedule for delivery? The job took much longer than we thought it would.

Why did it take so much longer? Because we underestimated the complexity of the job.

Why did we underestimate the complexity of the job? Because we made a quick estimate of the time needed to complete it, and did not list the individual stages needed to complete the project.

Why didn't we do this? Because we were running behind on other projects. We clearly need to review our time estimation and specification procedures.

Key Points

The 5 *Whys* strategy is an easy and often effective tool for uncovering the root of a problem. Because it is so elementary in nature, it can be adapted quickly and applied to most any problem. Bear in mind, however, that if it doesn't prompt an intuitive answer, other problem-solving techniques may need to be applied.[3]

---

[3] http://www.mindtools.com/pages/article/newTMC_5W.htm.

FUNDAMENTAL TERRORISM KNOWLEDGE

Gary Berntsen

Gary Berntsen is a 20-year veteran in the CIA's clandestine service who was awarded the Distinguished Intelligence Medal and the Intelligence Star, commanded a team of CIA and special forces during the war in Afghanistan in 2001, and is the author, with Ralph Pezzullo, of *Jawbreaker: The Attack on bin Laden and Al-Qaeda: A Personal Account by the CIA's Key Field Commander.*[4] Here he discusses the fight in Afghanistan, including bin Laden's escape from Tora Bora; his earlier career with the Counterterrorist Center (CTC); and his thoughts on the organization of the CIA today. This is an edited transcript of an interview conducted on January 20, 2006, with *Frontline*; in it, Berntsen offers insight as to when Al Qaeda might have formed.

> Islamic extremists would come out of Pakistan. They'd fly to Katmandu. They would then arm themselves, prepare bombs, move them across the border into India and conduct attacks, many attacks. We captured one group after another during that period. It was quite alarming, the volume of players involved.... The sophistication led me to believe that it might be state-sponsored, but it wasn't.... It was probably Al Qaeda as I look back on it now, but at that point we didn't understand that. I didn't understand it. Even though I stopped many bombings, we didn't put it together.... I think that it was in the early '90s, and it was because Mike Scheuer had formed that group within CIA, the bin Laden Group and was talking about the Sunni terrorism and this individual, [Osama] bin Laden, this financier. It was Scheuer who first brought that up ... and he convinced me early on that this was a growing problem. Later, when the bombs in East Africa go off [in the American Embassies in Kenya and Tanzania in 1998], I'm sent to lead the team because we think this is possibly Hezbollah. Hezbollah had done the attacks on the embassy in Beirut, had done the Marine barracks [there]; they had done the Israeli Embassy in ... Argentina in '92 and '94. They had been involved in [the bombing of the] Khobar Towers [in Saudi Arabia] in '96. So it looked like yet another attack done by Hezbollah. Of course, I get out there on the ground, and it's not; bin Laden has gone big.[5]

---

[4] Gary Berntsen and Ralph Pezzullo, *Jawbreaker: The Attack on bin Laden and Al-Qaeda: A Personal Account by the CIA's Key Field Commander* (New York: Crown, 2005).

[5] http://www.pbs.org/wgbh/pages/frontline/darkside/interviews/berntsen.html *Frontline* Interview.

Peter L. Bergen

Peter Bergen is a CNN terrorism analyst and print and television reporter who has traveled to Afghanistan, Pakistan, Yemen, Egypt, Saudi Arabia, Jordan, and Indonesia to learn about Osama bin Laden and his followers. In his newest book, *The Osama bin Laden I Know: An Oral History of al Qaeda's Leader,*[6] he provides an unprecedented portrait of the world's most wanted terrorist. He gives readers a glimpse into the life of bin Laden, beginning with the early days before he became the world's most wanted terrorist. In 1997, Peter Bergen traveled to Afghanistan to interview a young Saudi who, word had it, was using his family wealth to finance international terrorism. Bergen listened for an hour as the tall, thin man in camouflage quietly declared war against the West. Asked about his plans, he replied, "You'll see them and hear about them in the media, God willing."[7]

Michael Scheuer

One of the Central Intelligence Agency's foremost experts on Osama bin Laden has stepped out of the shadows and joined the public debate over past mistakes and future strategy in the war on terror. Michael Scheuer is the senior intelligence analyst who created and advised a secret CIA unit in tracking and eliminating bin Laden since 1996. What is new for Scheuer is that he is now free to comment and enlighten us on the culture that we are dealing with today. He was one of the Central Intelligence Agency's foremost experts on Osama bin Laden. He authored *Imperial Hubris: Why the West Is Losing the War on Terror* under the pen name Anonymous.[8] The book, written with the CIA's blessing, is critical of the Bush administration's counterterrorism policy, and was viewed by some at the White House as a thinly veiled attempt by the CIA to undermine the president's reelection. What are essential about this expert's material are that he was the first intelligence resource to detect the "threat" in Osama bin Laden and his reporting of how the threat thinks is important to understand how to better implement security strategies about the threat.

---

[6] Peter L. Bergen, *An Oral History of Al Qaeda's Leader: The Osama bin Laden I Know* (New York: Free Press, 2006).

[7] http://www.peterbergen.com/bergen/articles/details.aspx?id=256 review of OBL I Know in Books in Canada.

[8] Michael Scheuer, *Imperial Hubris: Why the West Is Losing the War on Terror* (New York: Brassey's, 2004).

Steven Emerson

In Steve Emerson's *American Jihad: The Terrorists Living among Us*, the author enlightens us to activities that have been going on inside our borders to plan and execute the attacks against us. How we could have been played this way and deceived by the terrorists is unbelievable, but their activities could have been easily headlined as follows[9]:

"Terrorist Joins U.S. Army Special Forces, Steals Methods"

"Terrorist Takes U.S. Special Operations Training to Al Qaeda Afghan Training Camps"

"Terrorist Buys Satellite Phone in America and Talks to bin Laden to Plan 1998 Kenya and Tanzania U.S. Embassy Attacks"

"To Avoid FBI & CIA Detection, Terrorist Volunteers as FBI Informant"

"Active Terrorist Registered as FBI Informant"

"Active Terrorist Informant Goes into Protective Status"

"Terrorist Sets up Training Camp in New Jersey"

"Terrorist Sets up Training Camp in Connecticut"

This demonstrates that much of the work carried out by Al Qaeda networks has been going on for years right under our noses, and yet somehow we missed the red flags. Some of the reasons why we seem to be unaware of the Jihadist extremist networks are that we hover in naïveté, we cannot imagine that it could happen inside our borders, and we have not evolved with terrorist threats to develop the capacity to imagine such activities in our neighborhoods. We generally stop learning once we leave school, but we are creatures of adaptation and the world we live in is in a constant state of change that we cannot seem to keep up with. It was never our job before 9/11 to be concerned with such matters, but we cannot think that way now. We should choose to change, or someone else will make us change.

Brian Jenkins

Brian Jenkins is an expert on terrorism and transportation security. During his nearly four decades of analysis, Jenkins has advised governments, private corporations, the Catholic Church, the Church of England, and many other international organizations on terrorist threats. Jenkins joined the army at 19. He served with the 7th Special Forces Group in the Dominican

---

[9] Steven Emerson, *American Jihad: The Terrorists Living among Us* (New York: Free Press, 2002).

Republic and with the 5th Special Forces Group in Vietnam. He subsequently served as a civilian with the Long Range Planning Task Group advising General Creighton Abrams, commander of military operations in Vietnam. Jenkins is the author of many books, including *Unconquerable Nation*, which explores the most pressing questions about terrorism. Brian Jenkins currently serves as Senior Advisor to the President of the RAND Corporation. He also served as a member of the White House Commission on Aviation Safety and Security and as an advisor to the National Commission on Terrorism. In an interview with *Security Management*, Jenkins offers insight — here are extracts from his interview.

SM: You note that in the Cold War we spent a lot of intelligence resources trying to get to know our enemy, whereas we tend to dismiss the Jihadists as mad dogs and evildoers, no further inquiry needed. This, you argue, has prevented us from understanding our enemy. What should we do instead?

Jenkins: We must begin by actually looking at what they say about themselves. They flood the Internet and the airwaves with their speeches, with discussions of their strategy, with discussions about tactics. We should be familiar with this because this tells us a great deal about why they think they're fighting; the messages that they use to radicalize and recruit young men and persuade them to turn themselves into weapons; how they plan to go about pursuing this struggle. I'm fond of quoting the movie *Patton*. After a triumph over the German forces, George C. Scott, playing the role of Patton[,] says, "Rommel, you magnificent bastard. I read your book." And in a sense that's a good place to begin. These people are out to get us. They write volumes. They write books, and we should read them.[10]

Jessica Stern

"A few years ago I decided to do something scholars rarely do: I decided to talk with terrorists" is how Jessica Stern begins her remarkable book.[11] Stern, an expert on terrorism and a Lecturer in Public Policy at Harvard University teaching courses on terrorism and counterterrorism, did something no one else has done. She decided to learn more about what makes

---

[10] Joseph Straw, *Security Management*, http://www.securitymanagement.com/article/what-s-wrong-war-terrorism.

[11] Buzzflash Interview, http://www.buzzflash.com/interviews/04/05/int04024.html.

terrorists tick by going to the source and interviewing them. Stern, in her introduction, is frank about her goals and her fears in traveling around the world, at risk to herself, in order to talk firsthand with individuals who "kill in the name of God." And she is an equal opportunity researcher: she interviews Christian, Jewish, and Islamic terrorists. As someone who from time to time consults for the government, Stern does not have a partisan political agenda. But she does have the desire to understand the motivations of terrorists in order to better fashion an effective strategy for reducing their omnipresent threat. In short, although Stern does not take political sides, she does take a strategic position. And her position, after interviewing terrorists and gleaning insights, is that trying to reduce terrorism requires a thoughtful, multifaceted approach, because the causes of terrorism and the motivations of terrorists are varied. She is the author of *Terror in the Name of God: Why Religious Militants Kill; The Ultimate Terrorists;* and numerous articles on terrorism and the proliferation of weapons of mass destruction. She served on President Bill Clinton's National Security Council Staff in 1994–1995. Stern was selected by *Time* magazine in 2001 as one of seven thinkers whose innovative ideas will change the world. Stern advises a number of government agencies on issues related to terrorism, and has taught courses for government officials.[12]

Wafa Sultan

Wafa Sultan (Arabic: وفاء سلطان) is a Syrian-born American psychiatrist and a controversial critic of Islam. She offers a unique perspective on why terrorists think the way they do.

Following are excerpts from an interview with Arab American psychiatrist Wafa Sultan, "There Is No Clash of Civilizations but a Clash between the Mentality of the Middle Ages and That of the 21st Century."[13] The interview was aired on Al-Jazeera TV on February 21, 2006, and a 6-minute composite video of her remarks was subtitled and widely circulated by the Middle East Media Research Institute (MEMRI) on weblogs and through e-mail. In this video, she scolded Muslims for treating non-Muslims differently and for not recognizing the accomplishments of

---

[12] "Jessica Stern," http://www.hks.harvard.edu/about/faculty-staff-directory/jessica-stern.
[13] Excerpts from Middle East Media Research Institute (MEMRI), "There Is No Clash of Civilizations but a Clash between the Mentality of the Middle Ages and That of the 21st Century," interview with Arab American psychiatrist Wafa Sultan, clip no. 1050, February 21, 2006, http://www.memri.org (accessed February 10, 2008). These excerpts also appear in Appendix G at the end of this book.

non-Muslim society, while using its wealth and technology. The *New York Times* estimated that the video of her appearance was viewed at least 1 million times as it spread via weblogs and e-mail. Sultan revealed to the *Times* that she is working on a book to be called *The Escaped Prisoner: When God Is a Monster.*[14]

Wafa Sultan: The clash we are witnessing around the world is not a clash of religions, or a clash of civilizations. It is a clash between two opposites, between two eras. It is a clash between a mentality that belongs to the Middle Ages and another mentality that belongs to the 21st century. It is a clash between civilization and backwardness, between the civilized and the primitive, between barbarity and rationality. It is a clash between freedom and oppression, between democracy and dictatorship. It is a clash between human rights, on the one hand, and the violation of these rights, on other hand. It is a clash between those who treat women like beasts, and those who treat them like human beings. What we see today is not a clash of civilizations. Civilizations do not clash, but compete....

Host: I understand from your words that what is happening today is a clash between the culture of the West, and the backwardness and ignorance of the Muslims?

Wafa Sultan: Yes, that is what I mean.

Host: Who came up with the concept of a clash of civilizations? Was it not Samuel Huntington? It was not Bin Laden. I would like to discuss this issue, if you don't mind....

Wafa Sultan: The Muslims are the ones who began using this expression. The Muslims are the ones who began the clash of civilizations. The Prophet of Islam said: "I was ordered to fight the people until they believe in Allah and His Messenger." When the Muslims divided the people into Muslims and non-Muslims, and called to fight the others until they believe in what they themselves believe, they started this clash, and began this war. In order to stop this war, they must reexamine their Islamic books and curricula, which are full of calls for takfir and fighting the infidels.

The full translation of the interview can be found at Appendix G, which consists of this and other excerpts of the interview with Wafa Sultan.

---

[14] http://en.wikipedia.org/wiki/Wafa_Sultan.

WHY WORKFORCE BREAKDOWN IS CRITICAL (BY PERSONALITY TYPE, LEADERSHIP STYLE, AND TEAM ROLE)

It is imperative that organizations understand their workforce in terms of their personality type, leadership style, and team role. By understanding its workforce, an organization will be able to predict decision making, reactions, values, motivations, and skills of their employees and put these factors to their highest and best use for the organization's success. Organizations will also be able to understand and appreciate the differences between all of their employees and realize that each one has something different to contribute. In understanding their leadership type, an organization will be able to create a team of individuals who operate as a whole.

Another reason why it is important to understand your workforce breakdown is because your workforce will determine whether or not your organization will survive an attack. By realizing that all employees do not react in the same way to a crisis situation, or to chaos, employers will be better prepared to deal with the reactions and educate their employees so that they can survive an attack. In general, people will react in one of four ways to stress or crises: (1) the employee will be calm, take a leadership role, and direct others in a manner that would lead to survival; (2) the employee will follow a leader, do what he or she is told, and contribute to the survival; (3) the employee will be catatonic — he or she will not be able to function at any level, and someone else will have to physically move him or her in order for the latter to survive; and (4) the employee will be out of control and possibly create more stress and chaos. Clearly, if an organization understands this and provides education for its workforce so that they understand this too — everyone will benefit and the chances for survival of an attack increase.

Theory X and Theory Y

Employees come in many varieties — but can be generally divided into two groups: employees who take charge of their job, take responsibility for their actions, and operate with little or no supervision; and employees who are unmotivated by their job, lack focus, and are thought to operate only when tightly supervised and told what to do, when to do it, and how to do it. This all boils down to motivation.

Social psychologist Douglas McGregor of Massachusetts Institute of Technology (MIT) expounded two contrasting theories on human motivation and management in the 1960s.[15] Douglas McGregor's Theory X and Theory Y models make assumptions about how motivation affects different employees. In Theory X, employees are assumed to dislike working, are unmotivated, and therefore need constant pushing, tight supervision, and direction to complete their job tasks. Theory Y employees are assumed to like working, are motivated, and therefore do not need the push, tight supervision, or constant directions — they complete their job tasks on their own. While these are just theories, it is easy to understand how, in some circumstances where an exact product or outcome is expected, Theory X supervision with harsh controls and constant direction would be expected so that the product or outcome can be predicted. However, under Theory Y, supervision understands that most employees want to feel in control of their job, and they want to contribute to the organization. They want to be treated as responsible and valued employees, and when treated as such, they feel like a part of the organization and want to do an even better job.

As employees are the greatest asset an organization has, it is critical that management understands that most employees should filter under Theory Y if they want to have an organization that operates as a unit and comes together during times of chaos or crises. Employees, when properly motivated through education, pay increases, or other perks, can provide imagination, creativity, and ingenuity that can help organizations achieve their potential, solve work issues, and improve retention and recruitment. Management should never underestimate the employees' potential and should learn how to motivate all employees so that they can each reach their potential, be a part of the organizational team, and share in the successes of the organization that they helped to create by their efforts. Conversely, if a manager feels that an employee falls under Theory X, it would be wise to determine what role such a person could be counted on being in a crisis, where there is little room for tight supervision.

Myers-Briggs Type Indicator

The Myers-Briggs Type Indicator (MBTI) is a personality questionnaire designed to identify certain psychological differences according to the typological theories of Carl Gustav Jung, as published in his 1921 book *Psychological Types* (English ed., 1923).[16] The original developers of the

---

[15] "Douglas McGregor," http://www.mindtools.com/pages/article/newLDR_74.htm.
[16] Carl Jung, *Psychological Types*, trans. H. Godwyn Baynes (New York: Harcourt Brace, 1923).

indicator were Katharine Cook Briggs and her daughter, Isabel Briggs Myers, who initially created the indicator during World War II, believing that a knowledge of personality preferences would help women who were entering the industrial workforce for the first time identify the sort of war-time jobs where they would be "most comfortable and effective."[17] The test indicates a certain predisposition to being extroverted, introverted, sensing, feeling, judging, perceiving, and feeling or thinking. While there is much controversy about tests like this, there is value to be appreciated in a setting where one has to determine how responders are going to react in a crisis. I am not convinced that this test is appropriate as a hiring tool, but military officers have been tested using this tool. The test indicates that there are 16 personality types and there are sufficient people in the workforce who have taken the test and know what they scored. The purpose of knowing the composition of one's team is for the purpose of understanding who have the minds for details and who is not suited for it. For more informa-tion on the Myers-Briggs Type Indicator, go to the Myers Briggs Foundation Web site, http://www.myersbriggs.org. There are 16 personality types:

ISTJ — Introverted Sensing with Thinking	ESTP — Extroverted Sensing with Thinking
ISFJ — Introverted Sensing with Feeling	ESFP — Extroverted Sensing with Feeling
INFJ — Introverted iNtuition with Feeling	ENFP — Extroverted iNtuition with Feeling
INTJ — Introverted iNtuition with Thinking	ENTP — Extroverted iNtuition with Thinking
ISTP — Introverted Thinking with Sensing	ESTJ — Extroverted Thinking with Sensing
ISFP — Introverted Feeling with Sensing	ESFJ — Extroverted Feeling with Sensing
INFP — Introverted Feeling with iNtuition	ENFJ — Extroverted Feeling with iNtuition
INTP — Introverted Thinking with iNtuition	ENTJ — Extroverted Thinking with iNtuition

Keirsey Temperament Sorter

Another similar test to the Myers-Briggs is the Keirsey Sorter. It has taken what Myers and Briggs developed and modernized it with other dimensions.[18] All 16 personality types are narrowly focused on four types of temperaments.

Idealistic NFs, being *abstract* in communicating and *cooperative* in implementing goals, can become highly skilled in *diplomatic integration*. Thus, their most practiced and developed intelligent operations are usu-ally teaching and counseling (NFJ mentoring), or conferring and tutoring (NFP advocating). And they would if they could be sages in one of these

---

[17] http://en.wikipedia.org/wiki/Myers-Briggs_Type_Indicator.
[18] http://www.keirsey.com.

forms of social development. The Idealist temperament has an instinct for interpersonal integration, learns ethics with ever increasing zeal, sometimes becomes diplomatic leaders, and often speaks interpretively and metaphorically of the abstract world of his or her imagination.

Rational NTs, being *abstract* in communicating and *utilitarian* in implementing goals, can become highly skilled in *strategic analysis*. Thus, their most practiced and developed intelligent operations tend to be marshalling and planning (NTJ organizing), or inventing and configuring (NTP engineering). And they would if they could be wizards in one of these forms of rational operation. They are proud of themselves in the degree to which they are competent in action, respect themselves in the degree to which they are autonomous, and feel confident of themselves in the degree to which they are strong willed. Ever in search of knowledge, this is the "Knowledge-Seeking Personality" — trusting in reason and hungering for achievement. They are usually pragmatic about the present, skeptical about the future, and solipsistic about the past, and their preferred time and place are the interval and the intersection. Educationally they go for the sciences, avocationally for technology, and vocationally for systems work. Rationals tend to be individualizing as parents, mindmates as spouses, and learning oriented as children. Rationals are very infrequent, comprising as few as 5 percent and no more than 7 percent of the population

Artisan SPs, being *concrete* in communicating and *utilitarian* in implementing goals, can become highly skilled in *tactical variation*. Thus, their most practiced and developed intelligent operations are usually promoting and operating (SPT expediting), or displaying and composing (SPF improvising). And they would if they could be virtuosos of one of these forms of artistic operation. Artisans are proud of themselves in the degree to which they are graceful in action, respect themselves in the degree to which they are daring, and feel confident of themselves in the degree to which they are adaptable. This is the "Sensation-Seeking Personality" — trusting in spontaneity and hungering for impact on others. They are usually hedonic about the present, optimistic about the future, and cynical about the past, and their preferred time and place are the here and now. Educationally, they go for arts and crafts, avocationally for techniques, and vocationally for operations work. They tend to be permissive as parents, playmates as spouses, and play oriented as children. There are many Artisans to be found in many places where the action is, and they are at least 35 percent and as many as 40 percent of the population.

Guardian SJs, being *concrete* in communicating and *cooperative* in implementing goals, can become highly skilled in *logistics*. Thus, their most practiced and developed intelligent operations are often supervising and inspecting (SJT administering), or supplying and protecting (SJF conserving). And they would if they could be magistrates watching over these forms of social facilitation. They are proud of themselves in the degree to which they are reliable in action, respect themselves in the degree to which they do good deeds, and feel confident of themselves in the degree to which they are respectable. They are in search of security as they are the "Security-Seeking Personality" — trusting in legitimacy and hungering for membership. They are usually stoical about the present, pessimistic about the future, and fatalistic about the past, and their preferred time and place are the past and the gateway. Educationally they go for commerce, avocationally for regulations, and vocationally for material handling work. They tend to be enculturating as parents, helpmates as spouses, and conformity oriented as children. There are even more Guardians than Artisans around, at least 40 percent and as many as 45 percent of the population.

If you have any coworkers who you feel are strange, it could be that they slipped into a work environment where they may not be a good fit. People tend to gravitate to like-minded people, and often tests show that they have similar personalities.

GROUP ROLES AND TEAM ROLES

Glenn Parker is an author and consultant on high performing teams and has developed tools to build and sustain such teams.[19] The Parker Team Player Survey (PTPS) is an easy-to-use self-assessment exercise that helps individuals identify their primary team player style — contributor, collaborator, communicator, or challenger. They discover how to best use their style for improved team performance and how to adjust the role they play on the team to meet the team's needs.[20]

Keep in mind that these categories are in no way fixed. A given person may show different behaviors in different groups or different behaviors in

---

[19] Parker, Glenn, *Team Players and Teamwork* (San Francisco: Jossey-Bass, 2008), http://www.glennparker.com/products/book-team-players-and-teamwork.html.
[20] http://www.cpp.com/products/parker/index.asp Parker Survey.

the same group at different points in time. However, most people tend to favor one of the four styles.

Knowing what styles exist in a group would help with appropriate assignments when teams meet to solve problems, design plans, or respond to threats or Homeland Security alerts, crises, disasters, or attacks. These are the four styles — which one do you think you are?

1. *Contributor*: The Contributor is described as a *task-oriented* team member who is willing and able to share knowledge and information. Contributors like to provide technical and clinical information to team members. The Contributor may frequently take on the role of "trainer" or "mentor" to new members. They are described as dependable, responsible, and helpful.

2. *Collaborator*: The Collaborator is described as a *goal-directed* team member who helps others remain focused on the overall purpose, mission, and goal of the team. Collaborators are "willing to extend themselves beyond their traditional boundaries or comfort areas"; they will "do whatever is necessary to get the job done." Collaborators do not mind working behind the scenes. They are willing to take on a variety of jobs and duties in order to meet a goal. They are hardworking, flexible, open-minded, and enthusiastic team members.

3. *Communicator*: The Communicator is described as a *process-oriented* team member. Communicators care more about team *process* than the end product. Communicators monitor the interpersonal climate of the team and take measures to improve relationships among team members. Communicators take an active role in facilitating consensus building and conflict resolution. They show concern for integrating new members and maintaining positive interactions among existing members. They take steps to ensure a supportive team environment.

4. *Challenger*: Challengers are described as questioning and critical. They express their opinions honestly and directly. They are very concerned with maintaining high ethical standards and high standards of quality. They are not afraid to express a dissenting opinion if they perceive a "higher good" in doing so. Challengers are willing to question authority "and will not accept decisions simply because 'that's the way it's always been done.'" Challengers force the team to think in new ways. Principled and candid, they have been described as the "conscience" of the team.

LOW-CONTEXT AND HIGH-CONTEXT COMMUNICATIONS

My experience of operating as a team member or leader of hundreds of teams in the United States and abroad in public and private sector critical infrastructure operations demonstrated that certain aspects of language are critical but not understood. Some cultures create people who are high-context communicators, while others create low-context communicators. These traits — while more prevalent in regions abroad — carry over into the culture of first-, second-, third-, or fourth-generation Americans. This varied method of communication can affect operational efficiency during normal operations and in a crisis if we do not understand this.

When workers from high-context and low-context cultures have to work together, often problems occur by the exchange of information. These problems can be categorized as differences in *direction*, *quantity*, and *quality*. Regarding differences in direction, employees from high-context cultures like China and France adapt to their good friends, families, and also close colleagues (in-group members). They communicate with them intensively (quantity difference) and exchange specific or detailed information about many different topics. The result is that every in-group member is constantly up-to-date with the facts around the business.[21]

In comparison to high-context cultures, low-context cultures like the United States and Germany orientate on many people of their daily life because they do not differentiate as much as high-context cultures between in- and out-groups. So their direction of communication is orientated on personal characters and refers to situations (direction difference). They mostly communicate within their out-groups in a broad and diffuse way (quantity difference). Within communication, they exchange information just to the necessary extent so that work can be done, and they don't discuss or exchange information constantly in their work environment and among colleagues (quality difference).

In China, communication tends to be very efficient because of their information flow at work and in privacy. The Chinese discuss everything in advance and consider meetings as an official "ceremony" where the already commonly agreed-on decision will be announced. This is important in the way of "giving and keeping face." The Americans and Germans, in contrast, inform the participating attendants in a meeting about the

[21] William B. Gudykunst and Young Yun Kim,"Communication with Strangers"; Lisa Hoecklin, "Managing Cultural Differences: Strategies for Competitive Advantage"; and "High Context versus Low Context Paper" on Web site: http://www.via-web.de/273.html (accessed March 2008).

Table 8.2 Reactive versus Proactive Language

Reactive Language	Proactive Language
There's nothing I can do about it.	Let's look at our alternatives.
That's just the way I am.	I can choose a different approach.
They won't allow that.	I can control my feelings.
I have to do that.	I can create an effective presentation.
I can't.	I choose.
I must.	I prefer.
If only ...	I will.

hard and necessary facts. The decision-making process takes place within the meeting. In France, it is similar to their Asian counterparts. They are also well informed before they meet each other. Many explicit and detailed discussions would probably be seen as an insult because everything is already clear.

REACTIVE VERSUS PROACTIVE LANGUAGE

Being proactive may be the single most important habit change that a person could ever achieve. By being proactive, a person takes control and chooses what life is about. Life is not "happening" to them anymore. Dr. Covey explains that when he was attending university, he found the following quote in one of his marketing books[22]:

There are 5 types of companies:

- *Those who make things happen*
- *Those who think they make things happen*
- *Those who watch things happen*
- *Those who wonder what the heck happened*
- *Those that didn't know anything had happened*

He thought this was true for people as well. Being proactive is about making things happen. But in this case, it can help organizations adopt proactive approaches that instill confidence in their operations or Homeland Security roles — thus building a strong foundation for any program. Table 8.2 is an example of how Dr. Covey feels reactive language could be reframed to make it proactive.

---

[22] Stephen Covey, *The 7 Habits of Highly Effective People*, (New York: Simon and Schuster, 1989).

Active Listening

What to Avoid

When we encounter people with a problem, our usual response is to try to change their way of looking at things—to get them to see their situation the way we see it or would like them to see it. We plead, reason, scold, encourage, insult, prod — anything to bring about a change in the desired direction, that is, in the direction we want them to travel. What we seldom realize, however, is that, under these circumstances, we are usually responding to our own needs to see the world in certain ways. It is always difficult for us to tolerate and understand actions that are different from the ways in which we believe we should act. If, however, we can free ourselves from the need to influence and direct others in our own paths, we enable ourselves to listen with understanding and thereby employ the most potent agent of change available.

What We Achieve by Listening

Active listening is an important way to bring about changes in people. Despite the popular notion that listening is a passive approach, clinical and research evidence clearly shows that sensitive listening is a most effective agent for individual personality change and group development. Listening brings about changes in people's attitudes toward themselves and others; it also brings about changes in their basic values and personal philosophy. People who have been listened to in this new and special way become more emotionally mature, more open to their experiences, less defensive, more democratic, and less authoritarian.

How to Listen

Active listening aims to bring about changes in people. To achieve this end, it relies upon definite techniques — things to do and things to avoid doing. Before discussing these techniques, however, we should first understand why they are effective. To do so, we must understand how the individual personality develops.

What to Do

Just what does active listening entail, then? Basically, it requires that we get inside the speaker — that we grasp, from his point of view, just what it is he is communicating to us. More than that, we must convey to the speaker that we are seeing things from his point of view. To listen actively, then, means that there are several things we must do. First, we must listen for total meaning. Any message a person tries to get across usually has two components: the content of the message, and the feeling or attitude underlying this content. Both are important; both give the message meaning. It is this total meaning of the message that we try to understand. For example, a machinist comes to his foreman and says, "I've finished that lathe setup." This message has obvious content and perhaps calls upon the foreman for another work assignment. Suppose, on the other hand, that he says, "Well, I'm finally finished with that damned lathe setup." The content is the same, but the total meaning of the message has changed — and changed in an important way for both the foreman and the worker. Here, sensitive listening can facilitate the relationship. Suppose the foreman were to respond by simply giving another work assignment. Would the employee feel that he had gotten his total message across? Would he feel free to talk to his foreman? Will he feel better about his job, and more anxious to do good work on the next assignment? Now, on the other hand, suppose the foreman were to respond with "Glad to have it over with, huh?" or "Had a pretty rough time of it?" or "I guess you don't feel like doing anything like that again," or anything else that tells the worker that he heard and understands. It doesn't necessarily mean that the next work assignment need be changed or that he must spend an hour listening to the worker complain about the setup problems he encountered. He may do a number of things differently in the light of the new information he has from the worker — but not necessarily. It's just that extra sensitivity on the part of the foreman that can transform an average working climate into a good one.

THE FORMING, STORMING, NORMING, PERFORMING MODEL

The "Forming, Storming, Norming, Performing" four-stage model, introduced by Bruce W. Tuckman in 1965, explains that when teams or groups come together for the first time, they inevitably go through a predictable development process before they are able to work efficiently and effectively. The four stages are depicted in Table 8.3.

The model evolved out of Tuckman's observations of group behavior in a variety of settings.

Table 8.3   Forming, Norming, Storming, Performing Model

Stage	Activity
Forming	High dependence on leader for guidance and direction. Little agreement on team aims other than those received from leader. Individual roles and responsibilities are unclear. Leader must be prepared to answer lots of questions about the team's purpose, objectives, and external relationships. Processes are often ignored. Members test tolerance of system and leader. Leader directs (similar to Situational Leadership® 'Telling' mode).
Storming	Decisions don't come easily within group. Team members vie for position as they attempt to establish themselves in relation to other team members and the leader, who might receive challenges from team members. Clarity of purpose increases, but plenty of uncertainties persist. Cliques and factions form, and there may be power struggles. The team needs to be focused on its goals to avoid becoming distracted by relationships and emotional issues. Compromises may be required to enable progress. Leader coaches (similar to Situational Leadership® 'Selling' mode).
Norming	Agreement and consensus largely form among team, who respond well to facilitation by leader. Roles and responsibilities are clear and accepted. Big decisions are made by group agreement. Smaller decisions may be delegated to individuals or small teams within group. Commitment and unity are strong. The team may engage in fun and social activities. The team discusses and develops its processes and working style. There is general respect for the leader, and some of leadership is more shared by the team. Leader facilitates and enables (similar to the Situational Leadership® 'Participating' mode).
Performing	The team is more strategically aware; the team knows clearly why it is doing what it is doing. The team has a shared vision and is able to stand on its own feet with no interference or participation from the leader. There is a focus on overachieving goals, and the team makes most of the decisions against criteria agreed with the leader. The team has a high degree of autonomy. Disagreements occur, but now they are resolved within the team positively and necessary changes to processes and structure are made by the team. The team is able to work toward achieving the goal, and also to attend to relationship, style, and process issues along the way. Team members look after each other. The team requires delegated tasks and projects from the leader. The team does not need to be instructed or assisted. Team members might ask for assistance from the leader with personal and interpersonal development. Leader delegates and oversees (similar to the Situational Leadership® 'Delegating' mode).

After completing his doctorate, Tuckman worked with the industrial psychology lab at Princeton University and then undertook research on small-group and organizational behavior as a Research Psychologist at the Naval Medical Research Institute in Bethesda, Maryland. He postulated that groups were likely to go through four distinct stages as they come together and begin to function.[23] These characteristics of human behavior in each stage might well be recognized by participants — but there may only be a limited consciousness of the changes and their implications. The obvious implication was that if people could develop a better appreciation of the processes surrounding group development, then it would be possible to enhance group effectiveness and functioning.

All models and theories have elements of information that can be critiqued or valued. The model is not included here because we are conducting psychological analysis or testing or endorsing or attacking reliability or validity. What is clearly logical is that we need not be concerned too much with why it has been critiqued — what we should do is take the value of this model for its simplicity. Instead of struggling with the idea that people on the team do not see eye to eye on all group ideas, embrace the fact that this is normal and acceptable. But hurry up and experience the attributes of the early stage so that the team can get to the *Performing* stage. You can almost see how all the pieces come together — moving in synchronicity because every team member knows his or her role and simply performs it. Figure 8.1 ("Teams and Groups") shows some of the most common work groups who would benefit from this model.

As you can see from the characteristics of each stage in the Tuckman model, it is typical for private and public sector team members, task forces, working groups, working committees, Red Teams, Tiger Teams (if they still exist), joint military forces, and coalition forces to exhibit the behavior dynamics associated with each stage.

It is important to understand that team member behaviors and emotions are likely to get in the way of collaboration when they first come together. This is normal and to be expected. But once each stage has been normalized — so to speak — the group can move to the next stage and be more effective. Each time it progresses to the next stage, the group learns valuables lessons about its members' abilities and strengths and about ways to capitalize on strengths to achieve the group's objectives. Nearly all work in the future can be expected to be performed by groups. All

---

[23] M. K. Smith, "Bruce W. Tuckman: Forming, Storming, Norming and Performing in Groups," *Encyclopaedia of Informal Education*, 2005, http://www.infed.org/thinkers/tuckman.htm.

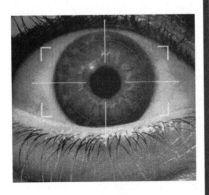

- DHS and the Private Sector

- Public to Public Sector Workgroup

- Corporate Incident Response Team

- Homeland Security Preparedness Plan Committee

- Business Continuity Plan (BCP) and Disaster Recovery Planning Team

- Emergency Planning Team

- Government Contractor Support Team

Figure 8.1 Teams and Groups

groups will experience conflict and chaos. Now, instead of allowing conflict to escalate and impede group progress, the group can demonstrate an opportunity to proactively address how to move forward.

Change is not permanent. If a group learns to apply Tuckman's model to be more effective in meeting its corporate goals or Homeland Security goals, the change needs constant reinforcements and nurturing. Often corporations will be proud that they brought a change agent consultant or a facilitator to help implement change. A few months later, managers complain that they wasted thousands of dollars because everything went back to the way it was before. They are very disappointed, and you can see it in their faces: the cost, the time spent, and the glory of the moment — all seemed very promising but went nowhere.

The reason that this change did not take effect is because the behaviors need constant reinforcement. They need to be repeated regularly. Someone needs to measure the change and log down moments of deviation. Intervening forces need to be launched when groups start deviating back to their old, normal behaviors.

CHAPTER EXERCISE

Utilizing Figure 8.2 ("Current Team Stage"), apply the model to one of our group activities. How is your group performing? What stage of

STAGE

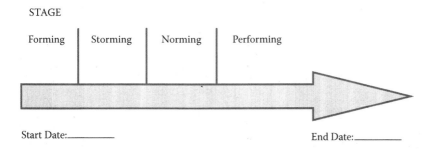

Figure 8.2 Current Team Stage

development would you say your group is in? Check the space that best illustrates what stage your group is in at this time. How many days, months, or years does this group have before the intended project should be completed? Does everyone in the group have a clear understanding of the group's vision, mission, objectives, milestones, deadlines, and success measures? What is the end goal? Given the group deadline, how much time does the group have to progress through the following stages? What can the group do to effectively achieve the desired goal in time?

9

Training and Exercises
Touch It, Feel It, Live It, Breathe It!

The free world is now consumed with a global and fateful struggle against terrorism! If terrorism is defeated under the leadership of the United States, a foundation for positive interaction will be built among diverse societies and a new plateau of human progress may be achieved. But if terrorism prevails — the potential exists for the regression of humanity into an age of darkness.

Lebanon General Michel Naim Aoun

OVERVIEW

Training needs to be a "constant" in the workplace — to broaden an individual's perspective, obtain job-specific knowledge and skills, obtain state-of-the-art knowledge and skills, and prepare people to perform a job, a new function, or a new procedure. Of all the things that can be done for prevention, preparedness, and response to a terrorist attack, the most important "proactive activity" includes the conduct of effective training and continuous education of people.

Millions of dollars are spent daily in the public sector for security prevention, detection, and response technologies. It is not understood why very little effort and time are set aside for employee training, education, and plan exercising. Manufacturers of security technology and managers of organizations that purchase technology seem to forget that no matter how sophisticated high-tech technology is, the weakest link is the "human factor" either as the operator of the technology or as the employee circumventing it and using his or her own shortcuts — because it's too hard to get used to or it created extra work.

Employees are our greatest assets in protecting our organizations. They should be considered the "organization's neighborhood watch." The real value of their potential capabilities is rarely recognized. Properly trained employees can provide "early warning" and create an atmosphere of a "hard target" just by being aware and reporting suspicious activities (i.e., strangers showing undue interest or asking "out-of-the-blue" questions that usually cause people to scratch their head afterwards). In this context, strangers who show this type of interest are probably conducting "reconnaissance and surveillance" as part of the terrorist operations cycle to assess vulnerabilities, and gathering intelligence to determine if the facility or organization makes a good target. Proper training can educate employees on threats, specifically terrorists' capabilities and methods of "gathering intelligence about the target" (their facility), as discussed in Chapter 5. The information gathered may not be secret or confidential, but it can be useful in the wrong hands. But to know what to do and how to do it requires training and education.

When the terrorist plotters of the Fort Dix attack were captured, it was discovered that they had considered a list of targets — one of them was McGuire Air Force Base (AFB), the next-door neighbor to Fort Dix. McGuire AFB was not selected because it was too hard of a target. The whole aim of this book will be missed if people do not "deduce, conclude, and put two and two together" to deny terrorists the ability to attack. We need education so we can figure out what needs to be done to protect ourselves from attacks like 9/11. We need tools and new ways to frame the problems we face today and will continue to face in the coming years. Well, we can always consider how the terrorists think (or the hackers or any other threats). The reason why hackers and other criminals are rarely mentioned in this book is because they have not declared to take on the whole world and threaten to destabilize world order, as Jihad extremists and Osama bin Laden have.

BENEFITS OF TRAINING

Effective training programs produce many benefits. They can decrease the time it takes to perform a task, increase effectiveness and efficiency for maximum productivity and positive "bottom-line" impact, improve the quality of products or services, reduce accidents and lower insurance premiums, implement new systems or procedures, and even reduce employee illness and stress through health-oriented work approaches. Effective training can also help deter terrorist attacks. The Israelis rely extensively on humans and less on technology. They use technology but only to complement what humans do. The Israeli population has an advantage on their side — everyone has to serve a short tour of duty in the military. A former Israeli officer once told me that someone's grandmother was responsible for providing as early a warning as possible in the face of an imminent attack. A suicide bomber was getting ready to get on a bus, and the lady was sitting opposite of the entry with full view of people entering the bus. "His rank was upside-down on his uniform. I thought something was off about his uniform, and that caused me to alert the bus driver," she would later report. The bus driver could only react by jumping out of his seat and pushing the guy out of the bus with his body. The suicide bomber and the driver died, but the rest of the passengers lived. Can we expect our citizens to be that alert and educated? We can strive and aim for it. Maybe our society is not there yet, but we can start today.

ADULT LEARNING

Training and exercises are essential in transferring knowledge that is critical and discovering human weaknesses that are sure to exist — and to do it right requires understanding adult learning: how adults sense information, how they receive it, how they process it, and how they recall it.

One interesting point is that if the training fails — and conditions are extremely dire — the body will unleash the brain's potential to enable survival. For example, adrenaline gets released, and the body slows down nonessential functions (cell renewal, hunger, etc.) to enable all body systems to concentrate on the required task — survival by means of running to safe ground or getting to where help is available. The body will even tell itself to start eating its own flesh, if the person is in a situation where he or she is stranded at sea for days or trapped in a cave while cave diving and starving to death.[1] I am not sure that the hidden brain rarely comes

---

[1] Discovery Channel: "The Human Body: Pushing the Limits" aired March 9, 2008, http://dsc.discovery.com/tv/human-body/more-about-human-body/more-about-human-body.html.

out when we are in normal everyday situations or in situations of less than dire need — therefore, we still need to learn and receive education.

Research has consistently shown that there are considerable differences between adult and child-adolescent learning styles. Additionally, since adults do not learn in the same manner as children, one cannot teach adults using techniques that were originally developed for use with children. Teaching adults requires the utilization of the process model rather than the content model.[2] Remarkably, people can learn from the moment of birth. Learning can and should be a lifelong process. We constantly make sense of our experiences and consistently search for meaning. In essence, we continue to learn. We can learn from everything the mind perceives (at any age). Our brains build and strengthen neural pathways no matter where we are, and no matter what the subject or the context.

In today's business environment, we must find better ways to learn — learning propels organizations forward. Strong minds fuel strong organizations. We must capitalize on our natural learning styles and then build systems to satisfy needs. Only through an individual learning process can we recreate our environments and ourselves to be a more highly evolved society.

Adults vary tremendously in how they acquire knowledge. Table 9.1 ("Children versus Adult Learning") gives a good comparison of how adult learners' needs eventually change in adulthood. Anyone who is still using what is used for children will not have success.

TRAINING METHODS

Adults learn by various methods — listening, seeing, music-based activities, numbers-based activities, feeling, touching, experiential, interactive activities (design more antiterror games — like PDR for the average American), social interaction, technical details, creative colorful images, and computers. Sometimes the learning styles are so dominant — people do not know this — that it will show in the training evaluation results.[3]

Instructor-led training (Figure 9.1) is most effective when interaction is required and educational material is being introduced or provided.

---

[2] http://www.utoledo.edu/colleges/education/par/Adults.html; and S. Stroot, V. Keil, P. Stedman, L. Lohr, R. Faust, L. Schincariol-Randall, A. Sullivan, G. Czerniak, J. Kuchcinski, N. Orel, and M. Richter, *Peer Assistance and Review Guidebook* (Columbus: Ohio Department of Education, 1998).

[3] From Malcolm Knowles, *The Adult Learner: A Neglected Species* (1984).

Table 9.1   Children versus Adult Learning

Assumptions	Children	Adults
Learner's concept	Dependent	Independent, self-directed
Learner's experience	Inconsequential	Rich in resource learning
Learner's readiness	Based on physical, mental, and social development	Based on need
Relevancy	Later application	Immediate application
Curriculum environment	Subject centered, authority oriented, formal, and competitive	Problem entered, collaborative, informal, and respective
Planning	By teacher	Mutual
Determination of needs	By teacher	Mutual and self-diagnosis
Lesson design	Sequenced in terms of subject matter, content focused	Sequenced in terms of need, problem focused
Activities techniques	Transmittal of information	Experiential
Evaluation	By teacher	Mutual

Figure 9.1   Instructor-Led Training

Table 9.2 ("Training Methods") provides a list of options to consider when you develop your training. Whatever you do, systematize it — if a threat causes damage, you may be asked to bring your training records to court.

Table 9.2   Training Methods

Training Methods	A Advantages	Disadvantages
Class instruction	Revised easily	Scheduling is difficult
	Developed quickly	Travel costs
	Face-to-face contact	Differences from class to class
Online group training	No travel costs	Requires computer equipment
	Developed quickly	No face-to-face contact
Videoconferencing and video/online	Supports large groups and multiple sites	High equipment costs
	No travel costs	Logistically challenging
On-the-job coaching	Effective knowledge transfer	Differences from instructor to instructor, session to session
	Related to trainee's job	Costly in terms of instructor-to-trainee ratio
	Face-to-face contact	
Online self-directed training	Consistent training content	High development costs
	Convenient access to training	Lengthy development time
Printed material	Portable	Less interesting
	Trainee sets own pace	Requires computer equipment
	Reuse does not require trainer participation	
Web-based training	Easy to modify	Limited bandwidth causes slow download times
CD-ROM/DVD	Supports complex multimedia	Difficult to modify
	Trainee sets own pace	
	Developed quickly	

Table 9.2 Training Methods

	B	
Training Methods	**Advantages**	**Disadvantages**
Video DVD or audio CD	Consistent training content	Requires playback equipment
	Can share copies	Can be costly to develop
	Trainee sets own pace	Difficult to modify
Just-in-time training	Available when needed at trainee's convenience	Costly to develop
	Related to trainee's job	Requires computer equipment
Continuous improvement	Promotes employee involvement	Requires training resources that are readily available on a continuous basis
	Promotes creative solutions	Differences from instructor to instructor
Computer-mediated	Accessible at the trainee's convenience	Requires computer equipment
Asynchronous collaboration	Promotes creative solutions	Can require computer software
	Promotes employee involvement	

CRAWL WALK RUN METHODOLOGY

Well-developed training supports the crawl, walk, run methodology for effective learning. This methodology has been successfully used for many years by the military. Table 9.3 ("Crawl Walk Run") details the three steps in this methodology, what they mean, and how they work. In every step, learning is verified before moving to the next step.

Table 9.4 ("Crawl Walk Run Description") details the type of scenarios and conditions that are used in each phase.

This methodology is easy to apply and is used extensively in business and military environments. Many people train this way without ever realizing it. This methodology makes sense, like a child developing and growing up — they crawl first and learn it before they walk, and they have to know how to walk before they can run.

To make training successful, it must be integrated into the corporate culture. Training must be a recurring event that is funded, planned, and supported by management with full commitment and buy-in by all involved.

Table 9.3 Crawl Walk Run

Phase	Meaning	Description
Crawl	Explain and demonstrate.	Describe the task step by step, indicating what must be done to successfully complete the task.
Walk	Practice what was learned with some assistance if required.	Provided a scenario or task, use knowledge learned to complete the task step by step.
Run	Perform the task to standard without assistance.	Provided a realistic scenario or task, use knowledge learned to complete the task to standard or be able to meet the objective.

Table 9.4 Crawl Walk Run Description

Phase	Description of Exercise to Support the Phase
Crawl	Situational training exercises that require coaching by the trainer, consultant, or O/C.
Walk	Situational training exercises using few tasks and favorable environmental conditions (e.g., day).
Run	Situational training exercises using multiple complex tasks, developing situations, and unfavorable conditions (e.g., environmental, lack of communications, or key personnel missing).

One thing we can learn from Al Qaeda is that if they apply money, time, and resources to train their people to attack, shouldn't we spend as much money, time, and resources to train our people to defend? Their effective use of training methods is evidenced by their standardized methods no matter where the terrorists are trained — Malaysia, Syria, the Philippines, the United States — and regardless of what language the training is taught in. They use curricula that are "modular": self-contained and focused on the basics. If you learn the basics of anything you want to learn, and learn them well, they will be second nature when needed.

Over the years, Al Qaeda has expanded the use of the Internet from a means of spreading propaganda to communicating with operatives to educational purposes. Over the Internet using roving Web sites, biweekly electronic journals, blog sites, and Web-based training also provides for the sharing of lessons learned immediately after they are learned and makes an ideal training medium for personnel located all over the world. The access to training also includes non-Al Qaeda Web sites that play a major role in providing security, intelligence, military, and emergency response training to interested Muslims and U.S militant groups. If it is beneficial to them, obviously it can be used to effectively train employees to benefit us in the fight against terrorism. But don't forget that they follow training with practical exercise.

VIDEO EXAMPLE FOR TRAINING

Videos are one of the best methods for training (seeing). Depending on the topic, there are many good videos that can teach the desired security skills or other skills needed to be productive or security conscious employees.

The movie *Catch Me if You Can* is a great display of effective training material for "social engineering" in action. Social engineering is the ability of a human being to be able to trick others into unwittingly giving up something — generally information. In the movie, the main character — a real person — tricks those around him into believing that he is whatever he wants to be. One day, he is a pilot; the next day, he is a doctor. With confidence, the main character does his "due diligence" to learn what he must know in order to carry off the ruse. He becomes comfortable in the skin of the person he is going to be, and then he prepares himself to be that person. The people around him never question him because he never gives them a chance to question any of his actions. He is able to stay in character, and therefore be completely believable. Social engineering is a powerful tool in the terrorist's arsenal — we are all vulnerable to a nice-looking face, a confident demeanor, and a lovable character. Why should we question those qualities when they are qualities we admire?

Another Show Solving a Problem

Attention to detail and awareness of your surroundings are critical to solving problems. A kidnap victim on the CBS series *Numbers* is rescued because the investigators paid attention to the details and the victim made herself aware of her surroundings. The victim is a journalist reporting on a shady real estate developer who is about to close escrow on a very large deal with the city. The journalist has found information about the developer that showed he had suppressed the price of certain parcels of land so that he could buy them at a reduced rate and have the land to proceed with his large deal. The developer has the journalist kidnapped to keep her out of the way so that his escrow can close. The investigators paid attention to the details of the recent reporting that the journalist had done, they investigated the stories that she had been working on, they talked to colleagues about her stories, and they found the link between her stories and the developer. By using math, the investigators were able to correlate recent land purchases the developer made with a list of numbers that was found at the journalist's house. The list of numbers turned out to be the parcel numbers of the land that had been purchased. There were two parcel numbers for land that the developer had purchased that did not appear on the journalist's list. By researching these two parcels, the investigators discovered that one of the parcels was a piece of vacant land, and the other parcel was located a distance from the other parcels and had a building on it — they deduced that this could be where the journalist was being held. It turned out that she was there. She heard the investigators and began making noises so they would find her. She was rescued.

You can probably come up with your own films for training tools. They draw interest and appeal to both visual and audio learners. This is just an example of how films can speed up the learning process — it is almost like being there. The learning needs to involve touching, feeling, and breathing it, as if the person being trained is there — experiencing the event!

EXERCISES

People go into exercises thinking they already know everything and they know how everything works; you get to throw them for a loop. Exercises work because people get to breathe it and live it as if it were the real thing. For example, in a red team exercise that was conducted at a critical infrastructure — the security guys were overwhelmed, alarms did not work, they did not know what to do next, their faces turned white, and soon they just stopped functioning due to everything going wrong. You can make a mistake here because it is safe ... but you can have a heart attack too! And you can get arrested and use up valuable cop time if your actions are not properly coordinated. One person did have a mild heart attack, and they had to deal with the emergency immediately — this left no reserves to deal with any other emergency had there been any more. The exercise showed that people could not seem to make basic or common-sense decisions — in settings like this, the environment is primed for "groupthink."

Many have an idea of what the Department of Homeland Security (DHS) expects in the way of training and exercises for terrorism preparedness. DHS provides extensive funding and support. Those exercises have standards and guidelines that need to be met, and many participants from government agencies to private companies participate; see the guidelines in Appendix H, "Homeland Security Exercise and Evaluation Program" (HSEEP). One can get an idea of what these exercises might entail by watching the movie *Dirty War*,[4] a film about how many component pieces need to come together quickly — efficiently and effectively — or people could cause the ordeal to worsen. It begins with ...

> In a post-9/11 world, how do you prepare for the unthinkable? Is it possible to stop a coordinated radioactive-weapons attack by determined terrorists in an international city? And what, if anything, should the public be told about such a threat? This HBO Films thriller shows how a "dirty bomb" attack might be planned and executed in London, despite the best efforts of police and intelligence forces — as well as how devastating the consequences of such an attack could be.[5]

Exercising complements training and education, and validates that training was effective. It is the one method of training that invariably opens the eyes of the organization to the fact that they may not be as prepared as they thought to detect and respond to a serious event. Terrorist organizations such as Al Qaeda spend just as much funds, effort, and time on training and exercising their plans as they do on developing them. They understand the importance of training and exercising, and if personnel are not trained properly and the plan is not exercised, the risk for failure increases exponentially. So why don't we seem to have the same approach?

Too often, the word *test* is used to validate plans and preparedness. From our early childhood school days, we have been programmed to fear this word. The mere sound of test leads one to believe that it means *pass* or *fail*. No wonder it is avoided. To promote a learning environment, the word *exercise* should be used to evaluate and validate training and security and response plans.

Regardless of what many executives and managers may think of how good their plans are, they are not prepared unless they rehearse and practice (henceforth referred to as *exercising their plan*). We do not mean exercising just the bits and pieces of the plan, performing a tabletop drill, or doing the exercise when all the cell phones are working and all the key players show up and the skies are blue. Organizations should exercise enough to build to the point where they can honestly say that their exercise

---

[4] HBO Films, *Dirty War*, http://www.hbo.com/films/dirtywar/.
[5] HBO Films, *Dirty War*.

was an intense experience and things went wrong, the way they would in real life, and leaders had to make tough decisions. Exercises should not be conducted just to say they were done to check a block or meet an audit requirement. Why? Because practice makes perfect.

In truth, everyone wants to be prepared for the worst-case terrorist scenario, so why is it so difficult to get organizations to complete preparation plans and follow through with training? Sometimes there is a "bias" that serves as a barrier to conducting an effective exercise. Why? Because management does not understand the true purpose of an exercise and does not want to look bad for all the money and effort that have been put into a plan or a program or department. Departments have to compete for the budget. What if someone strong and influential — a secret favorite department — gets funding and purchases many fancy gadgets that in the end did not serve their purpose, and now there is no budget? Or what if the training budget was used to buy equipment, pagers, or golf carts that security personnel thought they needed to do their job — and now there is no budget for training? The human factor enters the picture, and suddenly people realize that the funds were misspent, so the training component gets undercut and the company or organization just has to get by. This is the result of poor leadership and poor management. Management is supposed to be able to manage, control, track, and report — leaders are supposed to inspire others to achieve a vision through many of the "manager" processes. Often decision-making skills and "people-managing" abilities are lacking in the workplace. How many of the 200 million or so adults in our population do you think have been trained or mentored by good leaders and managers? If you want to know what will happen to societies that do not continue to learn, the next time you go to a video rental store, please rent a "must-watch" film called *Idiocracy*. Even if it's not your style of humor, you should watch this film. It portrays what will happen if people stop learning.

Essentially, today's managers develop scenarios for success instead of realism, results and identified gaps in a plan are toned down, and excuses are developed that include, "If this was a real incident, we would have done …"

It is interesting evaluating exercises and watching people go into them thinking they are ready; and then, as the exercise scenario develops and evolves, they find out how complex the scenario is, the cascading effects of decisions that are made, and how much coordination with other agencies and organizations is required. They walk away with new insight and the realization that it is easy to make mistakes. There is no better place to make a mistake than under a controlled environment where it is safe rather than during a real incident where lives are at stake. Exercises are a learning vehicle. Knowledge is gained and skills are developed. People learn to communicate and coordinate the necessary support and logistics needed. They develop the ability to make complex high-risk decisions in a changing environment filled with ambiguities.

A senior consultant for top *Forbes* companies in security and emergency preparedness who has conducted evaluations of organizations' preparedness across the nation in the private sector (technology, transportation, water, and financial), and in government (the Department of the Army and Department of Homeland Security), had several observations on the topic of exercises.

> Across the industries I evaluated, there were similar responses when senior management and executives were asked why their plans had not been exercised.
> Funding
> Lack of time
> High turnover of key management personnel (KMP)
>
> Companies that conducted training and exercises fell into two distinct categories:
> Table-top exercises only
> Exercises with unrealistic scenarios

He said the mere idea that they attempted exercises deserved applause. At least they had conducted some sort of exercise. It was more than what some of their competitors and counterparts did to evaluate the effectiveness of their plans, but despite the attempt, they failed in the execution.

Over the years, DHS has administered $22.7 billion in federal grants to states, territories, urban areas, and transportation authorities to strengthen prevention, protection, response, and recovery capabilities at all levels of government and critical infrastructures. In 2008, grant program allocations are $1.69 billion for the Homeland Security Grant Program (HSGP) and $852.4 million for the Infrastructure Protection Program (IPP). The money can be used for infrastructure protection (e.g., technology for intrusion detection and hardening), training, and exercising to strengthen prevention, protection, response, and recovery capabilities.[6] So, how much do

---

[6] Department of Homeland Security, http://www.dhs.gov/xnews/releases/pr_1201882312614.shtm.

you think will be used for training versus technology improvements, and will the money used for training and exercising be used effectively?

For too many organizations, developing a security or response plan ends when the plan is developed and written and is placed on the shelf for auditor reviews. To effectively have the capability for prevention, detection, and response plans, participants must be trained in their roles and rehearsed in the procedures they are expected to perform. Effective security to terrorism is a multiphase process that has to include internal and external feedback loops, management sponsorship, and activity relationships with all levels of an organization — effective training and exercising.

One of the most effective methods of evaluating security plans is conducting "red team" exercises — originally developed by the military as a game theory exercise to evaluate plans; increase understanding of the enemy's abilities, equipment, and tactics; and develop tactics to defeat them. Today, they are also used as a method of evaluating security plans, policies, and procedures. Experienced role-players are used to simulate the threat — they are competent, completely understand the methodologies used by the threat, and use them to challenge the customer's security.

The purpose is to validate perceived vulnerabilities or weaknesses in the overall security of a facility to test security operations and procedures, tactics, and equipment, and evaluate employee training by testing their security awareness. The Department of Homeland Security and several other federal departments and agencies have long used red team exercises to test security. The Department of Energy uses red teams to evaluate security and test response plans. The Federal Aviation Administration uses red team exercises to evaluate security and the ability to detect attempts at smuggling contraband onto aircraft. These exercises evaluate not only the human factor but also the technology used to detect threats. The National Strategy for the Physical Protection of Critical Infrastructure and Key Assets, published by the White House in February 2003, calls on DHS to use red teams to "evaluate preparedness" based on an "accurate assessment of national-level critical assets, systems, and functions."

One of the failures of red team exercises is that their results are often skewed by senior management and government officials suppressing findings; they reject the red team's conclusions or do not follow through with recommendations. Someone, usually management prewarns those being evaluated so that after the exercise, the results don't look bad. Other problem areas include not using qualified role players — this usually happens when exercises are conducted internally to save money. An effective red team exercise requires specially qualified and experienced people.

They should thoroughly know the methodologies used by the threat; have training and experience in gathering information, surveillance, and elicitation; be able to think like the threat; be able to think on their feet when the situation changes; and be able to live the lies they develop to play out their roles in the exercise. Another problem is unrealistic scenarios, or developing scenarios that are too restrictive or are not based on threat assessments. These problems are not exclusive to any single industry. They really stand out when you have had a chance to serve as an exercise controller or role player.

Red teams have been used for years in the corporate world to evaluate information technology security, plans, policies, and procedures. They are often referred to as ethical hacking. Kevin Mitnik is well-known for his knowledge and experience in using social engineering, and has written several books on the subject of organization vulnerabilities and how easy and vulnerable information security systems and people are in the corporate world — thus making it easy for "threats" to exploit vulnerabilities — threats being terrorists, spies, hackers, or others who wish to inflict harm or loss.

There are plenty of critical infrastructures that would benefit from red team exercises — for example, water treatment facilities, chemical plants, and transportation systems.

BUILDING AN EXERCISE

An exercise plan should be developed. At a minimum it should include the development of scope and objectives, exercise duration, management buy-in, and budget approval to meet the exercise scope and objectives.

Other Key Factors

- Having the right participants — internal and external.
- Having adequate supplies and equipment.
- Building the scenario — probably the most time-consuming scenarios are those developed to be based on threat and vulnerably assessments that have already been conducted.
- Postexercise reviews identify gaps, identify follow-ups, assign responsibility with deadlines, update plans — and plan for the next exercise.

To plan and conduct an exercise to validate a security or response plan, organizations should ensure that the following steps (at a minimum) are performed:

1. Obtain management sponsorship (funding and forecasting).
2. Initiate project.
3. Collect data: vulnerability assessments and threat assessment.
4. Select a project development team.
5. Develop realistic and measurable objectives (no more than 3 to 5).
6. Develop a safety plan.
7. Identify exercise participants.
8. Develop the scenario.
9. Select an exercise controller, evaluator, and observer group who are nonplayers and unbiased — external and internal.
10. Identify logistics and external support required.
11. Implement the exercise.
12. Document the results.
13. Conduct a "hot wash" — a postexercise brief that includes both participants and observers.
14. Identify good points and gaps of the exercise, plans, training, and logistics.
15. Document findings.
16. Develop a realistic and measurable project plan to improve procedures and plans.
17. Plan for follow-on training and the next exercise.

How Often Should You Exercise?

There are many variables that affect a response to this question, including the regulatory requirements of each industry, that is if the organization is a critical infrastructure (CI), and of course budget. But at a minimum, based on experience and best practices, a plan should be fully exercised at least annually. This does not include the tabletop or walk-through exercises that should be performed to lead up to the full exercise.

Exercises should provide challenges to the participants that require innovative problem solving in a time-effective manner. Exercises provide participants with a skill that would be impossible to obtain in any other way without risking injury in a real event.

TRAINING EVALUATION

Adults learn though various methods. Whether there is a formal training program, a corporate university, or a "train-as-needed" program, one important element is to get feedback. Training evaluations need to be performed in order to accomplish the following:

- Ensure that the material that was supposed to be learned was learned.
- Ensure that knowledge transfer occurred.
- See if information learned was retained so it can be recalled and applied.
- See if there is a return on investment (ROI).

Often, this is accomplished by asking the participants to fill out a critique form, but other methods include administering a test, conducting random spot-checks and testing knowledge. Random knowledge testing was often included as part of a red team exercise or as the information-gathering component of vulnerability assessments in much of my experience.

We would determine that a certain percentage of the organization would be randomly quizzed — the persons selected would be scheduled for "employee survey interviews." We would not tell them we were evaluating their knowledge; we would tell them we were conducting a survey on different aspects of their organization and wanted to gather some information — and we were always introduced by their managers. We would use a questionnaire similar to the one below, tally the results, and report them to top management as well as include in final reports.

1. What is your job in this organization?
2. Tell me a little bit about what that entails.
3. What would you consider to be an obstacle in this job?
4. Can you tell me what the corporate policy is on talking to the media?
5. Can you tell me how your company conducts training on security topics?
6. What is the regulation on (fill in the blank; e.g.,. list a policy, guideline, or directive) that you would refer to if the threat level suddenly changed from Bravo to Charlie (or from Yellow to Orange, or to Code Red)?
7. What is "Code Red?"
8. How do you get informed that the threat level has changed?

213

9. In an emergency evacuation, where do you go to assemble?
10. Would you know where the emergency kits are located if you had to go retrieve one right now?
11. Do you have a copy of the evacuation plan (or bomb threat checklist)? May I see?

Sometimes, if the scores were really bad, we had to share the information with other stakeholders besides the senior executives of the organization. In our environment, the results of training evaluations or feedback could feasibly be required to be presented in court if a catastrophe occurred (i.e., a terrorist attack). This is especially true in public sector organizations. In the aftermath, it is often labeled "fact finding," but really it is meant to be "Who's at fault for this?" and "Can they be held liable for this disaster?" In such a case, the results of your feedback may and often do end up on the Internet because if court records are not sealed, they become public information. These days it is not uncommon to find court records posted to the Internet.

There are more comprehensive methods for evaluation that can be better addressed by a company's training department. It can be performed as a large group or one-on-one, as in Figure 9.2. The random testing method provided above could easily be adapted and customized when there's no method in place to test knowledge learned or knowledge that one received

Figure 9.2 Training Evaluation Feedbacks

through training in their recent past. People need periods of "knowledge" reinforcement where the knowledge is allowed to settle and then the recall ability can be assessed. Evaluation does not have to be done in one session immediately following the training. But it is critical to perform it, more than most people realize — otherwise, the training could end up being wasted money that did not serve the purpose, and in the worst-case scenario, the training will be questioned in a court of law after an attack or other catastrophe.

"Give me your worst scorers and your best scorers" is one method that some organizations prefer for evaluation. In this method, they ask the ones who scored high and retained information why they thought they did so well. Often it was "The method in which the training was delivered was engaging," but sometimes it was that they had some knowledge already and this training served as a refresher. The ones who scored low often say, "It did not hold my interest" or "It was not explained very well." This type of response reinforces that adult learners learn "by doing" or by methods other than what teachers use in schools — where mostly it's one-way delivery with little time to deviate from the method of instruction.

TRAINING FAILURES

Critical infrastructures and other regulated industries are under the scrutiny of evaluators and investigators reviewing their training frequency and methods. Most of the time, it is a paperwork drill that is until something happens or they "test" the effectiveness of security using role players to attempt to defeat security during a "red team" exercise. Over the years, airport security and training has come into the limelight. One of the most common comments by investigators has been that poor employee training and weak compliance to security procedures has led to the defeat of security measures.

Other training failures include the executive or employee who travels overseas frequently and either avoids required foreign travel training that could protect him or her abroad or perhaps attends but does not pay attention to the training provided. Why? Is it complacency — or was it that the employee felt it was not important, did not have the time, and has traveled overseas for many years and never experienced an incident? The result of not taking this type of training seriously could result in death or facing other hazards.

215

In evaluating security training for over 20 years, I found it amazing how many people are motivated during training because what they learned was an eye-opener, yet within days to weeks they forgot everything they had learned. Most of the time, it is because the training was ineffective and was not reinforced once it was over.

Many organizations make attempts to comply with regularly scheduled training. But less than half are successful because they are not skilled in this arena.

A SUBJECTIVE METHOD FOR CALCULATING RETURN ON INVESTMENT (ROI)

Return on investment is important, and very few companies take the time to evaluate and analyze costs and benefits. It is only prudent to see "what you got for your money." So if the training is being conducted to protect business, people, critical functions, and assets, and it cost $5,000, $10,000, or $20,000 — what do you have to show for it? How many terrorists did you stop? How many hackers were identified on your network? How many disgruntled employees or potential workplace violence events did you identify and preempt? How many security violations decreased? Do you know how many you had in the first place?

Hypothetically speaking, let us posit that in the last year, your company spent $20,000 on training, $50,000 on physical security technology, $500,000 in security labor, and $10,000 on risk insurance premiums. The cost of your security can be summed up as $580,000. What was the cost of incidents responded to in the previous year? In a typical year, it would be conceivable for a company to experience the following incidents. For the sake of this high-level subjective exercise, let's calculate at the high end what the losses might have been if resources cost $120,000 [per employee compensation] and they work an average of 1,920 hours per year. The purpose of this exercise is not to be precise but to suggest one quick method of estimating the costs:benefits ratio. The first nine events are the security issues followed in the next section by the estimated cost of each line item:

1. Damage from one successful network intrusion from an outsider (3 days of labor of 12 resources to investigate and remediate).
2. Theft of five laptops with critical information (without data, $6,000; with privacy information, $25 to $300 per identity for 200

identities; trade secrets loss or loss of market share, a $35,000 to $1,000,000 loss of market share).

3. Labor to investigate and remediate 25 incidents of potential workplace violence (25 days of labor of one resource; compensation rate divided by 1,920 annual labor hours).
4. Labor to reinstall firewalls and other equipment (three resources for 2 weekend days and downtime; only calculating the labor cost of two resources).
5. Labor to respond to a virus attack (3 days of the labor of 20 resources).
6. Labor to file police reports and appear in court as a witness to an incident on your property (2 days of labor of one resource).
7. Brand damage from negative publicity (loss of market share or business, $100,000).
8. Turnover of security personnel five times in the year (average cost of turnover is $100,000 per person in loss of productivity from gap and time to get trained).
9. The insurance premium increased this year by $5,000 due to thefts.

Hypothetically, let's say the cost of these events was as follows:

1. $18,000
2. $1,012,000
3. $12,500
4. $8,000
5. $30,000
6. $1,000
7. $100,000
8. $500,000
9. $5,000

Estimated cost of security issues was: $1,686,500

These numbers are one method of attempting to determine the cost of security. To perform it more comprehensively would require input from several sources and your "numbers" people. The point of this exercise is — does technology provide a good return on investment over training? Simply stated, training employees is an absolute necessity that is often not given the importance it warrants in order to be profitable, productive, efficient, effective, compliant, and good corporate Samaritans who prepare and equip employees to succeed in the workplace. The benefits are often not quantifiable.

10

You Can Deter But You Can't Interdict
Don't Cross the Line!

I, Elsa Lee, do solemnly swear that I will support and defend the Constitution of the United States against all enemies, foreign and domestic; that I will bear true faith and allegiance to the same; and that I will obey the orders of the President of the United States and the orders of the officers appointed over me, according to regulations and the Uniform Code of Military Justice. So help me God.

Elsa Lee

KNOW THY LIMITS

We have arrived at a point where hopefully everyone knows much more on the topic of threat Prevention, Detection, and Response and the many activities that go into the processes of achieving preparedness. The greatest place to be is here — with perhaps, newly acquired knowledge to actually contribute in measurable ways to Homeland Security. It is also the most dangerous place to be, having just received a dose of privileged information that at one time was reserved for elite units and senior government leaders — but which we all now have a need to know because of the world we live in today. Of course, on that note everything shared with you is publicly available information. Nevertheless, you are either trying to help protect this country or you had ulterior motives — in which case, I hope you now see the light. Perhaps you can join the rest of us who are trying to preserve humanity and precious resources.

There is a fine line between security awareness, proactive preparedness measures, and crossing the line and breaking the law or acting in a manner that is unethical. If that line is crossed, there are serious consequences — the least of which is personal safety. Nothing is worth breaking the rules of the law.

DISTINCTIONS BETWEEN COLLECTING INFORMATION AND COLLECTING INTELLIGENCE

I mentioned in earlier chapters that we do not all speak the same language. Please understand that this can create problems, and we should all work to establish a few basic rules. The proper way to refer to the process of collecting information, in the private sector, should be "gathering information." The intelligence community will refer to it as "intelligence collection," and they have to undergo many levels of approval in order to collect. So for you to say, "I was doing my own intelligence collection last week and found…" — well, you may get a funny look in security or intelligence circles due to "intel types'" discomfort with this language. It is very specific to intelligence activities. In the intelligence community, if people are found to be engaging in such a task (intelligence collection) and then "blabbing" about it, people feel inclined to report them for possible compromise of security protocols.

In the private sector, we engage in activities for Prevention, Detection, and Response, and we may uncover suspicious activity. We are allowed to conduct an inquiry and conduct internal investigations, but our authority to perform those tasks ends inside the company premises. If the inquiry or investigative activities involved following people, it could turn into surveillance, and now the person's privacy is being violated. If a person had to be followed, it should be for something reasonable, such as the person is in danger or the police have been called and you are only following — at normal speeds — until you can "do a handoff." I have never encountered a situation where we had to engage in this activity, except for one time — and it was because the person feared for his safety and needed a second party to witness a financial transaction so he had to be followed to a bank.

Employees do not conduct surveillance. "They monitor their perimeter or facilities." They maintain situational awareness. They follow someone safely — if possible and if necessary just to obtain a license number — otherwise, they do not follow anyone. Terrorists and criminals conduct surveillance against their targets to collect intelligence (not to be confused with intelligence collection). Terrorists perform reconnaissance — they recon the area. Companies can recon too, but companies do not conduct surveillance. Law enforcement and intelligence conduct surveillance. Terrorists are not supposed to conduct surveillance, either — but they do.

Employees do not interdict; they monitor, and if something suspicious is noted or discovered, it gets reported to law enforcement. Employees do not conduct interrogations. They do not talk to subjects. They do not secretly tape-record conversations. They do not engage in search and seizure unless it involves property they own — for example, computers — and it is on their premises.

Some of the worst things that will happen if your company breaks the law or is perceived to have broken the law include the following:

- Brand damage.
- It will not be considered a minor violation, and you will get more than a slap across the hand.
- Botch up a possible lawful ongoing investigation or operation.
- Let the bad guys get away.
- Get hurt or killed.
- Get sued.
- Get prosecuted.
- Pay a fine.

HOW TO AVOID BOTCHING UP AN INVESTIGATION

The investigative process is very thorough and sensitive in nature requiring discretionary actions. A great deal of complexity is a constant because of resources that have to be pulled together, coordination that has to take place by multiple agencies, measures to avoid a compromise, and legal obligations to ensure that a case does not fall apart because of a technicality.

All lawful investigations and subjects of investigations require an extraordinary amount of diligence and planning. Law enforcement agencies spend endless liaison meetings coordinating the various aspects of their operations, areas of responsibilities, and dedication of investigative assets and equipment to ensure the desired end result. Prosecutors and private sector experts also have similar ongoing efforts when acts that can cause the loss of life, the unauthorized disclosure of defense information, and corporate crimes are being committed. Imagine how a security manager working for a corporation can complicate an investigation when he or she, or the corporation, takes matters into their own hands as if they had the same authority or power.

There are many former military intelligence personnel, ex-law enforcement officers, and private security officers who may have experience, former training, and a certain skills set to conduct an investigation; but what they lack that officials have are technical resources, investigative teams, legal permission, authority, and the proper training to conduct specific investigations. As a former counterintelligence agent, and having been trained in intelligence matters, it would be out of my scope and training to conduct a criminal investigation. Similarly, ex-investigators who have been trained in certain disciplines would not be equipped to investigate matters outside of a theft or a violation of a company's Internet policy.

Law enforcement agencies also face similar concerns in their own investigation to ensure they do not interfere with a covert operation by another agency. This type of scenario is not uncommon when local (county or municipal) agencies are investigating crimes within their jurisdiction while a federal agency is running an undercover investigation or operation.

Where corporations, private security companies, and investigative consultants run a risk is when they go beyond the steps of preliminary fact-finding activities to detect a problem, if indeed a crime has been committed. The reason the above-mentioned entities run a risk is because they may actually hurt a required set of circumstances that investigators need to conduct a thorough and effective investigation and tamper with evidence or obstruct justice.

An example of how a company may be outside of its scope of investigation is if it has a department store where there is shrinkage in inventory and perhaps other crimes also being committed, but the security manager investigates further and inadvertently alerts suspicious individuals that the company is aware of their activities. In a situation like this, it is best and imperative to bring in law enforcement officials immediately so that the perpetrators can be appropriately arrested and also so that the level of the threat can be fully identified.

Companies that hire ex–law enforcement, counterintelligence personnel, or special operations forces should provide special training to their
hires and review the position's scope of duties with them to clarify any
ambiguities or assumptions. These resources bring exceptional skills, but
sometimes these resources may cross certain lines because they are not
familiar with the way things work in the private sector and they have
been used to having authority in a previous career.

STUMBLING ACROSS EVIDENCE OF A CRIME: HOW TO PRESERVE IT AND RELINQUISH IT TO LAW ENFORCEMENT AGENCIES

The advent of the Internet has in many ways helped us to make our globe
smaller — and at the same time, it has made it easier to commit crimes.
Many companies have strict guidelines and policies on the usage of the
Internet for business purposes. Unfortunately, some people will also use
the Internet to surf pornographic sites or conduct illegal or unethical activities. When users access child pornography sites, they are putting their
company at risk in many ways (disrupting business when all computers
are seized or servers are shut down for an investigation by law enforcement) and also committing a federal crime. 18 USC 2252 makes it a federal
offense to knowingly receive child pornography. Companies may be more
apt not to report this because of the "fallout" that may occur as a result,
such as loss of customers or business, a loss of consumer confidence in
procedures, and ethical questions on how a business is operating. People
with information about a crime like this may also be more reluctant to
report it for fear of losing their jobs. A perfect case study happened in
California, where a librarian reported a man for accessing child pornography to police authorities and was consequently fired for reporting it.

Obtaining digital evidence of suspicious activities over the Internet
or crimes being committed over the Internet is crucial for investigators to
determine the level of damage and harm that has been done. Such evidence
helps prosecutors to arrest and bring to justice perpetrators or criminal elements who are committing fraud, violent acts, or white-collar crimes like
stealing proprietary information and selling it. Other crimes or activities
taking place in the workplace may include the following:

- Sexual harassment by employees
- Theft of company resources

- Sabotage of company property (intellectual)
- Securities and Exchange Commission (SEC) or Sarbanes-Oxley Act of 2002 (SOX) violations
- Unethical or questionable activities

We are living in a world with an uncertain future, but we can determine the outcome. It doesn't have to be "every man for himself." Through unified efforts and communities of teams we can all be gainfully employed, productive, prosperous, and contributors to our nation's Homeland Security.

Going forward, these should be common goals:

- Understanding the fundamentals and more about terrorism
- Hardening all facilities
- Building the pillars of preparedness
- Using simple models to relearn skills and reframe problems
- Relying more on the human factor before it becomes a lost art

We should consider the use of tools and models to help us organize better, solve problems more efficiently, and leverage the natural abilities and skills of team members to help in the overall effort to protect our country from terrorist attacks and other threats. We all have strengths, but that is not enough to perform all the tasks that go into preparedness. Imagine how far we can get when people with diverse skills and abilities take one idea and keep building it to the next step. Khalid Sheikh Mohammed (or KSM), the mastermind behind 9/11, considered himself an entrepreneur, and he applied "One idea leads to another" until he evolved the 9/11 plot.

Now we know what needs to done to protect our businesses, our critical infrastrucures, and our nation. If you don't know how or can't, hire someone to help you. The last point in this book is to keep all operations and activities aboveboard.

APPENDIX A

National Infrastructure Protection Plan — Table of Contents

LIST OF FIGURES AND TABLES

Figures

Tables

APPENDIX B
ASCE Report on Critical Infrastructure

2005 Grades

Subject	2001 Grade	2005 Grade	Comments
Aviation	D	D+	Gridlock on America's runways eased from crisis levels earlier in the decade due to reduced demand and recent modest funding increases. However, air travel and traffic have reportedly surpassed pre–Sept. 11 levels and are projected to grow 4.3% annually through 2015. Airports will face the challenge of accommodating increasing numbers of regional jets and new super-jumbo jets.
Bridges	C	C	Between 2000 and 2003, the percentage of the nation's 590,750 bridges rated structurally deficient or functionally obsolete decreased slightly from 28.5% to 7.1%. However, it will cost $9.4 billion a year for 20 years to eliminate all bridge deficiencies. Long-term underinvestment is compounded by the lack of a Federal transportation program.

Subject	2001 Grade	2005 Grade	Comments
Dams	D	D	Since 1998, the number of unsafe dams has risen by 33% to more than 3,500. While federally owned dams are in good condition, and there have been modest gains in repair, the number of dams identified as unsafe is increasing at a faster rate than those being repaired. $10.1 billion is needed over the next 12 years to address all critical non-federal dams—dams which pose a direct risk to human life should they fail.
Drinking Water	D	D	America faces a shortfall of $11 billion annually to replace aging facilities and comply with safe drinking water regulations. Federal funding for drinking water in 2005 remained level at $850 million, less than 10% of the total national requirement. The Bush administration has proposed the same level of funding for FY06.
Energy (National Power Grid)	D+	D	The U.S. power transmission system is in urgent need of modernization. Growth in electricity demand and investment in new power plants has not been matched by investment in new transmission facilities. Maintenance expenditures have decreased 1% per year since 1992. Existing transmission facilities were not designed for the current level of demand, resulting in an increased number of 'bottlenecks' which increase costs to consumers and elevate the risk of blackouts.

Subject	2001 Grade	2005 Grade	Comments
Hazardous Waste	D+	D	Federal funding for 'Superfund' cleanup of the nation's worst toxic waste sites has steadily declined since 1998, reaching its lowest level since 1986 in FY05. There are 1,237 contaminated sites on the National Priorities List, with possible listing of an additional 10,154. In 2003, there were 205 U.S. cities with 'brownfields' sites awaiting cleanup and redevelopment. It is estimated that redevelopment of those sites would generate 576,373 new jobs and $1.9 billion annually for the economy.
Navigable Waterways	D+	D	A single barge traveling the nation's waterways can move the same amount of cargo as 58 semi-trucks at one-tenth the cost — reducing highway congestion and saving money. Of the 257 locks on the more than 12,000 miles of inland waterways operated by the U.S. Army Corps of Engineers, nearly 50% are functionally obsolete. By 2020, that number will increase to 80%. The cost to replace the present system of locks is more than $125 billion.
Public Parks & Recreation	—	C	Many of our nation's public parks, beaches and recreational harbors are falling into a state of disrepair. Much of the initial construction of roads, bridges, utility systems, shore protection structures and beaches was done more than 50 years ago. These facilities are anchors for tourism and economic development and often provide the public's only access to the country's cultural, historic and natural resources. The National Park Service estimates a maintenance backlog of $6.1 billion for their facilities. Additionally, there is great need for maintenance, replacement and construction of new infrastructure in our nation's state and municipal park systems.

Subject	2001 Grade	2005 Grade	Comments
Rail	—	C	For the first time since World War II, limited rail capacity has created significant chokepoints and delays. This problem will increase as freight rail tonnage is expected to increase at least 50% by 2020. In addition, the use of rail trackage for intercity passenger and commuter rail service is increasingly being recognized as a worthwhile transportation investment. Congestion relief, improved safety, environmental and economic development benefits result from both freight and passenger market shifts to rail creating a rationale for public sector investment. The freight railroad industry needs to spend $175–$195 billion over the next 20 years to maintain existing infrastructure and expand for freight growth. Expansion of the railroad network to develop intercity corridor passenger rail service is estimated to cost approximately $60 billion over 20 years. All told, investment needs are $12–13 billion per year.
Roads	D+	D	Poor road conditions cost U.S. motorists $54 billion a year in repairs and operating costs — $275 per motorist. Americans spend 3.5 billion hours a year stuck in traffic, at a cost of $63.2 billion a year to the economy. Total spending of $59.4 billion annually is well below the $94 billion needed annually to improve transportation infrastructure conditions nationally. While long-term Federal transportation programs remain unauthorized since expiring on Sept. 30, 2003, the nation continues to shortchange funding for needed transportation improvements.

Subject	2001 Grade	2005 Grade	Comments
Schools	D–	D	The Federal government has not assessed the condition of America's schools since 1999, when it estimated that $127 billion was needed to bring facilities to good condition. Other sources have since reported a need as high as $268 billion. Despite public support of bond initiatives to provide funding for school facilities, without a clear understanding of the need, it is uncertain whether schools can meet increasing enrollment demands and the smaller class sizes mandated by the No Child Left Behind Act.
Security	—	I	While the security of our nation's critical infrastructure has improved since Sept. 11, the information needed to accurately assess its status is not readily available to engineering professionals. This information is needed to better design, build and operate the nation's critical infrastructure in more secure ways. Security performance standards, measures and indices need to be developed, and funding must be focused on all critical infrastructure sectors, beyond aviation.
Solid Waste	C+	C+	The nation's operating municipal landfills are declining in total numbers, but capacity has remained steady due to the construction of numerous regional landfills. In 2002, the United States produced 369 million tons of solid waste of all types. Only about a quarter of that total was recycled or recovered.

Subject	2001 Grade	2005 Grade	Comments
Transit	C−	D+	Transit use increased faster than any other mode of transportation — up 21% — between 1993 and 2002. Federal investment during this period stemmed the decline in the condition of existing transit infrastructure. The reduction in federal investment in real dollars since 2001 threatens this turnaround. In 2002, total capital outlays for transit were $12.3 billion. The Federal Transit Administration estimates $14.8 billion is needed annually to maintain conditions, and $20.6 billion is needed to improve to "good" conditions. Meanwhile, many major transit properties are borrowing funds to maintain operations, even as they are significantly raising fares and cutting back service.
Wastewater	D	D	Aging wastewater management systems discharge billions of gallons of untreated sewage into U.S. surface waters each year. The EPA estimates that the nation must invest $390 billion over the next 20 years to replace existing systems and build new ones to meet increasing demands. Yet, in 2005, Congress cut funding for wastewater management for the first time in eight years. The Bush administration has proposed a further 33% reduction, to $730 million, for FY06.

Subject	2001 Grade	2005 Grade	Comments
America's Infrastructure G.P.A. = D **Total Investment Needs = $1.6 Trillion** (estimated 5-year need—does not include security investment needs)	A = Exceptional B = Good C = Mediocre D = Poor F = Failing I = Incomplete		Each category was evaluated on the basis of condition and performance, capacity versus need, and funding versus need.

APPENDIX C
Bomb Threat Checklist

KEEP THE CALLER ON THE LINE AS LONG AS POSSIBLE!
EXACT TIME AND DATE OF CALL: _____
EXACT WORDS OF CALLER: _____
_____

Voice	Accent	Manner	Background Noise
❏ Loud	❏ Local	❏ Calm	❏ Factory Machines
❏ High-Pitched	❏ Foreign	❏ Rational	❏ Bedlam
❏ Raspy	❏ Race	❏ Coherent	❏ Music
❏ Intoxicated	❏ Not Local	❏ Deliberate	❏ Office Machines
❏ Soft	❏ Region	❏ Righteous	❏ Mixed
❏ Deep		❏ Angry	❏ Street Traffic
❏ Pleasant		❏ Irrational	❏ Trains
❏ Other	Speech	❏ Incoherent	❏ Animals
	❏ Fast	❏ Emotional	❏ Quiet
Language	❏ Distinct	❏ Laughing	❏ Voices
❏ Excellent	❏ Stutter		❏ Airplanes
❏ Fair	❏ Slurred	Familiarity with Threatened Facility	❏ Party Atmosphere
❏ Foul	❏ Slow		
❏ Good	❏ Distorted	❏ Much	
❏ Poor	❏ Nasal	❏ Some	
❏ Other	❏ Lisp	❏ None	
	❏ Other		

Questions to Ask the Caller

When is the bomb going to explode?

_____

Where is the bomb right now?

_____

What does it look like?

_____

What kind of bomb is it?

_____

What will cause it to explode?

_____

Did you place the bomb?

_____

Why did you place the bomb?

_____

Where are you calling from?

_____

What is your address?

_____

What is your name?

_____

****

If the voice is familiar, who did it sound like?

_____

Were there any background noises? PA system, street noises, machinery, booth, music, motors?

_____

Telephone number call received at:

_____

Person receiving call:

_____

Any additional remarks:

_____

_____

_____

DIAL 911 IMMEDIATELY, REPORT THREAT, AND CONTACT SECURITY FOR EVACUATION PROCEDURES.

APPENDIX D
Best Practices for Mail Center Security

There are millions of businesses that use the mail. The vast majority of these have only "one to a few" person(s) responsible for mail center–type operations. Of these millions of businesses, there are thousands of large, complex corporate mail center operations. The best practices listed below are a summary of well-developed mail center security procedures that can be used by any mail center. Procedures applicable primarily to large mail centers are identified as such, and in bold.

These recommendations come from businesses that use the mail and have been shared with the U.S. Postal Service (USPS) for distribution to its customers. Since needs and resources are often different, every suggestion may not apply to all businesses. Security managers should determine which are appropriate for their company and conduct periodic security reviews of their operation to identify needed improvements. The list below contains general security concepts and a few specific examples of how to accomplish them.

GENERAL MAIL OPERATION
PREVENTIVE RECOMMENDATION

- Appoint a Mail Security Coordinator (*and an alternate if a large mail center*).
- Organize a Mail Security Response Team, as practical, depending on the size of the mail center staff.
- Create, update, and/or review Standard Operating Procedures (SOPs), Security Procedures, Disaster Plans, and Operating Plans. Keep a backup copy of plan(s) off-site.
- Train personnel in policies and procedures relative to mail security, i.e., biological or chemical warfare, weapons, or natural disasters.

- Include from the staff, when possible, certified firefighters, bio-hazard handlers, and/or corporate safety, environmental, and health personnel, or train personnel in these duties.
- Members of the team should be equipped with cell phones or pagers and should be available up to 24 hours a day, 7 days a week, as is appropriate for the situation.
- Information and updates about the personnel and response procedures should be published and distributed company-wide.
- Publish an After-Action Report or Incident Report after every incident.
- Have senior management buy in and sign off on the company's mail security procedures.

EMPLOYEE SECURITY PROCEDURES

- Maintain good hiring practices.
- Provide in-depth screening and background checks when hiring new employees.
- Make arrangements with one or two temporary employment agencies to ensure that a restricted, prescreened group of individuals is available when needed to supplement the workforce.
- Enforce and institute a probationary period for the evaluation of employees.
- Establish a strict employee identification and personnel security program.
- Require employees to wear photo ID badges at all times.
- Instruct employees to challenge any unknown person in a facility.
- Where provided to employees, utilize uniforms with names and logos stitched on them for employees to wear at work.
- Provide a separate and secure area for personal items (e.g., coats and purses). Prohibit employees from taking personal items into the main workspace.
- Establish incoming-outgoing personal mail procedures.
- Hire or designate security personnel for the mail center area. (*Primarily for large mail centers.*)
- Establish health safety procedures.
- Have on-site medical personnel (*large mail centers*) or arrange for an off-site facility and personnel.

- Encourage employees to wash hands regularly, especially prior to eating.
- Encourage employees to see a doctor if suspicious symptoms occur.
- Encourage employee attendance in health seminars, talks, and info updates.
- As practical, establish or take advantage of company health programs (e.g., shots and checkups).
- Provide approved personal protection equipment according to Centers for Disease Control and Prevention (CDC) guidelines.

GENERAL SAFETY AND SECURITY PROCEDURES FOR INCOMING–OUTGOING MAIL AREAS

- Notify internal and external customers, as appropriate, of steps taken to ensure safety of mail.
- Control or limit access of employees, known visitors, and escorted visitors to the mail center with sign-in sheets, badges, and/or card readers. (*For large mail operations, include plant, workroom floor, etc.*)
- Subject to emergency exit safety requirements, lock all outside doors and/or prohibit doors from being propped open.
- Require deliveries to be made in a restricted, defined area.
- Restrict drivers to areas (rest areas) that are separate from the production and mail center facilities.
- Use video cameras inside and outside the facility and docks, as feasible.
- Keep the area for processing incoming and outgoing mail separate from all other operations, as feasible.
- If a separate processing area is used, it should not be part of the central ventilation system.
- Shutoff points of the processing area's ventilation system should be mapped and should be part of an emergency procedures handout.
- A separate processing area should include appropriate personnel protection equipment and disposal instructions for such equipment, as approved by the CDC.
- Designate, publish, and post evacuation routes for emergency situations.
- Conduct training, emergency preparedness drills, and information update meetings, as necessary.
- X-ray all incoming mail. (*Large mail centers.*)

- Maintain a Suspicious Package Profile.
- Ensure appropriate emergency access numbers are posted by or on every phone. Such numbers should include 911; the CDC at 770-488-7100; the local postal inspector; and the local police and/or fire department.
- Maintain updated employee lists (name, address, phone, and cell phone), and keep a backup copy off-site.
- Provide only vacuum systems for cleaning equipment, not forced-air systems.
- If not already done, alter receiving procedures to require a manifest with all shipments, and practice the acceptance of "complete" shipments only.
- Discarded envelopes, packages, and boxes should be placed in a covered container and transported to the loading dock for removal. (Ensure local arrangements are in place for the disposal of such material.)

ACCESS TO INFORMATION: EDUCATION AND COMMUNICATIONS

- Maintain a library of publications, videos, and brochures from appropriate information sources, and facilitate employee access to them as needed. Sources should include the USPS, CDC, and Occupational Safety and Health Administration (OSHA).
- Maintain and publish a list of useful Web sites from appropriate authoritative sources. Bookmark appropriate Web sites for easy access, i.e., those of the CDC, OSHA, the USPS, and the General Services Administration (GSA). Monitoring twice a day is a minimum recommendation, as situations warrant.
- Maintain and publish a list of phone numbers to call in an emergency: postal inspectors, the local fire department, the CDC, OSHA, the local police, etc.
- Present updated Best Practices from the CDC, OSHA, the GSA, the USPS, and the local Fire Department.
- Company-wide communications concerning mail center security procedures should be implemented.
- Require and encourage applicable employees to attend all local meetings pertaining to mail security issues.

GUIDELINES FOR MAIL CENTER THEFT PREVENTION

Mail is sometimes lost or stolen from company mail centers, or while en route to or from the Post Office. Much of this mail is quite valuable, containing cash, jewelry, and other high-value items. Needless to say, such losses are costly to the company and its investors. The following are some suggestions for improving theft prevention in your mail center operation:

- Know your employees. Don't put your new hires in your mail center without a criminal record check.
- Secure your mail center. Prevent access by unauthorized persons. Keep it locked whenever possible, especially when no one is on duty. Maintain a sign-in sheet for persons entering and leaving the mail center, including times of arrival and departure.
- Keep Registered Mail™ separate from other mail. Document transfer of Registered Mail by requiring the receiver to sign for custody.
- Protect company funds. If company funds are handled as part of the mail center operations, establish adequate controls to fix individual responsibility for any losses that may occur.
- Keep postage meters secure. Postage meters should be secured when not in use. Check mail periodically to determine if employees are using company postage meters for their personal mail.
- Vary times and lines of travel between the post office and plant. If currency or other valuable mail is sent or received, check periodically to see if mail messengers are making unauthorized stops or leaving mail unattended in unlocked vehicles.
- Employees caught stealing should be prosecuted. There is no greater deterrent to a potential thief than the fear that he or she may go to jail. The Postal Inspection Service will extend its full cooperation.

APPENDIX E
FY07 National Incident Management System (NIMS) Training Guidelines

Audience	Required Training
Federal/state/local/tribal/private sector and nongovernmental personnel to include the following: Entry-level first responders and disaster workers • Emergency medical service personnel • Firefighters • Hospital staff • Law enforcement personnel • Public health personnel • Public works/utility personnel • Skilled support personnel • Other emergency management response, support, and volunteer personnel at all levels	• ICS-100: Introduction to ICS or equivalent • FEMA IS-700: NIMS, An Introduction
Federal/state/local/tribal/private sector and nongovernmental personnel to include the following: *First-line supervisors*, single resource leaders, field supervisors, and other emergency management and response personnel who require a higher level of ICS/NIMS training.	• ICS-100: Introduction to ICS or equivalent • ICS-200: Basic ICS or equivalent • FEMA IS-700: NIMS, An Introduction

Audience	Required Training
Federal/state/local/tribal/private sector and nongovernmental personnel to include the following: *Required*: Midlevel management, including strike team leaders, task force leaders, unit leaders, division and group supervisors, and branch directors *Recommended*: Emergency operations center staff	• ICS-100: Introduction to ICS or equivalent • ICS-200: Basic ICS or equivalent • ICS-300: Intermediate ICS or equivalent • FEMA IS-700: NIMS, An Introduction • FEMA IS-800.A: National Response Plan (NRP), An Introduction*
Federal/state/local/tribal/private sector and nongovernmental personnel to include the following: *Required*: Command and general staff, select department heads with multiagency coordination system responsibilities, area commanders, and emergency managers *Recommended*: Emergency operations center managers	• ICS-100: Introduction to ICS or equivalent • ICS-200: Basic ICS or equivalent • ICS-300: Intermediate ICS or equivalent • ICS-400: Advanced ICS or equivalent • FEMA IS-700: NIMS, An Introduction • FEMA IS-800.A: National Response Plan (NRP), An Introduction*

* Not all persons required to take ICS-300 and ICS-400 will need to take IS-800.A. Emergency managers or personnel whose primary responsibility is emergency management must complete this training.

APPENDIX F
Fact Sheet on Dirty Bombs

BACKGROUND

A "dirty bomb" is one type of a radiological dispersal device (RDD) that combines a conventional explosive, such as dynamite, with radioactive material. The terms "dirty bomb" and "RDD" are often used interchangeably in the media. Most RDDs would not release enough radiation to kill people or cause severe illness — the conventional explosive itself would be more harmful to individuals than the radioactive material. However, depending on the scenario, an RDD explosion could create fear and panic, contaminate property, and require potentially costly cleanup. Making prompt, accurate information available to the public could prevent the panic sought by terrorists. A dirty bomb is in no way similar to a nuclear weapon or nuclear bomb. A nuclear bomb creates an explosion that is millions of times more powerful than that of a dirty bomb. The cloud of radiation from a nuclear bomb could spread tens to hundreds of square miles, whereas a dirty bomb's radiation could be dispersed within a few blocks or miles of the explosion. A dirty bomb is not a "Weapon of Mass Destruction" but a "Weapon of Mass Disruption," where contamination and anxiety are the terrorists' major objectives.

IMPACT OF A DIRTY BOMB

The extent of local contamination would depend on a number of factors, including the size of the explosive, the amount and type of radioactive material used, the means of dispersal, and weather conditions. Those closest to the RDD would be the most likely to sustain injuries due to the explosion. As radioactive material spreads, it becomes less concentrated and less harmful. Prompt detection of the type of radioactive material used will greatly assist local authorities in advising the community on protective measures, such as sheltering in place, or quickly leaving the immediate area. Radiation can be readily detected with equipment already carried by many emergency responders. Subsequent decontamination of the affected area may involve considerable time and expense.

Immediate health effects from exposure to the low radiation levels expected from an RDD would likely be minimal. The effects of radiation exposure would be determined by the following:

- The amount of radiation absorbed by the body
- The type of radiation (gamma, beta, or alpha)
- The distance from the radiation to an individual
- The means of exposure — external or internal (absorbed by the skin, inhaled, or ingested)
- The length of time exposed

The health effects of radiation tend to be directly proportional to the radiation dose. In other words, the higher the radiation dose, the higher the risk of injury.

PROTECTIVE ACTIONS

In general, protection from radiation is afforded by the following:

- Minimizing the time exposed to radioactive materials
- Maximizing the distance from the source of radiation
- Shielding from external exposure and from inhaling radioactive material

More detailed guidance can be found at the sources (see "Other Contact Information") provided at the end of this appendix.

SOURCES OF RADIOACTIVE MATERIAL

Radioactive materials are routinely used at hospitals, research facilities, and industrial and construction sites. These radioactive materials are used for such purposes as diagnosing and treating illnesses, sterilizing equipment, and inspecting welding seams. The Nuclear Regulatory Commission (NRC), together with 33 "Agreement" States that also regulate radioactive material, administers over 21,000 licenses of such materials. The vast majority of these materials are not useful for an RDD.

CONTROL OF RADIOACTIVE MATERIAL

NRC and State regulations require owners licensed to use or store radioactive material to secure it from theft and unauthorized access. These measures have been greatly strengthened since the attacks of September 11, 2001. Licensees must promptly report lost or stolen high-risk radioactive material. Local authorities also assist in making a determined effort to find and retrieve such sources. Most reports of lost or stolen material involve small or short-lived radioactive sources not useful for an RDD.

Past experience suggests there has not been a pattern of collecting such sources for the purpose of assembling an RDD. It is important to note that NPC states that the radioactivity of the combined total of all unrecovered sources in the United States over the past 5 years (when corrected for radioactive decay) would not reach the threshold for one high-risk radioactive source. Unfortunately, the same cannot be said worldwide. The U.S. Government is working to strengthen controls on high-risk radioactive sources both at home and abroad.

RISK OF CANCER

Just because a person is near a radioactive source for a short time or gets a small amount of radioactive dust on him or herself does not mean he or she will get cancer. Any additional risk will likely be extremely small. Doctors specializing in radiation health effects will be able to assess the risks and suggest mitigating medical treatment once the radioactive source and exposure levels have been determined.

There are some medical treatments available that help cleanse the body of certain radioactive materials. Prussian blue has been proven effective for ingestion of cesium-137 (a radioactive isotope). In addition, potassium iodide (KI) can be used to protect against thyroid cancer caused by iodine-131 (radioactive iodine). However, KI, which is available as an "over-the-counter" pill, offers no protection to other parts of the body or against other radioactive isotopes. Medical professionals are best qualified to determine how to best treat symptoms.

OTHER CONTACT INFORMATION

A number of Federal agencies have responsibilities for dealing with RDDs. Their public affairs offices can answer questions on the subject or provide access to experts in and out of government. Their Web sites and phone numbers are as follows:

Department of Energy: www.energy.gov; 202-586-4940

Department of Health and Human Services: www.hhs.gov; 202-690-6343

Department of Homeland Security: www.dhs.gov; 202-282-8010

Department of Justice: www.usdoj.gov; 202-514-2007

Environmental Protection Agency: www.epa.gov; 202-564-9828

Federal Bureau of Investigation: www.fbi.gov; 202-324-3691

Federal Emergency Management Agency: www.fema.gov; 202-646-4600

National Nuclear Security Administration: www.nnsa.doe.gov; 202-586-7371

Nuclear Regulatory Commission: www.nrc.gov; 301-415-8200

Transportation Security Administration: www.tsa.gov/public/; 571-227-2829

APPENDIX G
Arab American Psychiatrist Wafa Sultan
There Is No Clash of Civilizations But a Clash between the Mentality of the Middle Ages and That of the 21st Century

Following are excerpts from an interview with Arab American psychiatrist Wafa Sultan. The interview was aired on Al-Jazeera TV on February 21, 2006.

Wafa Sultan: The clash we are witnessing around the world is not a clash of religions, or a clash of civilizations. It is a clash between two opposites, between two eras. It is a clash between a mentality that belongs to the Middle Ages and another mentality that belongs to the 21st century. It is a clash between civilization and backwardness, between the civilized and the primitive, between barbarity and rationality. It is a clash between freedom and oppression, between democracy and dictatorship. It is a clash between human rights, on the one hand, and the violation of these rights, on other hand. It is a clash between those who treat women like beasts, and those who treat them like human beings. What we see today is not a clash of civilizations. Civilizations do not clash, but compete.

[...]

Host: I understand from your words that what is happening today is a clash between the culture of the West, and the backwardness and ignorance of the Muslims?

Wafa Sultan: Yes, that is what I mean.

[...]

Host: Who came up with the concept of a clash of civilizations? Was it not Samuel Huntington? It was not Bin Laden. I would like to discuss this issue, if you don't mind...

Wafa Sultan: The Muslims are the ones who began using this expression. The Muslims are the ones who began the clash of civilizations. The Prophet of Islam said: "I was ordered to fight the people until they believe in Allah and His Messenger." When the Muslims divided the people into Muslims and non-Muslims, and called to fight the others until they believe in what they themselves believe, they started this clash, and began this war. In order to stop this war, they must reexamine their Islamic books and curricula, which are full of calls for takfir and fighting the infidels.

My colleague has said that he never offends other people's beliefs. What civilization on the face of this earth allows him to call other people by names that they did not choose for themselves? Once, he calls them Ahl Al-Dhimma, another time he calls them the "People of the Book," and yet another time he compares them to apes and pigs, or he calls the Christians "those who incur Allah's wrath." Who told you that they are "People of the Book"? They are not the People of the Book, they are people of many books. All the useful scientific books that you have today are theirs, the fruit of their free and creative thinking. What gives you the right to call them "those who incur Allah's wrath," or "those who have gone astray," and then come here and say that your religion commands you to refrain from offending the beliefs of others?

I am not a Christian, a Muslim, or a Jew. I am a secular human being. I do not believe in the supernatural, but I respect others' right to believe in it.

Dr. Ibrahim Al-Khoul[1]: Are you a heretic?

Wafa Sultan: You can say whatever you like. I am a secular human being who does not believe in the supernatural....

Dr. Ibrahim Al-Khouli: If you are a heretic, there is no point in rebuking you, since you have blasphemed against Islam, the Prophet, and the Koran....

Wafa Sultan: These are personal matters that do not concern you.
[...]

---

[1] Dr. Ibrahim Al-Khouli was indentified as an Egyptian professor of religious studies at Al Azhar University.

Wafa Sultan: Brother, you can believe in stones, as long as you don't throw them at me. You are free to worship whoever you want, but other people's beliefs are not your concern, whether they believe that the Messiah is God, son of Mary, or that Satan is God, son of Mary. Let people have their beliefs.

[...]

Wafa Sultan: The Jews have come from the tragedy (of the Holocaust), and forced the world to respect them, with their knowledge, not with their terror, with their work, not their crying and yelling. Humanity owes most of the discoveries and science of the 19th and 20th centuries to Jewish scientists. 15 million people, scattered throughout the world, united and won their rights through work and knowledge. We have not seen a single Jew blow himself up in a German restaurant. We have not seen a single Jew destroy a church. We have not seen a single Jew protest by killing people. The Muslims have turned three Buddha statues into rubble. We have not seen a single Buddhist burn down a Mosque, kill a Muslim, or burn down an embassy. Only the Muslims defend their beliefs by burning down churches, killing people, and destroying embassies. This path will not yield any results. The Muslims must ask themselves what they can do for humankind, before they demand that humankind respect them.

REFERENCE

http://www.memritv.org/clip_transcript/en/1050.htm. The Middle East Media Research Institute (MEMRI) is an independent, nonprofit organization providing translations of the Middle East media and original analysis and research on developments in the region. Copies of articles and documents cited, as well as background information, are available on request. MEMRI holds copyrights on all translations. Materials may only be used with proper attribution.

APPENDIX H
Homeland Security Exercise and Evaluation Program

Homeland Security Exercise and Evaluation Program
━━━ *Terminology, Methodology, and Compliance Guidelines* ━━━

HOMELAND SECURITY EXERCISE AND EVALUATION PROGRAM (HSEEP)

The Homeland Security Exercise and Evaluation Program (HSEEP) is a capabilities and performance-based exercise program which provides a standardized policy, methodology, and terminology for exercise design, development, conduct, evaluation, and improvement planning. The HSEEP Policy and Guidance is presented in detail in HSEEP Volumes I-III. Adherence to the policy and guidance presented in the HSEEP Volumes ensures that exercise programs conform to established best practices, and helps provide unity and consistency of effort for exercises at all levels of government.

This document provides terminology, methodology, and compliance guidelines for all entities involved in exercises, including Federal, State, and local governments, departments, and agencies; private sector entities; and Non-Governmental Organizations.

The purpose of this document is to define the key requirements for an entity to be considered HSEEP-compliant. Section I of this document describes the key elements of the HSEEP exercise terminology and methodology. Section II provides a checklist which an entity can use to ensure its exercise program is HSEEP-compliant.

SECTION I: HSEEP TERMINOLOGY AND METHODOLOGY

A consistent terminology and methodology for exercises is critical to avoiding confusion, and to ensuring that entities can exercise together seamlessly. This section provides a high-level overview of key components of HSEEP terminology and methodology.

Exercise Types

There are seven types of exercises defined within HSEEP, each of wh ich is either discussions-based or operations-based.

Discussions-based Exercises familiarize participants with current plans, policies, agreements and procedures, or may be used to develop new plans, policies, agreements, and procedures. Types of Discussion-based Exercises include:

- *Seminar.* A seminar is an informal discussion, designed to orient participants to new or updated plans, policies, or procedures (e.g., a seminar to review a new Evacuation Standard Operating Procedure).

- *Workshop.* A workshop resembles a seminar, but is empl oyed to build specific products, such as a draft plan or policy (e.g., a Training and Exercise Plan Workshop is used to develop a Multi-year Training and Exercise Plan).

- *Tabletop Exercise (TTX).* A tabletop exercise involves key personnel discussing simulated scenarios in an informal setting. TTXs can be used to assess plans, policies, and procedures.

- *Game.* A game is a simulation of operations that often involves two or more teams, usually in a competitive environment, using rules, data, and procedure designed to depict an actual or assumed real-life situation.

Operations-based Exercises validate plans, policies, agreements and procedures, clarify roles and

responsibilities, and identify resource gaps in an operational environment. Types of Operations-based Exercises include:

- *Drill.* A drill is a coordinated, supervised activity usually employed to test a single, specific operation or function within a single entity (e.g., a fire department conducts a decontamination drill).

- *Functional Exercise (FE).* A functional exercise examines and/or validates the coordination, command, and control between various multi-agency coordination centers (e.g., emergency operation center, joint field office, etc.). A functional exercise does not involve any "boots on the ground" (i.e., first responders or emergency officials responding to an incident in real time).

- *Full-Scale Exercise (FSE).* A full-scale exercise is a multi-agency, multi-jurisdictional, multi-discipline exercise involving functional (e.g., joint field office, emergency operation centers, etc.) and "boots on the ground" response (e.g., firefighters decontaminating mock victims).

Exercise Documentation

The list below briefly describes the important document types associated with most exercises. The types of documentation described here are all discussed in more detail in *HSEEP Volume II: Exercise Planning and Conduct*.

- A *Situation Manual (SitMan)* is a participant handbook for discussion-based exercises, particularly TTXs. It provides background information on exercise scope, schedule, and objectives. It also presents the scenario narrative that will drive participant discussions during the exercise.

- The *Exercise Plan (ExPlan)*, typically used for operations-based exercises, provides a synopsis of the exercise and is published and distributed to players and observers prior to the start of the exercise. The ExPlan includes the exercise objectives and scope, safety procedures, and logistical considerations such as an exercise schedule. The ExPlan does not contain detailed scenario information.

- The *Controller and Evaluator (C/E) Handbook*[1] supplements the ExPlan for operations-based exercises, containing more detailed information about the exercise scenario and describing exercise controllers' and evaluators' roles and responsibilities. Because the C/E Handbook contains information on the scenario and exercise administration, it is distributed only to those individuals specifically designated as controllers or evaluators.

- The *Master Scenario Events List (MSEL)* is a chronological timeline of expected actions and scripted events (i.e., injects) to be inserted into operations-based exercise play by controllers in order to generate or prompt player activity. It ensures necessary events happen so that all exercise objectives are met.

- A *Player Handout* is a 1-2 page document, usually handed out the morning of an exercise, which provides a quick reference for exercise players on safety procedures, logistical considerations, exercise schedule, and other key factors and information.

- *Exercise Evaluation Guides (EEGs)* help evaluators collect and interpret relevant exercise observations. EEGs provide evaluators with information on what tasks they should expect to see accomplished during an exercise, space to record observations, and questions to address after the exercise as a first step in the analysis process. In order to assist entities in exercise evaluation, standardized EEGs have been created that reflect capabilities-based planning tools,

---

[1] *For large-scale/complex exercises, a separate Controller Staff Instruction (COSIN) and Evaluation Plan (EVALPLAN) may be necessary; but for most exercises a combined Controller/Evaluator Handbook is appropriate.*

such as the Target Capabilities List (TCL) and the Universal Task List (UTL). The EEGs are not meant as report cards. Rather, they are intended to guide an evaluator's observations so that the evaluator focuses on capabilities and tasks relevant to exercise objectives to support development of the After Action Report/Improvement Plan (AAR/IP).

- *An After Action Report/Improvement Plan (AAR/IP)* is the final product of an exercise. The AAR/IP has two components: an AAR, which captures observations and recommendations based on the exercise objectives as associated with the capabilities and tasks; and an IP, which identifies specific corrective actions, assigns them to responsible parties, and establishes targets for their completion. The lead evaluator and the exercise planning team draft the AAR and submit it to conference participants prior to an After Action Conference (see below). The draft AAR is distributed to conference participants for review no more than 30 days after exercise conduct. The final AAR/IP is an outcome of the After Action Conference and should be disseminated to participants no more than 60 days after exercise conduct.

Planning and After Action Conferences

The HSEEP methodology defines a variety of planning and after action conferences. The need for each of these conferences varies depending on the type and scope of the exercise. They include:

- Concepts and Objectives Meeting
- Initial Planning Conference (IPC)
- Mid-Term Planning Conference (MPC)
- Master Scenario Events List (MSEL) Conference
- Final Planning Conference (FPC)
- After Action Conference (AAC)

HSEEP Volume II: Exercise Planning and Conduct provides details on the outcomes, products, and associated timelines for each of these planning conferences.

SECTION II: HSEEP COMPLIANCE

For the purpose of this document, HSEEP Compliance is defined as adherence to specific HSEEP-mandated practices for exercise program management, design, development, conduct, evaluation, and improvement planning. In order for an entity to be considered HSEEP compliant it must satisfy four distinct performance requirements:

1. Conducting an annual Training and Exercise Plan Workshop and developing and maintaining a Multi-year Training and Exercise Plan.

2. Planning and conducting exercises in accordance with the guidelines set forth in HSEEP Volumes I-III.

3. Developing and submitting a properly formatted After-Action Report/Improvement Plan (AAR/IP). The format for the AAR/IP is found in HSEEP Volume III.

4. Tracking and implementing corrective actions identified in the AAR/IP.

The checklist provided below is intended to serve as a guide entities can use to assess whether or not their particular exercise program is HSEEP compliant.

1. Training and Exercise Plan Workshop (T&EPW)

- All HSEEP compliant entities conduct a T&EPW each calendar year in which they develop a Multi-year Training and Exercise Plan, which includes:
    - The entities' training and exercise priorities (based on an overarching strategy and previous improvement plans).
    - The capabilities from the TCL that the entity will train for and exercise against.
    - A multi-year training and exercise schedule which:
        - Reflects the training activities which will take place prior to an exercise, allowing exercises to serve as a true validation of previous training.
        - Reflects all exercises in which the entity participates.
        - Employs a "building-block approach" in which training and exercise activities gradually escalate in complexity.
- A new or updated Multi-year Training and Exercise Plan must be finalized and implemented within 60 days of the T&EPW.
- All scheduled exercises must be entered into the National Exercise Schedule (NEXS) System.
- The Multi-Year Training and Exercise Plan must be updated on an annual basis (or as necessary) to reflect schedule changes.

2. Exercise Planning and Conduct

- The type of exercise selected by the entity should be consistent with the entity's Multi-year Training and Exercise Plan.
- Exercise objectives should be based on capabilities and their associated critical tasks, which are contained within the EEGs. For example, if an entity, based on its risk/vulnerability analysis, determines that it is prone to hurricanes, it may want to validate its evacuation capabilities. In order to validate this capability it would first refer to the "Citizen Protection: Evacuation and/or In-Place Protection" EEG. Tasks associated with this capability include: "*make the decision to evacuate or shelter in place;*" "*identify and mobilize appropriate personnel;*" and "*activate approved traffic control plan.*" An entity may wish to create its own Simple, Measurable, Achievable, Realistic, and Task-oriented (S.M.A.R.T.) objectives based on its specific plans/procedures associated with these capabilities and tasks, such as: 1) "Examine the ability of local response agencies to conduct mass evacuation procedures in accordance with Standard Operating Procedures; and 2) Evaluate the ability of local response agencies to issue public notification of an evacuation order within the timeframe prescribed in local Standard Operating Procedures.
- The scenarios used in exercises must be tailored toward validating the capabilities, and should be based on the entity's risk/vulnerability assessment.
- Exercise planners should develop the following documents, in accordance with HSEEP Volume IV, to support exercise planning, conduct, evaluation, and improvement planning:
    - For Discussion-based exercises:

- Situation Manual (SITMAN)
- For Operations-based Exercises this requires:
  - Exercise Plan (EXPLAN)
  - Player Handout
  - Master Scenario Events List (MSEL)
  - Controller/Evaluator Handbook (C/E Handbook)

  Templates and samples of these documents can be found *in HSEEP Volume IV: Sample Templates and Formats*, available on the HSEEP website (http://hseep.dhs.gov).
- Exercises should adhere to the planning timelines laid forth in HSEEP Volume I.
- Exercises must reflect the principles of the National Incident Management System (NIMS).

3. After-Action Reporting

- AAR/IPs created for exercises must conform to the templates provided in *HSEEP Volume III: Exercise Evaluation and Improvement Planning*.
- Following each exercise, a draft AAR/IP must be developed based on information gathered through use of Exercise Evaluation Guides (EEGs).
- Following every exercise, an After-Action Conference (AAC) must be conducted, in which:
  - Key personnel and the exercise planning team are presented with findings and recommendations from the draft AAR/IP.
  - Corrective actions addressing a draft AAR/IP's recommendations are developed and assigned to responsible parties with due dates for completion.
- A final AAR/IP with recommendations and corrective actions derived from discussion at the AAC must be completed within 60 days after the completion of each exercise.

4. Improvement Planning

- An improvement plan will include broad recommendations from the AAR/IP organized by target capability as defined in the Target Capabilities List (TCL).
- Corrective actions derived from an AAC are associated with the recommendations and must be linked to a capability element as defined in the TCL.
- Corrective actions included in the improvement plan must be measurable.
- Corrective actions included in the improvement plan must designate a projected start date and completion date.
- Corrective actions included in the improvement plan must be assigned to an organization and a point of contact (POC) within that organization.
- Corrective actions must be continually monitored and reviewed as part of an organizational Corrective Action Program. An individual should be responsible for managing a Corrective Action Program to ensure corrective actions resulting from exercises, policy discussions and real-world

events are resolved and support the scheduling and development of subsequent training and exercises.

ADDITIONAL INFORMATION

The HSEEP website, http://hseep.dhs.gov, provides additional information regarding HSEEP Policy and Guidance. Available on the website are the revised versions of HSEEP Volumes I-III, which provide detail and context regarding many of the terms, processes, and requirements described above. Volume IV is a searchable library that provides many of the sample materials described above. The HSEEP Toolkit, which includes the National Exercise Schedule (NEXS) System, Design and Development System (DDS), and Corrective Action Program (CAP) System, allows users to schedule, plan, evaluate and track corrective actions from exercises. In addition, there are several exercise training courses, including independent study (IS-120a, IS-130, etc.), mobile (HSEEP Mobile Course), and residence courses (Master Exercise Practitioner Program) that teach students the principles of exercise planning, conduct, evaluation, and improvement planning.

INDEX